Postabortion care

POSTABORTION CARE

LESSONS FROM OPERATIONS RESEARCH

EDITORS

DALE HUNTINGTON

NANCY J. PIET-PELON

Population Council

The Population Council is an international, nonprofit, nongovernmental institution that seeks to improve the wellbeing and reproductive health of current and future generations around the world and to help achieve a humane, equitable, and sustainable balance between people and resources. The Council conducts biomedical, social science, and public health research and helps build research capacities in developing countries. Established in 1952, the Council is governed by an international board of trustees. Its New York headquarters supports a global network of regional and country offices.

Population Council
One Dag Hammarskjold Plaza
New York, NY 10017 USA
www.popcouncil.org

Library of Congress Cataloging-in-Publication Data

Postabortion care : lessons from operations research / editors, Dale Huntington,
Nancy J. Piet-Pelon.
p. cm.
Includes bibliographical references.
ISBN 0-87834-100-5 (pbk. : alk. paper)
1. Abortion—Complications—Treatment—Developing countries. 2. Birth control—Developing countries. I. Huntington, Dale. II. Piet-Pelon, Nancy J.

RG734.P682 1999
616.8'8—dc21 99-049051

Chapter 3 is reprinted with permission from *Studies in Family Planning* 1999; 30(1): 17–27.

This publication was made possible by the Office of Population of the United States Agency for International Development (USAID) under the terms of the Frontiers in Reproductive Health Cooperative Agreement number HRN-A-00-98-00012-00. The opinions expressed herein are those of the author(s) and do not necessarily reflect the views of USAID.

Printed in the United States of America

Contents

Tables and Figures

Tables

Figures

Foreword

Delegates to the 1994 Cairo International Conference on Population and Development (ICPD) agreed on a landmark Programme of Action designed to raise the quality of life and promote the development of the world's poor, especially women. Sadly, in the somewhat stilted words of the 1999 Report to the UN General Assembly, the "translation of commitment to the goals of the Conference into commensurate levels of donor funding has not been forthcoming." Probably only about half the donor money hoped for in 1994 is available. With the absolute number of women at risk of pregnancy growing at an unprecedented rate, some critical measures of women's health are actually deteriorating. Between 1994 and 1999, the World Health Organization (WHO) raised its estimate of the annual number of maternal deaths from 500,000 to 585,000. It is a tragic statistic with which to exit a century of such wealth and explosive medical progress.

This volume deals with one central but until now intransigent aspect of women's health: how to reduce the toll of death and morbidity associated with unsafe abortion. For the first time in the history of international decisionmaking, Cairo established a consensus on abortion. This was clearly reaffirmed in the 1999 United Nations General Assembly statement:

> Women who have unwanted pregnancies should have ready access to reliable information and compassionate counselling. Any measures or changes related to abortion within the health system can only be determined at the national or local level according to the national legislative process. In circumstances where abortion is not against the law, such abortion should be safe. In all cases, women should have access to quality services for the manage-

> ment of complications arising from abortion. Post-abortion counselling, education and family planning services should be offered promptly, which will also help to avoid repeat abortions.[1]

Where abortion is illegal, many women use herbal remedies, take modern drugs (such as Cytotec) in unsupervised ways, attempt to physically self-induce an abortion, or seek the help of abortion providers working outside the law. Such activities are common on a large scale. Some of those operating outside the law are motivated by a genuine desire to help women, but others are highly exploitative. A recent study in Ethiopia, where abortion is illegal, found that for some women the "cost" of obtaining an abortion includes being raped by a male abortionist. Where abortion is illegal, women are exposed to painful, dangerous procedures and many fall so sick that they need to be admitted to a public hospital or private clinic for treatment of uterine bleeding or infection following an incomplete abortion.

On average, a woman now living will have one induced abortion before she reaches menopause. Obviously, many women will go through life without inducing an abortion, while others will have several, but whatever way we look at it abortion is common and will remain common in the twenty-first century. This book provides the evidence-based studies to help health professionals meet the ICPD goal of providing women "access to quality services for the management of complications arising from abortion."

As the chapters demonstrate, progress has been made in improving access to postabortion care (PAC). It is a key area where practical achievements are possible, even in resource-poor situations with highly constrained budgets. Manual vacuum aspiration (MVA) has proven to be an appropriate and cost-effective treatment for women who come to hospitals or clinics with incomplete abortions. MVA is impeccably validated for incomplete abortion, and in many situations it actually saves money. MVA under local anesthesia is far superior to D&C under general anesthesia.

---

1 ICPD +5 has made an additional recommendation: "63. iii. In recognizing and implementing the above, and in circumstances where abortion is not against the law, health systems should train and equip health-service providers and should take other measures to ensure that such abortion is safe and accessible. Additional measures should be taken to safeguard women's health."

Combined with counseling and ready access to contraceptive and other reproductive health advice and services, the complete package of PAC presents a proven, win-win situation that helps women and reduces the pressure on overstretched health services.

Sincere and informed people are always likely to come to different conclusions concerning the ethical questions posed by abortion. Uninformed people are likely to continue to adopt viewpoints that are simplistic but strident, making a complicated subject even more difficult to confront. On the one hand, PAC represents the one step where reasonable and humane individuals should be able to establish a consensus, whatever their ethical perspective on induced abortion. On the other, while many ideas in medicine spread rapidly, change in relation to any aspect of abortion often takes place with glacial slowness.

Some will be tempted to say that the PAC techniques described in this volume are "impossible." The careful documentation and objective discussion this book provides should go a long way toward overcoming the common reluctance of health professionals and policymakers to confront the public health issues raised by abortion.

Malcolm Potts
Bixby Professor
School of Public Health
University of California, Berkeley

Acknowledgments

Many individuals contributed to the postabortion care studies reported on in this volume. Each study was based in a community or hospital that supported the research. We acknowledge and thank all of the local government officials and caregivers who agreed to work in this sensitive area, as well as the women and their families who consented to interviews during a difficult time in their lives.

The researchers who guided these studies and completed these chapters deserve our special thanks. Through their work they have contributed greatly to our knowledge of postabortion care—what works, what does not—and provided a direction for future research.

We acknowledge our USAID/Washington colleagues who supported these projects from the beginning—Marjorie Horn and Sarah Harbison. Forrest Greenslade, former president of Ipas, has had an important role in placing postabortion care in the mainstream of reproductive health care. Each chapter was reviewed by two or more anonymous referees who contributed their expertise to the finished work. Robert Heidel and Jared Stamm from the Population Council in New York did an able job of editing.

We envision this volume as a starting point for many who are seeking ways to enable women to gain access to appropriate postabortion care services. It may also be a guide for caregivers who work each day to improve the reproductive health of the women they serve.

Dale Huntington and Nancy J. Piet-Pelon

1

Introduction

Dale Huntington

Women who have experienced complications from incomplete abortion are among the most neglected of reproductive health care patients. The medical care that is provided to them commonly involves the use of dilation and curettage (D&C), often under inappropriate and insufficient anesthesia. Manual vacuum aspiration (MVA) is not widely available in many developing countries, even though use of MVA with local anesthesia for treatment of an incomplete abortion performed in the first trimester has been demonstrated to reduce health risks to the patient, lower the hospital's costs, and lead to quicker recovery. Too often, scant attention is paid to other health conditions with which the patient presents (e.g., reproductive tract infections, sexually transmitted diseases, and repeated miscarriages). In addition to the generally poor quality of medical care, interpersonal communication during postabortion treatment is substandard in most settings. Counseling on the medical procedure required and the course of postoperative recuperation is usually not provided. Linkages to family planning services—either by service provision during the postabortion hospital visit or by referral to nearby family planning clinics—are not a customary element of discharge procedures for most postabortion patients.

The change in the United States government administration in 1992, followed by the recommendations of the 1994 International Conference on Population and Development (ICPD), lessened constraints on research surrounding issues of induced abortion and the improvement of emergency medical services. A number of programs and operations research activities investigated the ways and means of improving the medical care provided to women with incomplete abortion. These developments served to bring the concept of postabortion care into the mainstream of women's reproductive health programs.

The postabortion care initiative is an international effort founded on a public health perspective of women's reproductive health that focuses on the rapid transfer of knowledge and materials to reduce high rates of maternal mortality and morbidity from unsafe abortion. Although some public health professionals worldwide have been working on the issue of unsafe abortion for decades, the sequence of events in the years preceding the 1994 ICPD and immediately thereafter drew attention to the important contribution made by the postabortion care concept to the field of women's reproductive health.

The elaboration of a postabortion strategy within a quality-of-care framework has clearly facilitated its development. The reliance upon concepts drawn from a dominant paradigm for evaluating family planning programs makes the idea of improving postabortion medical services immediately accessible to both researchers and program managers. The introduction of MVA has been used to upgrade clinical practices related to pain control as well as infection prevention. A number of improvements in interpersonal communication practices, chiefly involving information and counseling, are bundled around the technology, drawing providers' attention to alternative case management procedures that involve a more woman-centered approach to postabortion care. The operations research studies included in this volume represent a substantial contribution to increasing our understanding of these issues.

Julie Solo and colleagues report on a study in Kenya that examined three service-delivery models in hospital settings, each based upon holistic case management procedures for postabortion patients but with alternative approaches to providing family planning services. In two of the service delivery models contraceptive methods were provided in the OB/GYN inpatient department. One variation of this model had OB/GYN staff providing contraceptives, and the second had maternal and child health/family planning (MCH/FP) outpatient staff coming to the hospital's OB/GYN department to provide the methods. The third experimental model referred postabortion patients from the OB/GYN department to the hospital's MCH/FP clinic for family planning services (patients who indicated a desire for contraceptives were escorted to the family planning clinic prior to discharge).

Solo and her colleagues report that substantial changes in the quality of postabortion services were noticed in each of the sites. The provision of family planning in the OB/GYN department by the same staff who provided postabortion care was most effective in terms of reaching more women with counseling, increasing family planning acceptance, and providing contraceptive methods. The addition of family planning services to the inpatient OB/GYN department necessitated a reconfiguration of the physical space (for counseling and storage of contraceptives) that caused additional resources to be expended. There was some evidence that patients who sought family planning services in the MCH/FP clinic did indeed receive higher-quality counseling than those who received counseling in the OB/GYN department, indicating that additional training in interpersonal communication skills should be provided to OB/GYN staff. A large number of referred patients were lost to follow-up, however, thereby limiting the effectiveness of the model based on referral.

As in Africa, abortion in much of Latin America is legally restricted and the subject of pervasive religious and cultural sanctions. In this setting some of the most innovative interventions have focused on improving provider–patient interaction, so that postabortion patients are treated with more compassion, and on changing surgical procedures and other aspects of medical treatment. The chapter by Ana Langer and her colleagues on work done in a large public hospital in Oaxaca, Mexico, is revealing of a regional variation within the global postabortion care initiative.

Oaxaca is the capital city of an impoverished, rural state in Mexico. The hospital in this study treats up to four postabortion patients daily, many of whom speak one of 20 local languages or dialects but do not understand Spanish (the language of the physicians). A quasi-experimental study designed to test service-delivery improvements included data collection on a wide range of quality-of-care indicators. In addition, the study conducted in-depth interviews with staff and patients to assess their perceptions of changes in postabortion services. The intervention's four essential steps were to: (1) modify hospital procedures to reduce waiting time, improve pain management, and ensure privacy; (2) switch from D&C to MVA; (3) improve provider–patient relations, by conducting a special course on counseling about postabortion contraception and counseling practices specific to postabortion patients; and (4) produce specially adapted printed materials to reinforce the counseling. The Oaxaca study's emphasis on improving interpersonal communication, particularly the need to address class and language barriers between providers and ethnic minority patients, is in the forefront of postabortion care behavioral change interventions.

The results from the Oaxaca study reveal several positive changes in the treatment and care of postabortion patients. The total amount of treatment time, particularly postoperative waiting time, decreased substantially. The immediate acceptance of MVA instruments was also evident: Before the study only about 10 percent of cases were treated with a combination of D&C and MVA, whereas after the intervention 78 percent of the appropriate cases were treated with MVA alone. The results in improving pain management were mixed. Although providers began to use a local instead of a general anesthetic more frequently after the study's intervention, clinical measures to relieve pain before and after the procedure were not affected—even though these measures had been repeatedly emphasized during the training and supervisory follow-up visits.

Remarkable changes occurred in the manner in which patients were treated and in the quantity and frequency of information exchange as a result of efforts directed toward improving interpersonal communication skills. One result of the improved interpersonal communication processes was a significant increase in the percentage of women who accepted a postabortion contraceptive method (from 30 percent previously to 60 percent following the study) and in the percentage of women who received the method at the hospital before discharge (from 29 percent to 57 percent). The authors note that despite these impressive gains, a degree of mistrust and fear remained in the relations between providers and patients. Overcoming culturally bound behaviors and beliefs regarding the provision of medical care will require sustained diligence and effort. The study in Oaxaca is instructive for addressing these issues.

The influence of the caregiving environment on the services provided to postabortion patients is again evident in a second study from Latin America included in this volume. Juan Díaz and colleagues report on how legal sanctions against abortion have negatively affected the care given to postabortion patients in three public-sector hospitals in Bolivia. Previous investigators had identified such problems as the routine interrogation of postabortion patients to identify cases of illegal abortion coupled with notification of judicial authorities for prosecution; charging higher fees to patients who present with signs of induced abortion (fees that are prohibitively high for many women, thus causing delays in seeking care); and other practices related to substandard case management protocols. Improving the quality of services from within this generally restrictive environment led the authors to concentrate on improvements in interpersonal communication. In contrast to most other postabortion care operations research studies, the Bolivia study did not change the surgical practice of D&C in favor of MVA. Change was introduced instead by moving the physical location of the treatment area into a newly refurbished room. The results clearly show substantial improvement in providers' technical competence with postabortion treatment and in contraceptive use following abortion. Coupling improvements in staff technical knowledge with an emphasis on improving interpersonal communication skills led to more of the medical staff providing more frequent counseling, with a greater breadth of information being discussed with postabortion patients. The effects of the training program's emphasis on value-free interpersonal behavior are shown in several indications that providers' treatment of women became more compassionate and caring. Anecdotal evidence suggests that the improvements in the interpersonal care led to an increase in adolescent patients as the surrounding communities became aware of the hospital's improved quality of care.

Nahla Abdel-Tawab and colleagues conducted an influential study in Egypt that examined the effects on the woman's recovery of counseling the husbands of postabortion patients. An experimental posttest-only control group design was used to measure the effect of the intervention on husbands' level of involvement and on patient outcomes one month after discharge. Husbands in the intervention group received several "health education" messages concerning their wives' health (based on formative research conducted earlier in Egypt): the need for rest and nutrition, warning signs, return to fertility, and the need for family planning methods to avoid undesired pregnancy. The effect of providing this information on the level of the husband's support (material and emotional), the patient's physical and emotional recovery, and the couple's contraceptive use was assessed through home interviews with patients and group discussions with a few husbands. The counseling had a positive effect on both husbands' behavior and patients' recovery. For example, patients whose husbands were counseled reported significantly lower levels of emotional distress related to the incomplete abortion than did patients whose husbands were not counseled. This study raises a number of ethical issues related to enforcing measures that protect the patient's right to privacy.

The cost-efficiency of the postabortion care initiative has been reported on previously.[1] These cost studies have suggested that considerable savings accrue with the introduction of MVA, and that most efficiencies are gained through reductions in the duration of hospital stay, less intensive use of hospital materials and supplies, and more effective use of staff time. The methodology for assessing the treatment of postabortion patients used in these early studies was refined by Ipas (an international reproductive health organization based in Chapel Hill, North Carolina) through its collaboration with the Population Council's INOPAL project (Investigación Operativa y Asistencia Técnica en Planificación Familiar y Salud Materno-infantil en América Latina y el Caribe). Reports of two applications of the cost-study methodology are presented in this volume.

The Ipas cost methodology is a standard approach to recording the utilization of resources and estimating a per-patient cost. Through an intensive review of a facility's financial, administrative, and personnel records, estimates are made of the costs of medical supplies, salaries, and relevant direct fixed costs. Overhead estimates are used to determine the average cost of bed use per minute and per day. Postabortion patients are also observed in order to assess the variable costs associated with their treatment. This time and motion study involves having trained observers use standardized checklists to record the amount of time spent by patients in each service department or treatment station, the time spent by medical and nonmedical personnel in direct patient contact, and the types of supplies and medications used in treating patients. By combining information taken from the review of hospitals' administrative data and the time and motion study, it is possible to derive estimates of the total average cost of treating a postabortion patient per unit of time (commonly the cost per bed minute) or the average cost per patient treated in a facility. These costs are then compared before and after changes have been made in the case management protocols for postabortion patients, in order to estimate the impact of improvements on the facility's costs.

Carlos Brambila and colleagues used this methodology to examine the costs associated with delivering postabortion services in a large public-sector hospital in Oaxaca, Mexico. The improvements to postabortion services in the Oaxaca general hospital are similar to changes made in other settings described in this volume. MVA instruments were introduced, counseling procedures were emphasized, and linkages with hospital family planning services were established through discussions with staff. The impact of these improvements on the quality of care provided to postabortion patients is comparable to the changes observed in other settings. The cost savings associated with these service-delivery improvements are equally impressive. The total cost per patient was reduced by 32 percent, from US$265 to $180 (including the costs associated with introducing the improvements). The most significant savings were achieved in the use of instruments, medicines, and supplies; costs were reduced by almost two-thirds, from $92 before the study to $32 after services were improved.

The Oaxaca cost study has contributed to the development of the Ipas methodology in its analysis of the allocation of staff time during the different stages of care. The study produced a ratio of personnel time that indicates the effort required to provide medical care at each of the station areas. Use of this ratio reveals that prior to the intervention the personnel effort required for patient assessment was 49 percent higher than after the intervention—clearly indicating that more efficient use of staff occurred as a result of the service-delivery improvements. The study showed that although the amount of staff time decreased, the amount of time spent by category of staff varied substantially. For example, after the intervention, doctors devoted more time to ultrasound diagnostics, but patients waited less for treatment. In a similar manner, increased reliance on MVA meant that nurses devoted proportionally more time to the care of the patient than doctors did: The amount of doctor time during the procedure decreased by 24 minutes per patient while the amount of nursing time increased by approximately 10 minutes. While the savings in personnel time are small compared to other sources of savings, detailed analysis shows that allocation of staff time is more efficient and relies less upon specialized medical personnel during nondiagnostic or therapeutic stages of care.

Another example of an analytic variation on the Ipas methodology is presented by Laila Nawar and her colleagues from Egypt. This cost analysis was part of a larger program to improve the postabortion medical care provided to Egyptian patients. Two of ten hospitals involved with the postabortion care improvement program were selected as sites for cost analysis. Prior to the postabortion operations research studies, these two sites were providing services at a very low level of quality. For example, approximately two-thirds of the postabortion patients at the district hospital underwent D&C with no anesthesia, and aseptic procedures were not commonly adhered to in either site.

Using the Ipas methodology, Nawar and her colleagues reported a 32 percent increase in the costs per postabortion patient in the district hospital and an 8 percent increase in the general hospital when MVA cannulas are discarded after a single use, which is government policy; assuming multiple use of cannulas, the cost increases in the district and general hospitals were reduced to approximately 6 percent. The hypothetical cost savings from reusing cannulas essentially compensated for the increased costs of using pain control medication and antiseptic supplies, as personnel time was little affected by the postabortion care intervention. The study also reported reductions in length of hospital stay (a 69 percent reduction in the district hospital and a 30 percent reduction in the general hospital), but the savings in direct fixed costs associated with the shorter length of stay did not offset the increased costs of supplies, materials, and medications. The Egypt cost study clearly shows that in settings with substandard postabortion quality, improvements will carry a price.

The savings generated by changing postabortion treatment are a type of "opportunity savings" (freeing up resources for use elsewhere) as opposed to reductions in costs that could lead to overall reductions in hospital expenditures. Most of these savings are actually associated with a reduced length of stay due to changing the care setting from inpatient to outpatient or using lower-level (local) anesthesia. While these savings are important some of the length-of-stay costs are up-front or relatively fixed and cannot be treated as being proportional to the duration of the hospitalization (e.g., 25 percent incurred during the first quarter of the stay, 25 percent incurred during the second quarter, etc.). Laundry and certain administrative costs (linked to admittance and discharge), among others, will not vary regardless of whether the patient stays four hours or two days. The next generation of cost studies will need to refine the analysis of costs associated with length of stay to avoid an overestimation of the savings. Future postabortion cost studies will also need to demonstrate how resources that are freed up can be reallocated, and to determine whether or not the types of costs that have been investigated are actually the most significant costs from a hospital manager's point of view (i.e., those under his control). For example, are the cost savings on routine cases being converted into making more resources available for the treatment of patients who present with severe complications? To the extent that postabortion cost studies can provide answers to these types of questions, the data they produce will have direct relevance to the management of medical services, and provide useful information for development of health care policy.

In the large majority of studies, the sites most commonly selected for experimenting with improved postabortion care services have been public-sector hospitals, where care is provided by teams of physicians and nurses. However, trained medical staff in primary care settings can also safely provide postabortion services using MVA with local anesthesia. This volume contains two studies that examine models of incorporating postabortion services into primary care settings. Both chapters have been produced under the leadership of Deborah Billings and involve different teams of researchers in Ghana and Mexico.

Billings first discusses an attempt to decentralize postabortion care services within rural areas of Ghana by training community midwives as postabortion care providers. Although Ghanaian law allows registered medical personnel in certified facilities to induce abortion under certain circumstances, many women continue to suffer the consequences of unsafe abortion because of the unavailability of providers and the stigma attached to having an abortion at a public clinic. It is widely acknowledged in Ghana that unsafe abortion is one of the primary causes of pregnancy-related mortality in the country. In addition, the availability of emergency medical services is extremely limited in rural areas. Ghana's Ministry of Health included references to providing accessible and safe postabortion services in its 1996 National Reproductive Health Service Policy and Standards. Implementation of this policy has included an experimental component for training some of the country's 6,000 community midwives as postabortion care providers.

A pre- and postintervention controlled study design was employed to examine improvements in the quality of care associated with training community midwives in postabortion care. Providers in local hospitals (who supervise community midwives) and midwives were interviewed, along with women who arrived at one of the six district hospitals for treatment of postabortion complications. Following the baseline data collection, 40 midwives and four physicians were trained together in improved case management procedures. Many benefits were gained by training the midwives along with their physician supervisors, including the development of a supportive and trustworthy supervisory system for the decentralized postabortion services.

The results show that training of midwives greatly improved access to postabortion services: Waiting time before treatment for women who sought care from midwives averaged 90 minutes, as compared to an average of 220 minutes among women who sought care at district hospitals. Women reported that they felt comfortable with the midwives' skills and abilities. An evaluation of the midwives' clinical skills indicated that they successfully used MVA—with no procedural complications—and consistently processed all instruments according to strict aseptic protocols. In addition to demonstrating their ability to follow case management protocols, the community midwives also ensured that follow-up appointments with their patients were routinely observed, including the provision of postabortion family planning. The study concludes that the collaborative links with district hospitals (where the physician supervisors reside) established with the postabortion training have provided the midwives with opportunities to improve their professional skills in other areas. In addition, their close proximity to the communities where they work and their in-depth understanding of the problems women face have led many of the midwives to convene community education activities to raise women's and men's awareness of unsafe abortion and unwanted pregnancy.

An alternative model of extending postabortion services to the primary care level is to enlist the support of lay professionals. Billings and her colleagues in Mexico report on the results from an ethnographic study in rural Morelos. As in Ghana, complications of unsafe abortion are responsible for a significant proportion of maternal mortality in Mexico: Routinely collected statistics from public-sector facilities suggest that abortion-related complications represent the third or fourth most important cause of maternal mortality. In large part this is because rural women have limited access to emergency medical services. Despite the Mexican government's attention to improving the skills of traditional midwives, prior to this operations research study no attempt had been made to provide training on postabortion care for these lay health care providers. Billings and her colleagues conducted a qualitative field study of traditional midwives' concepts and experiences regarding abortion, and explored differences in midwives' knowledge about abortion before and after their participation in a postabortion care training program that focused on stabilization of any complications and referral for postabortion treatment.

Earlier research had indicated that midwives' knowledge about abortion complications was insufficient and inaccurate. In addition, although training for midwives was shown to improve their knowledge about a range of medical conditions, their popular beliefs about risk factors for a miscarriage (such as passing by a cemetery or washing shawls) were little changed. Postabortion training for these traditional midwives was oriented to add to their existing treatments, while discouraging potentially harmful beliefs. Billings and colleagues point out that traditional midwives require training and evaluation models different from those used to teach hospital-based personnel: The process of integrating popular belief systems and indigenous pharmacopoeia within the Western conceptual framework of warning signs and follow-up care needs to be better understood before more effective use can be made of these lay professionals.

The strong normative sanctions against induced abortion in the Morelos communities, however, were found to constrain the effective use of traditional midwives as postabortion care providers. These constraints hindered the development of a referral network from the community to the nearby hospital for the prompt treatment of incomplete induced abortion. Midwives' fears of being labeled "abortionists" reportedly inhibited some from readily providing emergency medical treatment. In addition, the traditional midwives have experienced feelings of ostracism and condemnation by physicians in modern hospitals (where not all staff are familiar with and supportive of midwives) when they accompany women for emergency medical care. These perceptions and experiences contribute to the difficulties of creating a viable referral network for treatment of incomplete abortions in Morelos. Conducting joint workshops with midwives and physicians, as was done in Ghana, may be one way to break down barriers between the traditional and modern health care systems.

The WHO strategic approach to contraceptive introduction is a useful starting point for organizing a discussion of the issues surrounding the decentralization of postabortion services. Distinctions must be made between initiatives that seek to decentralize a technology (MVA) and those that develop autonomous centers of locally-based authority for the delivery of health care services. The ability to create policies on costs, commodity supply, personnel, and management systems in support of locally-controlled services is an indication of a decentralized program. The next generation of postabortion operations research studies that examine elements of decentralization will need to pay closer attention to these elements, in addition to the effort to make MVA technology more widely available. The development of sustainable sources of MVA supply in particular requires substantial attention.

Karin Ringheim addresses the ethical conduct of operations research related to postabortion care. She takes as the starting point of her discussion the 1964 Helsinki Declaration, which provided clear guidance on subordinating the interests of science to the welfare of research subjects. A consensus on the nature of ethical standards has evolved to include three fundamental principles: (1) respect for persons, including the right of self-determination of capable individuals and protection of persons with impaired or diminished autonomy; (2) beneficence, which implies an ethical obligation to maximize benefits and minimize harm and also includes the idea of nonmaleficence (or "do no harm"); and (3) justice for research subjects, which is attained through equal treatment of all subjects.

The challenge for operations research is to ensure that both interviewers and service providers adhere to strict ethical guidelines of the sort outlined by Ringheim. The requirements for confidentiality and valid informed consent do not typically draw attention to the importance of interviewer selection and often are not addressed in training programs for data collectors. Indeed, guidelines for the ethical training of interviewers and providers are notably lacking in the field of reproductive health operations research. Several issues are unresolved and poorly documented in the literature. For example, obtaining informed consent is not as straightforward as it may seem. Western, highly individualized language concerning the right to withdraw from a study, the right to refuse to answer questions, and so on is not easily adapted into non-Western, traditional cultural settings. The content of these statements needs to be clarified within each setting, and respondents should review and agree upon procedures to be followed. Supervision and close monitoring of provider–client interactions are necessary to ensure that interviewers and providers adhere to ethical procedures and do not abuse their power to influence and subvert client choice.

The importance of ensuring the ethical treatment of women by service providers is an unexplored area for operations research, where the focus has been on the ethical conduct of data collection activities. As Ringheim states, "Changing a lifetime pattern of paternalism toward women where the provider believes that he or she knows best is not easily accomplished. More particular to the provision of postabortion care is how to alter the hostility and negligence that may await clients, based on providers' negative attitudes toward abortion." These issues come to the fore in the administration of pain control medication, in the ethical necessity for the patient to be able to control her pain treatment, and in the responsibility of the service provider for ensuring that services do not result in physical or mental discomfort, harm, or danger.

The conduct of postabortion operations research with unmarried or adolescent women, which occurs in many settings, poses several ethical considerations particular to such subjects. It may be difficult to convince local providers that these younger women should participate in a study, or, if they do participate, that they have the same rights to informed consent and confidentiality as do older, married women. Attention to these ethical considerations should be increased with these subjects because of their heightened vulnerability to physical or psychological harm if their pregnancy or abortion is disclosed to family members. In some settings adolescents will be more apt to seek care in the private sector so as to ensure confidentiality, creating new challenges for researchers to expand their investigations beyond public-sector systems, as well as to establish the highest ethical standards for both service providers and data collectors.

Taken together, the chapters in this volume are indicative of the growing body of work on postabortion care research. It is hoped that they will be a stimulus to other researchers and clinicians to critically assess their assumptions about the care provided to postabortion patients and their abilities to improve the available services. Although substantial improvements in the medical care and counseling of postabortion patients can be achieved without significant investment of additional resources, these studies reveal the critical role of MVA instruments in the clinical care provided to postabortion patients—both the intrinsic value of the technology and the additional value of bundling improved ancillary clinical practices and interpersonal communication skills around a new surgical instrument. Unfortunately, in most of the studies reported on in this volume MVA instruments were donated, as their commercial availability is constrained by the lack of local regulatory approval. More work is needed to assist in efforts to increase the commercial availability of MVA instruments in developing countries worldwide.

There is a great need for improvement in the care provided to women who have suffered an incomplete abortion, whether it was a spontaneous miscarriage or an induced abortion performed by an unskilled provider in unsafe conditions. It is revealing to note that the quality of the services provided to postabortion patients in the baseline or control group settings in the studies reported on here are by and large substandard and unethical. For too long this essential medical service has been willfully neglected because of the polemics surrounding the abortion debate. These studies effectively demonstrate that improvements can be made to the services provided to postabortion patients without violating local norms or legal restrictions on the provision of induced abortion. It is time to move postabortion care into the mainstream of women's reproductive health care services; the studies in this volume are intended to further that goal.

Note

1 See, for example, B.R. Johnson, J. Benson, J. Bradley, and A. Rabago Ordonez. 1993. "Costs and resource utilization for the treatment of incomplete abortion in Kenya and Mexico," *Social Science and Medicine* 36(11): 1443–1453.

2

Effects of Husband Involvement on Postabortion Patients' Recovery and Use of Contraception in Egypt

Nahla Abdel-Tawab, Dale Huntington,
Ezzeldin Osman Hassan, Hala Youssef,
and Laila Nawar

Population-based studies on the incidence of abortion (spontaneous or induced) are lacking in Egypt, even though evidence suggests that abortion is a common medical procedure. A recent study of the postabortion caseload in Egyptian public-sector hospitals found that one out of every five admissions to the OB/GYN ward was to a postabortion patient (Huntington et al. 1998).

Although the proportion of postabortion patients admitted with serious complications is relatively small, their ability to recuperate after receiving emergency medical treatment is of concern, particularly because of evidence that postabortion patients in Egypt may not be receiving adequate care after hospital discharge.

A study examining psychosocial stress in the postabortion period found that postabortion patients (especially those in rural areas) resume their domestic labor shortly after the procedure (Huntington, Nawar, and Abdel-Hady 1997). Early resumption of hard work interferes with recovery and places a burden on postabortion patients' already compromised health. Moreover, many patients often have to deal with questions and doubts from their husbands or in-laws regarding their ability to conceive again or to carry a pregnancy to term. As a result, some patients may give in to family pressure for another pregnancy soon after their abortion in order to prove their fecundity.

Despite the documented role of husbands as decisionmakers in matters of reproductive health (Abdel-Aziz, El-Zanaty, and Cross 1992; Ali 1995), very little has been done to formally involve husbands in matters related to the health of their wives, particularly in relation to postabortion care. Current health services for postabortion patients seldom give any information to the patients themselves, let alone to their husbands. Studies that measure the effects of husbands' involvement have commonly been conducted in family planning settings. Moreover, most of the past research focused on a self-selected group of husbands who received counseling. Prior to the present study, it was not known in Egypt whether involving husbands would be feasible and acceptable, or whether it would have a positive impact on the health of their spouses.

The study examines the effects of counseling the husbands of postabortion patients on husbands' level of involvement in their spouses' recovery and on patients' recovery and subsequent use of contraception.

Study Hypotheses

The following hypotheses were tested in this study:

- Levels of positive husband involvement in spouses' postabortion recovery will be higher among husbands who receive counseling than among husbands who do not.
- Postabortion patients whose husbands receive counseling will report better physical and psychological recovery one month after discharge from the hospital than patients whose husbands do not receive counseling.
- Contraceptive use or intent to use in the near future, measured one month after discharge, will be higher among postabortion patients whose husbands receive counseling than among patients whose husbands do not.

Study Intervention

The study was conducted in six hospitals in Menia Governorate in southern Egypt. The component on husband counseling was added to an intervention that included improving postabortion clinical services through using manual vacuum aspiration (MVA), improving case management procedures, and enhancing counseling for postabortion patients (Nawar et al. 1997a).

Content of Counseling for Husbands

The counseling of husbands emphasized the important role they can play in their wives' recovery and in the adoption of a family planning method during the postabortion period. Although the manner in which this information was transmitted varied, each husband received, at the minimum, a "health education" message (although physicians were encouraged to have more lengthy exchanges with husbands). These messages were on the following five topics: (1) patient's need for rest and adequate nutrition (emphasizing inexpensive nutritious food); (2) postabortion warning signs indicating need for follow-up care; (3) the possibility of a return to fertility within two weeks; (4) the need for family planning to avoid unwanted or poorly timed pregnancy; and (5) cause of the miscarriage (if appropriate) and source of referral care (if necessary). Because abortion is illegal in Egypt, no attempt was made to differentiate between cases of spontaneous or induced abortion.

Procedures for Counseling Husbands

All postabortion patients received improved medical care and complete counseling about their health condition and family planning. Counseling of patients and husbands was done separately. This decision was based on findings from previous studies that showed women felt less free to ask questions or express concerns in the presence of their husbands (Kim and Awasum 1996). Counseling of husbands was done by the attending physician when the patient was ready to leave the hospital. Because of the sensitive nature of abortion and the possibility that by involving the husband he might gain information about his wife's medical condition that could pose a risk to the woman (e.g., a husband might learn that his wife induced the abortion without his knowledge or that she concealed her pregnancy from him), considerable attention was devoted to establishing strict ethical guidelines and procedures (Abdel-Tawab, Huntington, and

Nawar 1997). Counseling was given only to husbands of consenting patients. The following enrollment procedure was developed through extensive pretesting to ensure protection of patient privacy while maximizing the number of husbands who would receive the intervention.

Procedures on patient admission. If the patient was brought to the hospital by her husband, the nurse in charge asked him to return at discharge to pick up and assist his wife. Husbands did not receive counseling at this point; they were counseled only after the patient's consent was obtained.

Obtaining patient's informed consent. The nurse in charge sought the patient's permission to have the doctor speak to her husband about her medical condition. The nurse read a standardized consent statement to the patient after she had received complete medical treatment (including counseling) and only after it was determined that she was in stable physical and emotional condition.

Contacting the husband. The pilot test of the informed consent procedures showed that family members often go back and forth to the patient's home while she is in the hospital. Thus it was relatively easy to contact those husbands who did not accompany the patient at admission. Patients who agreed to have their husbands counseled were asked to tell their relatives or companions, who were already at the hospital, to send for the husband to pick her up at discharge.

Procedures at discharge. The attending physician commonly signs the discharge forms and gives the patient any remaining instructions for postabortion care. If the patient had agreed to have her husband counseled and if the husband was present at discharge, the nurse would ensure that he met with the physician. In all cases husbands received counseling by the attending physician in private, away from their wives.

Training Providers on Procedures for Counseling Husbands

Thirty physicians (five from each hospital) received one day of orientation on the content and procedures for counseling the husbands of postabortion patients. The orientation was done in conjunction with training for the "scaling-up" intervention already in place, which included training on use of MVA and basic patient counseling (Nawar et al. 1997b). The orientation strategy focused on creating a cadre of supervisors who would then train their colleagues and provide daily on-site supervision and follow-up for a period of three months.

Research Methodology

Study Design

A true experimental, posttest-only control group design (Campbell and Stanley 1963) was used to measure the effects of counseling husbands on their level of involvement in matters related to their spouses' health and, by consequence, on their wives' recovery and use of contraceptive methods. Consenting postabortion patients were randomly assigned to either an intervention or a control group. Husbands in the intervention group received counseling about the medical condition of their wives. Husbands in the control group did not receive such counseling (although their wives did receive improved postabortion medical care and counseling). A follow-up interview was conducted with both groups of patients one month after hospital discharge to assess their physical and psychological recovery and to determine whether they were currently using or intended to use contraception in the near future. The 30-day period was deemed sufficient to measure the effects of counseling on recovery and immediate postabortion contraceptive use, although it was considered too short to investigate medium- and long-term morbidity or the attainment of other reproductive intentions.

Study Sample

The sample size was initially estimated at 220 couples from each group (intervention and control) to account for losses to follow-up, statistical significance tests, and budget considerations. All consenting postabortion patients who were admitted to the study hospitals during a two-month enrollment period were eligible for the study; this length of time was anticipated to be sufficient for the enrollment of the desired sample of patients.

Variables and Measurement

Independent variable. The principal independent variable is whether or not the husband received counseling regarding his wife's medical condition. This was determined by the physician's signature on the patient discharge form attesting that counseling was provided.

Intervening or mediating variables. The effects of counseling husbands on their wives' recovery is assumed to be mediated by the degree to which counseling translates into husbands' support. The study measures husband support as perceived by wives (i.e., based on patients' self-reports), which may or may not be the same as that perceived by the husbands or a third person.

A review of relevant literature, consultations with experts in the field, and exploratory studies revealed two broad dimensions of improved husband support: instrumental and emotional support. Preliminary analysis of the two indexes used to measure these two dimensions, however, revealed that they were moderately correlated (r=0.29). Confirmatory factor analysis was conducted in which items from the two indexes were pooled together to explore patterning of the data. Rotated factor analysis revealed a third factor, family planning support, that had been initially contained within the emotional support index. Separated out, these three indexes of husband support (instrumental, emotional, and family planning) were less correlated with one another (r=0.143) (i.e., more independent and with greater internal consistency reliability for each index).[1] Items included in each index are shown in Table 2.1.

The index for instrumental support measured the degree of tangible or material support provided by husbands. The index tapped indicators of help provided by husbands in buying and preparing food for the patient and assisting with various household activities. The index had five items and an internal consistency reliability of 0.77.

The emotional support index measured the husband's reaction to the lost pregnancy, as well as his understanding of his wife's physical and emotional needs as reported by the patient herself. The index had eight items and an internal consistency reliability of 0.86.

TABLE 2.1
Items on instrumental, emotional, and family planning support indexes

Instrumental support index
- My husband buys nutritious food for me
- My husband helps prepare food for me
- My husband encourages me to stay in bed
- My husband prepares hot drinks for me
- My husband helps with cleaning the house

Emotional support index
- My husband was more concerned about my health than about the lost pregnancy
- My husband was willing to skip his work and stay with me
- My husband encouraged me to make a follow-up visit
- My husband reassured me about my health
- My husband was angry at me because I lost this pregnancy
- My husband was upset because we had to postpone sex
- My husband could not understand how exhausted I was
- I could not tell my husband how I was feeling

Family planning support index
- My husband would not let me use a family planning method
- I can talk freely with my husband about family planning
- My husband would let me choose any family planning method that I want
- My husband would agree to go with me to the family planning clinic
- My husband and I are in agreement with regard to family planning
- My husband encourages me to take a break from pregnancy and childbirth

The family planning support index measured aspects of family planning support by the husband, such as approval of his wife's use of family planning, openness to discussions about family planning with his wife, and willingness to accompany his wife to the family planning clinic. The index had six items and an internal consistency reliability of 0.85.

Dependent variables. The two principal dependent variables for the study are improved patient recovery and contraceptive use.

Three dimensions of the patient's health were measured to examine patient recovery: physical, emotional, and social health. Separate indexes were constructed for each dimension, using the same development process described above to identify the items on each index, followed by confirmatory factor analysis.

Physical health was measured through a "weakness index," which identified physical health problems that the patient might be having one month after her discharge from the hospital. Patients were asked whether they were having any of the following symptoms: fatigue, shortness of breath, or headache/dizziness. They were also asked whether they were having difficulty performing activities such as walking, standing, housework, and so forth. The index had eight items and an internal consistency reliability of 0.88. A high score on the weakness index was indicative of poor physical recovery.

Postabortion patients' emotional health status was assessed through the Psychological Distress Index (PDI), adapted from the Grief Scale developed by Peppers and Knapp (1980). Patients were presented with a list of emotional symptoms such as sleep difficulty, loss of appetite, anxiety, and so forth, and were asked to indicate whether they had experienced any of those symptoms in the past three days. The index had eight items and an internal consistency reliability of 0.88. A high PDI score indicated poor emotional recovery.

An index was constructed that included items on the patient's resumption of social activities such as talking with her husband about his work, visiting friends, resumption of sexual relations, and relations with her children. The index had a very low internal consistency reliability and was therefore dropped from subsequent analysis.

The second class of dependent variables that were measured in this study concerned contraceptive use. Respondents were asked whether they were currently using a family planning method. Those who said they were not were asked whether and when they intended to begin using a family planning method.

Control variables. Because of the potential effect of a great number of factors on husband involvement, patient recovery, or use of contraception, the study identified several control variables and utilized them in the analysis. The variables measured included patient's and husband's characteristics, husband–wife relationship characteristics, patient's medical characteristics, and characteristics of the index pregnancy. An autonomy index was used to measure husband–wife relations, composed of five items that measured the wife's ability to make a solitary decision on each of the following: visiting a neighbor, visiting her parents, going out with a friend, visiting the doctor, and choosing meals for the family. The patient's medical characteristics included presence of abortion complications as well as any preexisting medical conditions such as hypertension, kidney disease, parasitic disease, and so forth. With the exception of information on the patient's medical characteristics, which was collected by the discharging physician, information about all other control variables was collected at the home interview with the patient.

Characteristics of the hospital where the patient was treated was another control variable measured in the study. The six study hospitals were divided into two groups: Group A and Group B hospitals (three in each group). Group A hospitals were generally smaller (i.e., they had fewer physicians) and therefore a larger proportion of physicians in those hospitals were exposed to the training and orientation. It was expected that even with the study's monitoring and supervision visits, performance of physicians from Group A hospitals would be somewhat better than that of those from Group B hospitals.

Data Collection Activities

Patient enrollment and randomization. A patient who agreed to participate in the study was asked her full name and address for the follow-up interview. Patients who preferred to have their follow-up interview outside their homes were asked to come back to the hospital on an assigned date and time. A special logbook was used for randomization purposes. Access to this logbook was strictly controlled. Patients with an even log number were assigned to the intervention group while those with an odd number were assigned to the control group (i.e., every second consenting patient was assigned to the intervention group). Three or four nurses in each of the participating hospitals were in charge of patient enrollment and randomization procedures.

At discharge, an attending physician gave the patient instructions regarding her health condition and information on family planning and also documented on the patient's discharge form any complications or preexisting medical conditions. If the patient was in the intervention group, a nurse arranged for the meeting to take place between the physician and the husband. The physician then indicated that the counseling had taken place and provided basic sociodemographic information about him/herself, including age, medical degrees, and position.

TABLE 2.2
Patients who participated in study: Enrollment, attrition, and completion

Patients	Intervention group	Control group	(n)	Percentage
Completed the study	136	157	293	80
Husband did not show up at discharge	45	—	45	12
Husband away for entire month	1	14	15	4
Lost to follow-up	6	7	13	4
Total no. of patients agreeing to participate	188	178	366	100

Follow-up interviews. Follow-up interviews were conducted with patients in the intervention and control groups one month after discharge from the hospital. Unless the patient indicated a preference to have the interview at the hospital, follow-up interviews were conducted at patients' homes. To the extent that it was feasible, patients were visited 30 days after their discharge. If the patient was not available, revisits were made to her home, with a maximum of three callback visits within a four-day period. Five trained female interviewers conducted the follow-up interviews with patients. Interviewers were blinded as to the research group (i.e., intervention or control) to which the respondent belonged.

Results

Patients and Husbands Recruited for the Study

Of 381 postabortion patients who were admitted to the postabortion wards during the two months of data collection and who were approached for the study, 366 patients agreed to participate, yielding a refusal rate of 3.9 percent.

Table 2.2 shows the proportion of patients who completed the study and patients who were lost at different stages of the study; 12 percent of the patients who agreed to participate were excluded because their husbands did not show up at discharge and therefore did not receive counseling. Only patients in the intervention group were excluded from the study if the husband did not show up at discharge; 24 husbands of patients in the control group also did not show up at discharge (data not shown).

The following were reasons given for the husband's absence as explained by patients in the control group during the follow-up interview: husband out of town when the abortion happened (20 cases), husband arrived at hospital after patient's discharge (3 cases), husband was too busy at work (1 case). Unfortunately, similar information about husbands in the intervention group is lacking.

Very few patients were lost to follow-up (4 percent) and hence did not complete the follow-up interview. None of the patients who requested to have their follow-up interview at the hospital showed up on the assigned date and they were therefore lost to follow-up. Fifteen patients completed the follow-up interview but were later excluded from the analysis because their husbands were absent for the entire month of recovery. Thus the final sample was composed of 293 patients, 136 in the intervention group and 157 in the control group.

Patients' and Husbands' Characteristics

Table 2.3 shows that postabortion patients who participated in the study were more likely to be younger than 25 years or in their 30s, had little or no schooling, and had three or more living children. Forty-five percent of the patients reported previous use of contraception and 61 percent indicated a desire for more children in the future. According to 39 percent of the patients, the lost pregnancy was planned. Forty-three percent of patients said they lost their pregnancy at a gestational age of 12 weeks or higher. Seventy-seven percent of patients reported experiencing at least one complication such as excessive bleeding, fever, or offensive discharge during the 30-day recovery period. Sixty-five percent of patients were treated in a hospital that was classified in this study as Group B (i.e., a larger hospital with a smaller proportion of physicians who received direct training and orientation). On the patient autonomy index, the majority of patients scored a medium score (20–59 points out of 100).

Fifty-three percent of husbands of postabortion patients were 35 years or older and 63 percent had little or no schooling. Slightly more than half of the studied couples lived in a nuclear family setting (55 per-

TABLE 2.3
Percent distribution of selected sociodemographic and medical characteristics of postabortion patients and their husbands

Characteristic	Intervention (n=136)	Control (n=157)	Total (n=293)
Patient			
Age (years)			
<25	37	38	38
25–29	28	26	23
≥30	35	36	39
Education			
No school/less than primary	79	83	81
Primary or higher	21	17	19
No. of living children			
0	24	22	23
1–2	32	27	29
≥3	44	51	48
Preexisting medical conditions			
Yes	2	7	5
Gestational age of lost pregnancy*			
<8 weeks	14	20	17
8–11 weeks	48	30	39
≥12 weeks	38	48	43
Not known	0	2	1
Index pregnancy was planned			
Yes	37	40	39
Ever use of contraception			
Yes	46	45	45
Desire for more children			
Yes	62	60	61
Complications during recovery			
One or more	74	79	77
Hospital			
Group A	34	36	35
Group B	66	64	65
Autonomy level[a]			
Low	21	13	17
Medium	57	64	61
High	22	23	22

* $p<0.01$.

[a] The autonomy index range was 0–100. Scores were classified into <20, 20–59, ≥60 to denote low, medium, and high autonomy, respectively.

(continued)

cent) while the remainder lived with parents or in-laws. The majority of couples who participated in the study lived in rural areas (76 percent).

Table 2.3 shows that patients in the intervention and control groups were comparable on most of the above characteristics. However, patients in the control group were more likely to have lost the index pregnancy at

TABLE 2.3 ***(continued)***

Characteristic	Intervention (n=136)	Control (n=157)	Total (n=293)
Husband			
Age			
<30	28	27	28
30–34	20	19	19
≥35	52	54	53
Education			
No school/less than primary	62	64	63
Primary/preparatory	13	16	15
Secondary/college	25	20	22
Household composition			
Nuclear	50	59	55
Extended	50	41	45
Residence			
Urban	21	27	24
Rural	79	73	76

12 or more weeks than patients in the intervention group, who were more likely to have lost it between 8 and 11 weeks. This difference is statistically significant.

Support Given by Husbands During Recovery

The study posits that counseling will lead to greater involvement by husbands, which, in turn, will positively affect their spouses' recovery. The intervening variable, husband involvement, is operationalized through an expression of greater instrumental, emotional, and family planning support by the husband. This section presents the results of the intervening variable—the indicator of how the study's intervention was translated into action by the husbands. It also examines the effects of the control variables on these demonstrable actions as a prelude to investigating the impact of the intervention on the two dependent variables.

Figure 2.1 shows mean levels of the different types of support provided by husbands of postabortion patients. On average, husbands in the two groups provided a higher level of emotional and family planning support than instrumental support to their wives (mean 83, 65, and 17, respectively). Bivariate analysis showed no differences between the intervention and the control with regard to the degree of support provided by husbands.

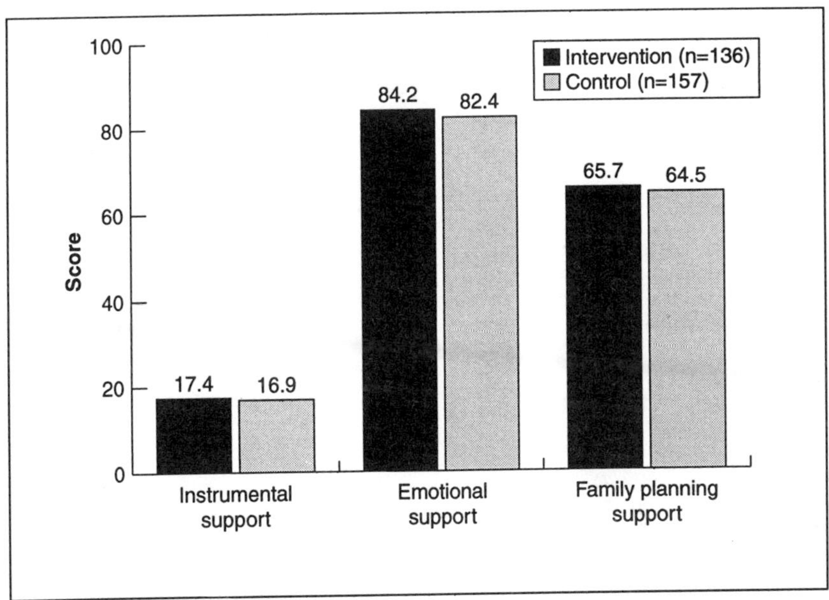

FIGURE 2.1 Mean score on three indexes of support provided by husbands of postabortion patients

Because of the relatively small sample size and skewness of observations, respondents were classified into two groups depending on the level of support provided by husbands (i.e., below mean corresponds to low support; above mean corresponds to high support). Logistic regression analysis was conducted to measure the association between counseling of husbands and each type of support provided, after controlling for potential confounders. A hierarchical modeling technique was used to enter variables into the model. Counseling of husbands was entered first and then other variables were entered for forward selection with alpha set at 1.0.

Table 2.4 shows that after adjusting for other patient characteristics, counseling of husbands was associated with an increase in the likelihood that the husband will provide high instrumental, emotional, or family planning support to his wife during recovery. Counseling was associated with a greater increase in family planning and instrumental support than emotional support. Other factors associated with increased instrumental support by the husband were: living in a nuclear family arrangement, patient's experience of complications during recovery, and higher education of the husband (i.e., secondary or above). Interestingly, receiving coun-

TABLE 2.4
Logistic regression analysis of variables associated with high level of instrumental, emotional, and family planning support provided by husbands[a] (n=293)

Variable	Adjusted odds ratio	90% confidence interval
Instrumental support[b]		
Household composition (nuclear)	2.6	1.7, 4.0
Complications during recovery (yes)	1.8	1.1, 3.2
Husband's education (secondary or above)	1.7	1.0, 2.5
Husband counseled (yes)	1.5	0.9, 2.4
Group A hospital and husband counseled (yes)	0.5	0.2, 0.9
Emotional support[c]		
Index pregnancy planned (yes)	2.8	1.8, 5.0
No. of living children (≥3)	2.0	1.2, 3.3
Husband and wife blood relatives (yes)	1.9	1.2, 2.9
Husband counseled (yes)	1.3	0.8, 1.9
Family planning support[d]		
Desire for more children (no)	5.0	2.5, 10.0
Husband's education (secondary or above)	2.5	1.4, 5.0
No. of living children (≥3)	2.5	1.4, 5.0
Group A hospital	1.7	1.1, 2.7
Husband counseled (yes)	1.6	1.1, 2.6

a Logistic regression analysis was used to measure association between counseling of husbands and each type of support after controlling for other patient characteristics. Dependent variable in each model was high level of that dimension of husband support.

b Reference categories are: couple lives with in-laws/parents, patient did not experience complications during recovery, husband completed less than secondary education, husband did not receive counseling, patient was admitted to Group B hospital and husband did not receive counseling.

c Reference categories are: index pregnancy was not planned, patient has fewer than 3 living children, husband and wife are not blood relatives, husband did not receive counseling.

d Reference categories are: patient wants more children in the future, husband completed less than secondary education, patient has fewer than 3 living children, patient was admitted to Group B hospital, husband did not receive counseling.

seling in a Group A hospital (i.e., a smaller hospital with more trained physicians) was associated with decreased instrumental support by husbands.

Emotional support by husbands was less likely to be affected by counseling than by patient and husband characteristics. Husbands were more likely to provide emotional support to their wives if the index pregnancy was planned. Patients who had three or more living children were more likely to receive emotional support from their husbands than patients with fewer children. Also, when patients and their husbands were blood relatives husbands were more likely to provide emotional support to their wives.

Husbands' support of family planning was mostly determined by the couple's demographic characteristics. When a couple did not want

TABLE 2.5
Logistic regression analysis of variables associated with good physical recovery of postabortion patients[a] (n=293)

Variable	Adjusted odds ratio	90% confidence interval
Emotional support by husband (high)	1.7	1.1, 2.6
Husband counseled (yes)	1.3	0.8, 2.0
Instrumental support by husband (high)	1.1	0.7, 1.7
Complications during recovery (yes)	0.2	0.1, 0.3

a Reference categories are: low level of emotional support by husband, husband did not receive counseling, low level of instrumental support by husband, patient did not experience complications during recovery.

more children in the future, the husband was five times more likely to provide family planning support to his wife than if the couple wanted more children. Also, if the couple had three or more living children, the husband was 2.5 times more likely to provide family planning support to his wife. Husbands with secondary or higher education were more likely to provide family planning support than husbands with fewer years of schooling. Patients who were treated in smaller Group A hospitals were 1.7 times more likely to receive family planning support from their husbands than patients who were treated in larger Group B hospitals.

Outcomes of Counseling

This section reviews the results of the two outcome indicators: patient's recovery and use of contraception.

Physical recovery. The aforementioned weakness index measured patients' physical recovery one month after discharge. Patients scoring less than 7 out of 14 on the weakness index were considered as having experienced good physical recovery while those with a score of 7 or above were considered to have poor physical recovery.

Table 2.5 shows results of logistic regression analysis of variables associated with good physical recovery. The variables husband counseled, instrumental support, and emotional support were entered first, then the following variables were entered for forward selection: gestational age, hospital group, experience of complications during recovery, number of

TABLE 2.6
Logistic regression analysis of variables associated with good emotional recovery of postabortion patients[a] (n=293)

Variable	Adjusted odds ratio	90% confidence interval
Patient's education (no school/less than primary)	2.5	1.4, 4.3
Emotional support by husband (high)	2.0	1.3, 3.0
Index pregnancy planned (yes)	1.7	1.1, 2.6
Husband counseled (yes)	1.0	0.6, 1.4
Complications during recovery (yes)	0.4	0.2, 0.7
Patient's autonomy index score		
Low	0.4	0.2, 0.8
Medium	1.0	0.6, 1.7

a Reference categories are: patient completed primary or higher education, low level of emotional support by husband, index pregnancy was not planned, husband did not receive counseling, patient did not experience complications during recovery, patient scored high (≥60) on autonomy index.

living children, and interaction between counseling of husband and hospital group. Interestingly, a high level of emotional support by the husband was significantly associated with improved physical recovery by the patient, whereas instrumental support by the husband was not. The strongest predictor of physical recovery, however, was absence of any complications during convalescence. Patients who experienced complications were five times less likely to report physical recovery than patients who did not experience complications.

Emotional recovery. The aforementioned Psychological Distress Index showed that slightly more than half of the study patients (53 percent) did not report any emotional symptoms, hence were considered as having experienced good emotional recovery. Table 2.6 shows results of logistic regression analysis of variables associated with good emotional recovery. The variables husband counseled and emotional support were entered first. The following variables were entered for forward selection (alpha=0.1): number of living children, desire for more children, whether index pregnancy was planned, patient's educational level, patient's autonomy level, experience of complications during recovery, hospital group, and interaction between hospital group and husband counseled.

As shown in the table, a positive association exists between emotional support by the husband and good emotional recovery. Patients who reported receiving a high level of emotional support from their husbands were twice as likely to experience good emotional recovery. Two additional variables were associated with improved emotional recovery: patients with little or no education and patients reporting that the index pregnancy was planned. Two variables were negatively associated with good emotional recovery: low level of patient autonomy and patient's experience of complications during recovery.

Family planning use. The second outcome indicator examined in this study was family planning practice. By the end of the one-month follow-up period, 14.7 percent of women reported having started using contraception. An additional 34.5 percent of patients said they were planning to use contraception within one month. Because of the small number of observations of patients in the first category, subsequent analysis combined the two groups into one, for a total of 49.2 percent of postabortion patients.

Logistic regression analysis was conducted to determine association between patient's use of family planning and counseling of husbands and degree of family planning support, while controlling for potential confounders. The following variables were entered into the model for forward selection: number of living children, desire for more children, patient's age, previous use of contraception, whether index pregnancy was planned, patient's experience of complications during recovery, hospital group, and interaction between hospital group and counseling of husband.

Table 2.7 shows that after controlling for other variables, husband support of family planning is highly predictive of contraceptive use or intention to use. Other variables that were predictive of use of contraception were previous use of family planning, husband receiving counseling at a Group A hospital, and couples with three or more children. On the other hand, if the index pregnancy was planned, the patient was less likely to use or to intend to use a family planning method in the near future.

Discussion

The study was the first to test an intervention for counseling the husbands of postabortion patients in Egypt. Its primary aim was to examine

TABLE 2.7
Logistic regression analysis of variables associated with use of or intention to use family planning by postabortion patients[a] (n=293)

Variable	Adjusted odds ratio	90% confidence interval
Family planning support by husband (high)	5.9	3.5, 10.0
Group A hospital and husband counseled (yes)	3.8	1.5, 9.4
Previous use of family planning (yes)	3.5	1.7, 5.6
No. of living children (≥3)	2.5	1.4, 5.0
Husband counseled (yes)	0.6	0.3, 1.2
Index pregnancy planned (yes)	0.4	0.2, 0.7

a Reference categories are: low level of family planning support by husband, patient was admitted to Group B hospital and husband did not receive counseling, patient has not used family planning before, patient has fewer than 3 living children, husband did not receive counseling, index pregnancy was not planned.

the effects of counseling on husbands' behavior and on postabortion patients' recovery and use of contraception. Other issues addressed included the feasibility of counseling husbands and of conducting follow-up assessments of postabortion patients while protecting their rights to privacy.

Overall the study findings show a positive association between counseling husbands and their involvement in their spouses' recovery. On average, patients in the two study groups received more emotional and family planning support than instrumental support from their husbands. Because the study was conducted in a traditional society, where men are often discouraged from participating in what are perceived as women's activities, this result is expected. It is interesting to note, however, that husbands were more likely to provide instrumental support to their wives when the couple lived within a nuclear family, implying that husbands are willing to help if no other women are available to provide such support.

The results show that support by husbands is crucial for patients' recovery and use of contraception. Emotional support by husbands is particularly important for women's physical and emotional recovery. Family planning support by husbands is the strongest predictor of family planning use by the patient. These findings are in agreement with those documented in the literature on the health effects of social support (Cohen and Syme 1985). The family planning literature also documents an association between husbands' support of family planning and adoption and continuation of contraception (Joesoef, Baughman, and Utomo 1988; Terefe and Larson 1993).

Also supported is the primary hypothesis of the study that counseling of husbands will result in positive changes in their behavior, which in turn will lead to better patient outcomes. Counseling of husbands is most likely to influence patient outcomes through changes in husbands' level of involvement.

Program managers in Egypt should consider including counseling of husbands as part of the medical services provided to postabortion patients. The content of counseling should highlight the importance of emotional and family planning support, because these two dimensions of support were associated with better patient outcomes. Counseling should be more vigorous with husbands of patients who are otherwise less likely to receive support from their husbands. According to the findings of this study these include patients with fewer living children and those with husbands who have less education. It is important that providers establish two-way communication during counseling in order to identify husband groups who are less likely to provide support to their wives.

The study also shows that counseling of husbands is associated with better outcomes in some hospitals than in others. This clearly suggests that having senior and better-trained staff provide the counseling leads to a stronger impact on husbands' behavior. It also suggests that the two-tiered system (training of trainers) may not be as effective as direct training of all service providers, although, obviously, the former is less expensive. It would have been helpful if counseling sessions were observed directly so that variations in quality of counseling given in different hospital groups could be ascertained.

Some administrative and logistic changes may be needed in each hospital in order to make counseling of husbands more feasible and effective. The current set-up in OB/GYN wards may need to be changed to make the hospital environment more husband-friendly and to encourage husbands to accompany their wives to the hospital. Providing family planning services at the OB/GYN ward would make it easier for couples to obtain a family planning method before discharge and hence translate their family planning intentions into action.

A final caveat needs to be made. Counseling of husbands should not be seen as a substitute for counseling of patients, but rather as an additional service for those patients who choose to involve their husbands. In future attempts to add counseling of husbands to the medical care of postabortion patients, mandatory precautions should be in place to protect patients' privacy.

Study Limitations and Recommendations for Future Research

The present study was conducted in one governorate in Upper Egypt. While one could argue that the patients and husbands who participated are not very different from those in other parts of the country, a study that examines regional variations on the effects of husband counseling is warranted. Another limitation relates to a potential selection bias concerning husbands who participated in the intervention group. Excluding from the study husbands who did not come to the hospital for their wives' discharge may have led to an exaggeration of the positive impact of the intervention, as these excluded husbands may in fact have been less caring toward their wives. On the other hand, these husbands, like their counterparts in the control group, may have been absent due to travel or other compelling reasons. It would be instructive to replicate this study in other parts of Egypt using a larger sample of postabortion patients and their husbands.

Acknowledgments

The study was a collaboration between the Population Council's Asia and Near East Operations Research and Technical Assistance Project in Cairo and the Egyptian Fertility Care Society. The study was conducted with funds from the United States Agency for International Development. We acknowledge with special thanks the support of senior officials at the Ministry of Health and Population and National Population Council in Egypt. The contributions made by the field coordinators and hospital staff in Menia Governorate were crucial for the conduct of this study. Special thanks are due to the patients and husbands who participated in the study. We are also grateful to our colleagues in the New York office for their helpful comments and suggestions on the study proposal and during implementation.

Note

1 Internal consistency reliability measures the degree of correlation among individual items in an index. Values close to 1.0 denote greater correlation among items (Green and Lewis 1986).

References

Abdel-Aziz, H., F. El-Zanaty, and A. Cross. 1992. *Egypt Male Survey, 1991.* Calverton, Md.: Demographic and Health Surveys/Macro International.

Abdel-Tawab, N., D. Huntington, and L. Nawar. 1997. "Ethical considerations in studying the effects of counseling the husbands of postabortion patients in Egypt," paper presented at 125th American Public Health Association Meeting, Indianapolis, Ind., 9–13 November.

Ali, K. 1995. "Notes on rethinking masculinities: An Egyptian case," in *Learning About Sexuality: A Practical Beginning,* eds. S. Zeidenstein and K. Moore. New York: Population Council, pp. 98–109.

Campbell, D. and J. Stanley. 1963. *Experimental and Quasi-Experimental Designs for Research.* Boston, Mass.: Houghton Mifflin Co.

Cohen, S. and S.L. Syme. 1985. *Social Support and Health.* Orlando, Fla.: Academic Press.

Green, L. and F. Lewis. 1986. *Measurement and Evaluation in Health Education and Health Promotion.* Palo Alto, Calif.: Mayfield Publishing Company.

Huntington, D., L. Nawar, and D. Abdel-Hady. 1997. "Women's perceptions of abortion in Egypt," *Reproductive Health Matters* 9: 101–107.

Huntington, D., L. Nawar, E.O. Hassan, H. Youssef, and N. Abdel-Tawab. 1998. "Postabortion caseload study in Egyptian hospitals," *International Family Planning Perspectives* 24(1): 25–31.

Joesoef, M., B. Baughman, and B. Utomo. 1988. "Husbands approval of contraceptive use in metropolitan Indonesia: Program implications," *Studies in Family Planning,* 19: 162–168.

Kim, Y.M. and D. Awasum. 1996. "What are the particular aspects of counseling male family planning clients? Case from Kenya," paper presented at the Men and Reproductive Health Task Force Workshop, 124th Annual Meeting of APHA, New York, N.Y., 17–21 November.

Nawar, L., D. Huntington, E.O. Hassan, N. Abdel-Tawab, and H. Youssef. 1997a. "Expanding improved postabortion care in Egypt is underway," paper presented at the 23rd IUSSP General Population Conference, Beijing, China, 11–17 October.

Nawar, L., D. Huntington, E.O. Hassan, H. Youssef, and N. Abdel-Tawab. 1997b. *Scaling-up Improved Postabortion Care in Egypt: Introduction to University and Ministry of Health and Population Hospitals.* Cairo, Egypt: Population Council Asia and Near East Operations Research and Technical Assistance Project.

Peppers, L. and R. Knapp. 1980. "Maternal reaction to involuntary fetal/infant death," *Psychiatry* 43: 155.

Terefe, A. and C. Larson. 1993. "Modern contraception use in Ethiopia: Does involving husbands make a difference?" *American Journal of Public Health* 83: 1567–1571.

3

Creating Linkages Between Incomplete Abortion Treatment and Family Planning Services in Kenya

Julie Solo, Deborah L. Billings,
Colette Aloo-Obunga, Achola Ominde,
and Margaret Makumi

Unsafe abortion constitutes a major public health problem throughout the world. Approximately 20 million women undergo unsafe abortions every year (WHO 1994). Unsafe abortion is defined by the World Health Organization as a procedure for terminating an unwanted pregnancy either by persons lacking necessary skills or in an environment lacking the minimal medical standards, or both (WHO 1993). The phrase "unsafe abortion" also refers to the inappropriate management of complications caused by spontaneous abortion or miscarriage. Approximately 70,000 women die annually from complications related to unsafe abortion (WHO 1994), making it one of the five main causes of maternal mortality.

In Kenya, as throughout the world, the health consequences of unsafe abortion for women of reproductive age are significant. Access to abortion is severely restricted in Kenya and is legally permitted only when it is necessary to save the life of the woman. Hospital-based studies in Nairobi have shown that unsafely induced abortion accounts for as much as 35 percent of maternal mortality and at least 50 percent of hospitals' gynecological admissions (Lema, Kamau, and Rogo 1989; Rogo 1993). These figures underestimate the true extent of the problem, however, because they represent only those women who are able to reach public hospitals for treatment; women who seek services from private providers or through other means are excluded from these estimates, as are women who do not seek or who lack access to services.

What these numbers represent are individual women, each with her own story. The following accounts from the study's in-depth interviews illustrate some of the circumstances that can lead to a woman's arriving at a hospital with an incomplete abortion, as well as some of the challenges of providing appropriate and effective services:

> A 20-year-old unmarried woman who was a farmer came to the hospital after an induced abortion. It had been her first pregnancy. She had a regular partner, but did not want to have children until she was married. When she arrived at the hospital, her cervix was torn because a quack had used scissors to perform the abortion. Asked why she was not using a family planning method at the time she became pregnant, she said that whenever she asked her boyfriend to use a condom, he bought a sweet and asked her to eat it with the wrapper on. This, he said, is the same way he would feel if he had sex with a condom on. She was afraid to use the pill because she thought it could make her barren.

> A 30-year-old married woman with four children came to the hospital after experiencing a miscarriage, her second one that year. She was emphatic that she did not want any more children. She had not wanted this last pregnancy, but her husband had insisted on having another child. She believed that her miscarriage resulted from her looking after her youngest child (19 months old), who had been continuously ill. She was determined to leave the hospital with a method and even requested that the providers talk to her husband and convince him that she should be discharged with a method, preferably tubal ligation.

Following the international endorsement of postabortion care at the International Conference on Population and Development (ICPD) in Cairo in 1994, the concept of postabortion care has gained wide acceptance as one way to improve services provided to women with complications from spontaneous or unsafely induced abortions, to help break the cycle of repeat abortions, and to help to reduce maternal morbidity and mortality. It consists of three elements (Greenslade et al. 1994): (1) emergency treatment for complications of spontaneous or unsafely induced abortion; (2) postabortion family planning counseling and services; and

(3) linkage of emergency abortion treatment services and comprehensive reproductive health care.

One way to improve emergency treatment, the first element of postabortion care, is through the introduction of manual vacuum aspiration (MVA), a technique that has been shown to be safer and less costly than dilation and curettage (D&C) (Baird, Gringle, and Greenslade 1995). Providing the second element, postabortion family planning, enables women to avoid repeated unwanted pregnancies and therefore also to avoid unsafely induced abortions. It allows women who have had spontaneous abortions a period of rest and waiting before their next pregnancy, should they want or need such rest. Anecdotal evidence and empirical data from this study illustrate the high prevalence of repeat abortions; almost one-fourth (24 percent) of women interviewed for this study had experienced previous pregnancy losses. Linking postabortion care (PAC) services to other reproductive health care services, such as management of sexually transmitted infections, improves women's health. Currently, linkages among the PAC components are rarely found in health care settings in most of the world.

Providers and policymakers in Kenya have been active in implementing PAC services since 1989, although most work has focused on introducing MVA to improve treatment services. In an effort to expand PAC activities to incorporate the second element—postabortion family planning—into its services, the Ministry of Health (MOH) supported the project presented in this chapter to determine the most effective, feasible, and acceptable way to deliver postabortion family planning counseling and methods in a hospital setting. The recently revised reproductive health guidelines of the MOH include a section on postabortion care, emphasizing the importance of providing counseling and services to postabortion patients (MOH, Kenya 1997b).

Study Design

The Population Council's Africa Operations Research and Technical Assistance (OR/TA) Project II, the Kenyan MOH, and Ipas collaborated on a study to test different ways of providing improved PAC services, includ-

TABLE 3.1
Postabortion family planning models tested, by hospital: Kenya, 1996–97

Model	Site
Model 1: FP services provided on the gynecological ward by ward staff	Coast Provincial General Hospital, Mombasa; New Nyanza Provincial General Hospital, Kisumu
Model 2: FP services provided on the gynecological ward by MCH/FP staff	Nakuru Provincial General Hospital; Meru District Hospital
Model 3: FP services provided in MCH/FP clinic by MCH/FP staff	Eldoret District Hospital; Nyeri Provincial General Hospital

MCH/FP=maternal and child health/family planning.

ing creating linkages between incomplete abortion treatment and family planning services. In addition to improving emergency treatment through either the introduction or upgrading of MVA services, three different models of providing postabortion family planning were tested, as illustrated in Table 3.1. These three models varied by where services were offered and by who provided the services.

This study aimed to test and compare the feasibility, acceptability, quality, and effectiveness of the three models, with each model being introduced and implemented at two hospitals. The goal of all of the models was to make postabortion family planning services more accessible to women immediately after treatment and before discharge from the hospital. These models were designed for Kenyan MOH hospitals, all of which have maternal and child health/family planning (MCH/FP) clinics on site. These clinics, however, are generally distant from the gynecological wards, and no formal linkages exist between the two units. Each model had different potential benefits: In Model 1, the distance between services is bridged, and the same provider can be responsible for all aspects of a patient's management; in Model 2, the distance is bridged, and providers with family planning experience can provide the services; and in Model 3, experienced family planning providers offer the services, commodities do not have to be moved from the clinic to the ward, and referral to a family planning clinic potentially could lead to easier follow-up.

The study consisted of four main components: (1) site selection; (2) preintervention data collection; (3) intervention; and (4) postintervention

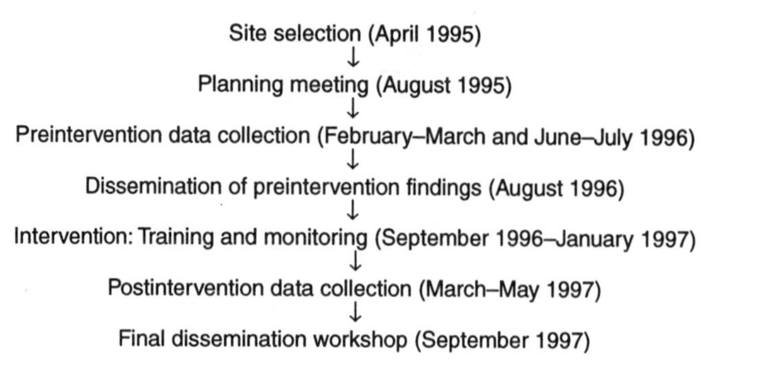

FIGURE 3.1 Project time schedule

data collection. Figure 3.1 outlines the time schedule for these main components, as well as for the dissemination and planning meetings.

During the site-selection phase, 18 public hospitals were visited and six were chosen as study sites. This selection was based primarily on the hospital's caseload of women presenting with incomplete abortion, so that adequate numbers of women could be interviewed to assess the differences in the models being tested. Figure 3.2 shows the proportion of gynecological ward admissions for the treatment of incomplete abortion for five of the hospitals.[1]

The intervention consisted of three elements: (1) training of staff in MVA and postabortion family planning; (2) provision of equipment and supplies; and (3) reorganization of services. Project monitors and Ipas trainers made monitoring and evaluation visits to the sites to help staff address problems in the delivery of services throughout the intervention period from September 1996 to January 1997.

Training in both MVA and postabortion family planning was conducted in September and October 1996. Each training course took place over a five-day period. Approximately five staff members at each facility were trained in MVA and five were trained in postabortion family planning. In Model 1, the gynecological ward staff members who participated in the MVA training also received training in postabortion family planning, whereas in Models 2 and 3, gynecological ward staff received MVA training and MCH/FP staff received postabortion family planning training.

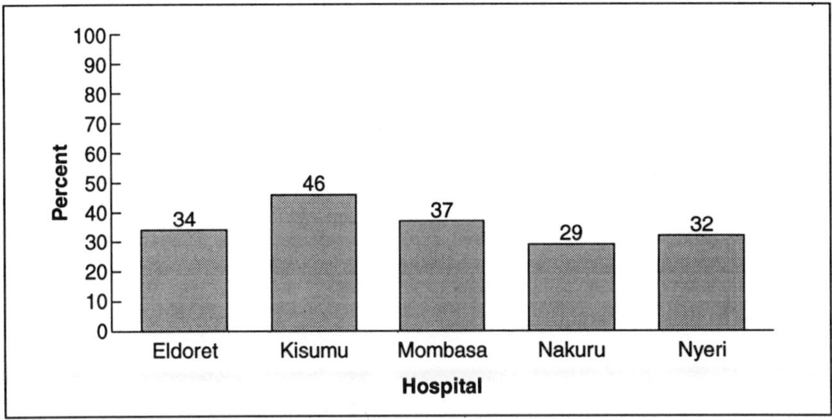

FIGURE 3.2 Percentage of gynecological ward admissions for treatment of incomplete abortion: Five Kenyan hospitals, 1997

To ensure that staff who were trained returned to their sites and implemented MVA and postabortion family planning services immediately, equipment and supplies were provided as part of the project and delivered to the sites directly after the training. These included MVA instruments,[2] sterilizers, portable lamps, gynecological couches, blood-pressure machines, kidney dishes, tenaculums, speculums, and surgical gloves. The equipment provided for each hospital differed somewhat according to the specific needs of the site.

Reorganization of services included two important aspects: either renovating or creating MVA rooms on or next to the gynecological wards and linking treatment of incomplete abortions to postabortion family planning services. The latter involved procedural reorganization, including reallocation of staff time and responsibilities to provide the new services. For sites implementing either Model 1 or Model 2, this linkage of services also required creating a private space for counseling postabortion patients and arranging for contraceptives to be available on the ward; this was accomplished in collaboration with the MCH/FP clinic at each site and posed no major problems.

Table 3.2 indicates the number of structured interviews conducted with patients, staff, and patients' partners during the pre- and postintervention periods. One interviewer was stationed at each hospital for the duration of data collection. Women arriving at the hospital with incom-

TABLE 3.2
Number of interviews conducted with patients, staff, and patients' partners, pre- and postintervention, by hospital: Kenya, 1996–97

Hospital	Patients (preintervention)	Patients (postintervention)	Staff (preintervention)	Staff (postintervention)	Male partners (postintervention)
Eldoret	80	50	26	20	15
Kisumu	51	50	22	11	22
Meru	75	45	22	19	16
Mombasa	93	71	17	9	19
Nakuru	121	60	20	18	6
Nyeri	61	43	33	29	14
Total	481	319	140	106	92

plete abortions, without additional serious complications, and with gestations of 16 weeks or less since their last menstrual period were selected to participate in the study. They were included after interviewers had obtained their verbal informed consent and were interviewed after having received all of their services and as close to the time of their discharge as possible. Interviews focused on the patient's evaluation of the services and the information she received, on her waiting times, family planning history, and intended contraceptive use. Interviews with staff members were conducted throughout the pre- and postintervention periods and focused on their responsibilities, attitudes, and knowledge of MVA and postabortion family planning.

In the postintervention period, women's husbands or partners were also interviewed if the woman, separate from the man, first consented to such an interview and the man provided his consent. In addition, researchers completed logsheets to document the daily gynecological ward admissions, daily bed occupancy, and daily caseloads of incomplete abortions. Researchers also kept diaries of their experiences at the hospitals, which added depth and context to the quantitative data collected. Feasibility questionnaires were administered to medical superintendents and hospital matrons in the postintervention period.

Results

During this study, information was collected from gynecological ward registers to assess the caseloads of incomplete abortion and the proportion of ward admissions related to this problem as an indicator of its magnitude.[3] On average, more than one-third (35 percent) of gynecological ward admissions during the two-month period of postintervention data collection at five hospitals in the study were the result of incomplete abortion (489/1,404). This proportion ranged from a low of 29 percent to a high of 46 percent (as shown in Figure 3.2). These figures, comparable to those found in other studies conducted in Kenya, demonstrate the extent of the problem of unsafe abortion. Clearly, the consequences of unsafe abortion pose a substantial problem for these hospitals. These data represent only a portion of the total problem of unsafe abortion, however, because they refer solely to women who came to the hospital for treatment. Although exact figures are lacking, the assumption that only a small proportion of women who undergo unsafe abortion come to a public health facility for treatment is widely accepted as reasonable.

Profile of the Patients

As Table 3.3 indicates, no major differences were found between the sociodemographic characteristics of the women interviewed in the pre- and postintervention periods. The variety among these patients is striking; the profile of an incomplete abortion patient goes beyond that of the young, single schoolgirl that is typically portrayed by providers. In particular, women presenting with incomplete abortions include a large number who are older than 30 years (22 and 17 percent in the pre- and postintervention periods, respectively) and a substantial number of married women. The majority of women interviewed, however, were between 20 and 29 years old, and a large proportion (18 and 17 percent, respectively) were adolescents (15–19 years old).

In both the baseline and the postintervention periods, a need for family planning was manifest among a substantial number of these patients. In the postintervention period, 16 percent reported that they did not want to have more children, whereas almost half stated that they would like to space their next birth: 22 percent said that they would like to wait one to two years for their next child, and 24 percent said that they would like to wait more than two years.

TABLE 3.3
Percentage of patients with incomplete abortion interviewed, pre- and postintervention, by selected characteristics: Kenya, 1996–97

Characteristic	Preintervention (N=481)	Postintervention (N=319)
Age		
15–19	18	17
20–24	38	42
25–29	23	24
30–34	11	9
≥35	11	8
Parity		
0	33	32
1	29	31
2	15	15
>2	23	21
Marital status		
Married (monogamous)	63	61
Married (polygamous)	8	8
Single	23	23
Other	6	8
Previous pregnancy losses		
1	15	17
≥2	9	7
Preferred timing of next birth		
Less than one year	18	20
Wait 1–2 years	22	22
Wait more than 2 years	20	24
No more children	23	16
Up to God	4	5
Don't know	13	13
Using contraceptive at time of last pregnancy		
Yes	22	17

Among the women interviewed in the postintervention period, just over half (51 percent) had ever used a family planning method, with the pill being the most common method used (31 percent) followed by injectables (18 percent), condoms (10 percent), and the IUD (9 percent) (data not shown). Seventeen percent of women had been practicing family planning at the time they became pregnant. The majority of these women had been using the pill (47 percent) or practicing periodic abstinence (19 percent) (data not shown). Compared with the women interviewed in the postintervention period, a slightly higher proportion of women interviewed before the intervention had ever used a method (59 percent, data not shown) and had been using one at the time they became pregnant (22 percent).

TABLE 3.4
Percentage of postabortion care providers interviewed, pre- and postintervention, by selected characteristics: Kenya, 1996–97

Characteristic	Preintervention (N=140)	Postintervention (N=106)
Occupation		
Nurse	67	72
Medical officer	16	18
Clinical officer	10	9
OB/GYN specialist	6	2
Location		
Gynecological ward	57	80
MCH/FP clinic	22	18
Operating room (main or voluntary surgical contraception theater)	16	1
Whole facility (matron)	5	1
Sociodemographic		
Age (mean years)	35	34
Marital status		
Married	69	71
Single	26	26
Other	5	3
Religion		
Protestant	65	71
Catholic	31	27
Muslim	3	1
Other	1	1

Profile of the Providers

Providers who were involved in the PAC process at each hospital were interviewed. As shown in Table 3.4, in both the pre- and postintervention periods, the majority of the providers interviewed were nurses, and the remainder included medical officers, clinical officers, and obstetric and gynecological specialists. Most providers were stationed on the gynecological ward or in the MCH/FP clinic. On average, providers were about 35 years old, more than two-thirds were married, and most were Protestant or Catholic.

No significant differences were found between the pre- and postintervention samples except for the location of staff within the hospital. During the baseline, operating room staff were interviewed, because at that time evacuations were performed in the main operating room in Meru and in the voluntary surgical contraception theater in Mombasa. Typically, they were no longer involved in providing these services in the postintervention period, because MVA services were being provided in a room on the ward instead of in the operation theater.

A little more than one-fourth (27 percent) of the providers were trained in postabortion family planning, whereas 37 percent were trained in MVA (data not shown). Both of these proportions had increased from the baseline rates of 6 percent and 27 percent, respectively, because training in postabortion family planning and in the MVA procedure was a part of the study intervention. Not all of the providers who were interviewed had taken part in this training, because only a small number of providers from each site were trained during the intervention.

Improved PAC Services

The intervention focused on two aspects of postabortion care: improving emergency treatment services through introducing or upgrading MVA services, and introducing postabortion family planning. Substantial improvements were gained in treatment services after the intervention, including improvements in providers' attitudes, information provision, and a dramatic decrease in the duration of patients' stay at the hospital. The following discussion focuses on the introduction of postabortion family planning services and a comparison of the three different models that were tested.

Postabortion Family Planning: A Comparison of the Models

Postabortion family planning counseling and provision of methods were introduced at each of the hospitals. Although family planning services were already offered at the hospitals involved in the study, they were provided at the MCH/FP clinic, which often was located far from the gynecological ward. Providing postabortion patients with family planning information and methods was not standard practice. Although this linkage was new to the hospitals, providers embraced it as an important addition, and patients indicated satisfaction at receiving family planning services as part of their hospital stay.

In the postintervention period, 68 percent of women interviewed received family planning counseling. Sixty-nine percent decided to begin using contraceptives, and of these, almost three-fourths (70 percent) received a method before leaving the hospital,[4] a substantial increase from the baseline, when only 7 percent received family planning counseling, 22 percent decided to begin using family planning, and of these, only 3 percent received a method.

Information for Nyeri Provincial General Hospital is excluded from the data given above, because the situation at this hospital was unique. After a preliminary planning meeting held in August 1995 at the beginning of this project, staff from Nyeri were so enthusiastic about the idea of postabortion family planning services that they began implementing their model immediately. Therefore, in the baseline, they were already offering these services, and 98 percent of women interviewed were receiving family planning counseling. Sixty-two percent had decided to begin using contraceptives. Almost all of these women (97 percent) received a family planning method before leaving the hospital. These services have continued successfully at Nyeri; in the postintervention period, 91 percent received counseling, 88 percent decided to begin practicing family planning, and 95 percent of these women received a method before discharge.

The three models of postabortion family planning tested were described in Table 3.1 above. In comparing the models, four dimensions are considered: effectiveness, feasibility, acceptability, and quality of care.

Effectiveness. Two primary measures were used to determine effectiveness: (1) the proportion of women who receive family planning counseling before discharge from the hospital, and (2) for those who decide to begin using family planning, the proportion who leave the hospital with a method. Model 1 was the most effective of the three models by both of these measures, with 92 percent of women receiving counseling, compared with 62 percent for Model 2 sites and 54 percent for Model 3. Not only did more women receive counseling with Model 1, but a higher proportion of those who decided to begin using contraceptives left the hospital with a method (82 percent for Model 1, compared with 63 percent and 75 percent for Models 2 and 3, respectively).

Feasibility. Information was collected on feasibility by focusing on the following components: facility upgrading, staffing required to provide postabortion family planning, procedural reorganization, and patient flow.

Sites implementing a model of postabortion family planning in which services were offered on the ward (Model 1 or 2) had to create a private space there for family planning counseling. This modification was accomplished in different ways; for example, by designating an unused room or by creating new space with partitioning. In all cases, existing facilities were adapted within limited budgets.

In spite of the additional investment to set up counseling on the ward, many providers noted the advantages of allowing the same nurse to be responsible for a patient's management at the facility, from treatment to counseling to discharge, as is possible in Model 1. This approach was viewed by many providers as optimal for staffing. In addition, because the staff offering postabortion family planning and their patients were located in the same place in Model 1, greater flexibility was available for offering services, explaining, in part, the greater effectiveness of this model. The coordination between different units required for the staffing of Model 2, in which clinic staff go to the ward to provide services, proved to be particularly difficult.

All sites needed to reorganize some procedures because postabortion family planning was new. Sites offering services on the ward were all able to obtain contraceptive methods (the combined pill, injectables—Depo-Provera and sometimes Noristerat—and condoms) from the MCH/FP clinic at the hospital. Other institutions that might choose to implement postabortion family planning and do not have supplies readily available on site would have to identify alternative methods of obtaining and maintaining a steady supply of contraceptives.

Patient flow is also affected by the model of postabortion family planning that is used. In Nyeri (a Model 3 site), where, typically, patients were treated within a couple of hours after they arrived at the hospital, they now must wait until the morning to be escorted as a group to the MCH/FP clinic to receive family planning services, adding to the time they spend in the hospital. An unanticipated problem arose: Bringing these women as a group to the clinic stigmatized them as "abortion patients." Clearly, greater flexibility in provision of postabortion family planning is possible when these services are offered on the ward.

Based on the findings described above, Model 1 is the most feasible of the three, given the infrastructure and setup of the hospitals in which this study took place. Ensuring a supply of contraceptives on the ward and setting up a private space for counseling proved to be less problematic than creating the support and logistics for escorting women to the family planning clinic or for coordinating family planning clinic staff so that they could be available on the ward.

Acceptability. Acceptability was measured by a series of questions posed to staff members about the timing, staffing, and location of postabortion family planning services, according to the model implemented in their hospital. Almost all found the timing, which was typically after treatment and before discharge (90 percent), and the staff delivering the services (93 percent) to be appropriate. No statistically significant variation was found by model.

Location of services, however, was not acceptable according to 23 percent of providers interviewed. Of these 24 providers, 21 worked at sites offering postabortion family planning services in the family planning clinic (see Model 3). The problem most commonly mentioned (71 percent of the 24 providers) was the long distance from the ward to the family planning clinic, which was viewed as a burden to both patients and staff. Although this model worked well in Nyeri, many of the providers there said that they would prefer to offer postabortion family planning on or near the ward, and currently they are exploring ways to create a counseling space.

When staff members were asked what advice they would give to hospitals wishing to set up similar services, in addition to stating the importance of training (43 percent) and of obtaining and maintaining the necessary equipment (32 percent), many emphasized that they should provide family planning after the MVA procedure (21 percent), that they should provide services on the ward (10 percent), and that they should set up a counseling room there (11 percent).

Many of the providers interviewed (58 percent) have been given additional responsibilities since the introduction of improved PAC services. The majority (89 percent) find these responsibilities acceptable. Of the seven providers who do not, five said that they feel overworked. These new responsibilities include counseling patients about family planning, assisting in MVA procedures and the maintenance of equipment, escorting patients to the MCH/FP clinic, training other providers on the job in postabortion care, and providing preprocedure counseling.

Quality of care. In examining quality of care in postabortion family planning services, the following elements are considered: women's evaluation of the services they received; choice of methods; and information provided about the method a woman receives (how the method is used, the possibility of changing methods, what to do if problems occur, and the method's side effects).

Almost all women felt that the staff providing family planning counseling to them were both acceptable (99 percent) and easy to understand (99 percent). Most (89 percent) said that the length of the consultation was about right, whereas 8 percent felt that it was too short, and 3 percent said it was too long. Of the 59 percent of women surveyed who said that they had questions, 90 percent said that they were given an opportunity to ask them, and almost all of these women (94 percent) felt that they had received satisfactory responses to their questions. Although these figures are encouraging, most likely some courtesy bias occurred in these answers. As other researchers have noted, women are often reluctant to express to interviewers their dissatisfaction with services.

About two-thirds (64 percent) of women who received a family planning method left the hospital with the combined pill. The second most commonly chosen method was an injectable contraceptive (20 percent), followed by the condom (11 percent). Only a few women chose Norplant® implants, the IUD, or female sterilization. This method mix varied somewhat by model; fewer women at Model 1 sites received the pill (55 percent, compared with 68 and 73 percent at Model 2 and 3 sites, respectively), and more women at Model 1 sites received condoms (14 percent, as op-

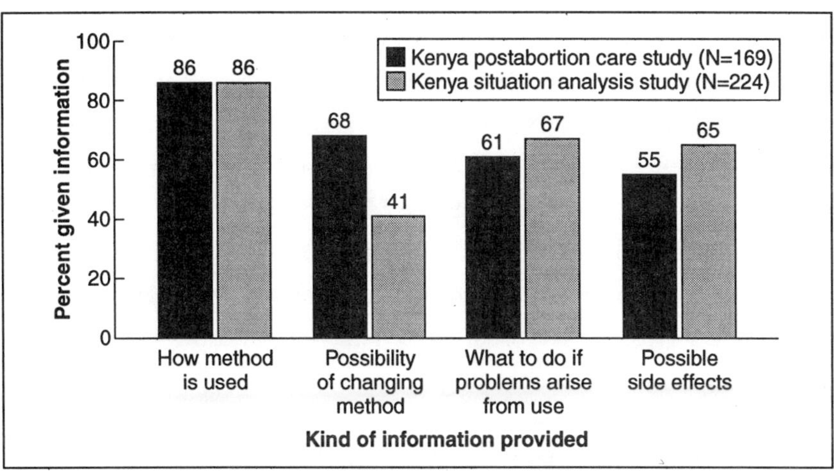

FIGURE 3.3 Information provided to women about contraceptive method chosen, postabortion care and situation analysis studies: Kenya, 1995–97

posed to 9 and 8 percent at Model 2 and 3 sites, respectively). A similar proportion at all sites received injectables (19, 23, and 19 percent, respectively, for the three models).

Figure 3.3 indicates that most women were told how their chosen method is used, and about the possibility of changing methods. Only slightly more than half of the women, however, were told about possible side effects of the methods offered. Providing this information is important, because the occurrence of side effects is a common reason for method discontinuation. In addition, this information enables women to make an informed choice of contraceptive methods. These results are fairly similar to data from the 1995 National Situation Analysis Study in Kenya, which assessed quality of care among family planning clients (Ndhlovu et al. 1997), although postabortion clients were told much more frequently about the possibility of changing methods and were less frequently informed about possible side effects.

Provision of information about the method a woman received varied substantially by model (data not shown); Model 3 generally performed better than both Models 1 and 2: 71 percent of women at Model 3 sites were told about the side effects of various contraceptive methods. This proportion dropped to 51 percent for Model 1 and to 45 percent for

Model 2 sites. Similarly, at Model 3 sites, 79 percent were told what to do if they experienced any problems with the method they chose; 64 percent received this information at Model 1 sites, and only 38 percent received it at Model 2 sites. Variation was found among sites, and, in fact, one of the Model 1 sites performed as well as the Model 3 sites.

That Model 3 tended to perform better in terms of family planning counseling is to be expected, because the nurses at these sites regularly provide this service in their usual setup. That one of the on-ward Model 1 sites performed as well is encouraging.

Summary: Which Model Works Best?

Model 1 (provision of postabortion family planning on the ward by ward staff) was the easiest to set up, the most effective, and the most acceptable to clients and staff. Model 3 ranked highest on various indicators of quality of care, although one of the Model 1 sites performed almost as well. At sites implementing Models 2 and 3, providers suggested as preferable that ward staff offer postabortion family planning on the ward—that is, shift to Model 1. Overall, Model 1 is recommended for sites planning to implement improved PAC services; emphasis on family planning counseling and method provision during the training of gynecological ward staff may be required. This model was most effective at ensuring that all women treated for abortion complications receive information about their rapid return to fertility and about a variety of methods they can use either to avoid another unwanted pregnancy or to rest before becoming pregnant again.

Male Involvement and Partner Communication

An unanticipated benefit to offering services on the gynecological ward occurred in terms of men's potential access to these services. In the baseline research, 41 percent of women were found to have visited the hospital accompanied by their husbands or partners. As a result, and because of increasing interest in involving men in reproductive health care, interviews with men were added to the postintervention research. Similarly, in the postintervention period, 42 percent of women were accompanied by their husbands or partners. Almost one-third (29 percent) of the women's husbands or partners were interviewed during the postintervention fieldwork. In addition to expressing a great deal of interest in and concern about learning more about their wives' or partners' conditions, the vast majority of men were also interested in receiving family planning information. Not all husbands or partners were interviewed, but only the ones who happened to accompany the women seeking care at the hospital; therefore, this sample is not representative of all partners of patients seeking treatment for incomplete abortion. As is always the case with male involvement, the necessity of protecting the confidentiality of a woman's care and assuring that she is consulted first before involving her partner is paramount.

Only 14 percent of the men interviewed said that they had received any information about their wives' condition, and almost all who did not (94 percent) would have liked to. They indicated that they were primarily interested in learning about what caused the problem (82 percent) and how to avoid the same problem in the future (47 percent).

Few men (15 percent) received family planning counseling. Men rarely receive any counseling, and providing it was not an official part of the intervention. Almost all of these men (10 of 14) were interviewed in Mombasa, a site providing postabortion family planning on the ward with ward staff. The staff at this hospital decided that a need existed to counsel men, because a common reason women gave for not using a family planning method was their having to consult with their husbands before doing so. Therefore, when men were present, the staff counseled couples together if the woman first agreed. This unexpected benefit came about from providing family planning services on the ward; providers have greater access to men there, compared with the MCH/FP clinics, which men rarely visit.

By providing information to men, the Mombasa hospital has begun to meet a need that exists elsewhere as well. At all of the sites, men expressed a desire for information; almost all men (92 percent) who did not receive family counseling indicated that they would have liked to have been included in these services. In addition, 93 percent of women said they would have liked to have had their husbands or partners receive these services. All of the men who received counseling received it together with their wives or partners as a couple, and most (86 percent) who would have liked to receive counseling would have preferred to receive it in this way, as a couple. A somewhat lower proportion of women (72 percent) said that they would like to be counseled together, whereas 20 percent said that they would like separate counseling (15 percent of the men said that they would prefer separate counseling), and 9 percent did not state a preference for either mode. Clearly, women should always be consulted first to determine whether they wish their partner to be counseled. Although most (93 percent) said that they would, 5 percent said that they would not and 2 percent didn't know.

Sustainability of Services

Providers were optimistic about the sustainability of postabortion family planning services. Most (89 percent) felt that these services would continue to be offered during the following year; only 1 percent said the services would not continue, 6 percent said maybe they would, and 5 percent did not know. Some of the reasons for continuing cited by providers were that the services had become part of the hospital routine (17 percent), that the staff was dedicated (14 percent), and that more providers were being trained on the job (20 percent). This continuity depends, however, on a constant availability of supplies, according to 24 percent of providers.

In order for postabortion family planning services to continue, hospitals must institute on-the-job training. Only a limited number of providers were trained at each site for the purposes of this study. Some of the sites have already proceeded to train more providers, and their initiative must be encouraged and continued. In addition, to maintain high-quality services and to continue training others, staff refresher courses should be offered. For long-term sustainability, postabortion care must be institutionalized as part of preservice training for all relevant staff.

Conclusions

The study's findings show that provision of postabortion family planning services on the gynecological ward by ward staff was the preferred model. A dissemination workshop was held in September 1997 in Nairobi with more than 80 participants, including representatives from the six hospitals, the MOH, provincial medical officers, and many organizations working in the reproductive health field. Much enthusiasm was expressed for the success of the project, and after the presentation of findings, participants developed provincial-level plans for expanding PAC services so that the MOH can achieve its goal of providing such improved services at all of its hospitals. Model 1 will be promoted for providing postabortion family planning services, but the ministry planners recognize that this model might not be feasible for all sites.

The authors of this study recommend that any health facility that plans to introduce postabortion family planning services conduct a needs assessment to determine whether certain conditions are met to facilitate implementation of Model 1: (1) adequate staff in the area of the hospital where postabortion patients are treated; (2) private space on or near the ward for counseling, or the potential to create this space; (3) space to store family planning commodities; and (4) a plan for keeping the ward stocked with contraceptives.

The feasibility of setting up services will vary depending on whether or not these conditions are met. For example, if the staff have no training in family planning provision, costs will accrue for providing training or the facility will have to consider transferring staff with this training (if they are available) to the ward. If space is available for a counseling room, setting one up on the ward is fairly easy and inexpensive. In some settings, however, doing so may not be possible. Finally, making methods available is essential for providing women with a full range of services. Contraceptives were easily available on site in Kenyan MOH hospitals, but in cases where they are not, additional costs will arise for developing the facility's ability to obtain and maintain supplies. Even if methods are not available on site, however, providing counseling and referring women to facilities where they could receive methods are still important services.

Overall, the authors found a great deal of support for improved PAC services and, therefore, strongly recommend that these services be promoted in efforts to improve women's reproductive health. Such services can address only one aspect of the overall problem of unsafe abortion, because only a small proportion of women who undergo such abortions seek services at hospitals. In addition, postabortion care can help women to avoid a repeat unplanned pregnancy, but it cannot prevent the unsafe abortions that lead women to seek treatment for complications in the first place. Therefore, increased efforts should be made to understand the circumstances causing unsafe abortion at the community level and to develop effective interventions.

A need remains for addressing the third element of postabortion care, linkages to more comprehensive reproductive health care. Such linkages could include primary prevention, detection, and management of sexually transmitted infections (STIs). STIs are an important contributor to spontaneous abortions, and this study, as well as other work in the area of postabortion care, indicates that a substantial proportion of incomplete abortion patients have experienced a spontaneous abortion (see Huntington et al. 1998). Providing more comprehensive care to these women could help identify the causes of their miscarriages and thereby help them avoid future pregnancy losses.

Further research is needed concerning what happens to women after they leave the hospital to determine whether they continue to use the family planning method the hospital provided (or another method) and are able to achieve their reproductive intentions. Knowing that the hospital provided them with a method is not enough. The concept of postabortion care has anticipated the benefits of reducing repeated unplanned pregnancies and thereby decreasing the number of unsafe abortions and the incidence of maternal mortality and morbidity. This impact should be documented, however, to determine its extent. Many methodological and ethical difficulties confront those conducting this kind of research, but some attempts are already underway. For example, preliminary findings from a study conducted in Zimbabwe indicate a high frequency of unplanned pregnancy within the six-month period following hospital discharge after women have received postabortion family planning services (Johnson et al. 1998). Research in social security hospitals in Mexico City for which women were interviewed after six months illustrates the importance of identifying women's concerns throughout the PAC process (Fuentes Velásquez et al. 1998). Findings from these two projects that included follow-up interviews with women underscore the importance of ensuring that counseling and method provision are sensitive, appropriate, and in accordance with their needs.

Acknowledgments

The authors would like to thank the project's researchers, who spent long periods of time in the hospitals collecting data: Elizabeth Achieng, Njeri Kagondu, Annabel Kihuha, Eugenia King'ori, Dorcas Kungu, Mumbi Kyalo, Elizabeth Mugwe, Millie Obel, Rena Otieno, Agnes Rinyiru, and Lilian Rono. We would also like to thank the women who allowed us to speak at length with them at such a difficult time and who provided us with so much valuable information. This work would not have been possible without the commitment and hard work of the providers at all of the hospitals involved in the study. We acknowledge as well the important contributions of the trainers, Solomon Orero and Monica Oguttu. Numerous colleagues at the Population Council, notably Ian Askew and Esther Muia, and at Ipas, including Janie Benson, Lisa Bohmer, Bertha French, and Khama Rogo, provided essential assistance throughout the project. Finally, we express our gratitude to the United States Agency for International Development, which provided funding and support without which this study would not have been possible.

Notes

1 Pertinent data were not available for one of the six hospitals involved in the study.

2 MVA equipment was supplied through the Postabortion Care Consortium drawdown account and was not purchased with USAID funds.

3 In a recent review of safe motherhood in Kenya (MOH 1997a), the authors note the difficulty of obtaining reliable data on the contribution that abortion makes to maternal mortality and morbidity. They point out that, in one study they reviewed, "abortion only featured as an important cause of admission but was omitted as a cause in the death register—a fact the authors attribute to the stigma attached to abortion-related mortality."

4 The proportion of women presented here includes only those who wanted to begin using contraceptives and who received a family planning method. A number of women wanted to become pregnant again or did not want to begin using a method for a variety of reasons. Therefore, the authors felt that it was more important to learn whether the women who wanted a method received one.

References

Baird, Traci L., Robert E. Gringle, and Forrest C. Greenslade. 1995. *MVA in the Treatment of Incomplete Abortion: Clinical and Programmatic Experience.* Carrboro, N.C.: Ipas.

Fuentes Velásquez, Jaime, Deborah L. Billings, Jorge Arturo Cardona Pérez, and Braulio E. Otero Flores. 1998. "Una comparación de tres modelos de atención post-aborto en México" [A comparison of three models of postabortion care in Mexico]. Documentos de Trabajo núm. 14. Mexico City: Population Council.

Greenslade, Forrest C., Harrison McKay, Merrill Wolf, and Katie McLaurin. 1994. "Post-abortion care: A woman's health initiative to combat unsafe abortion," *Advances in Abortion Care* 4(1): 1–4.

Huntington, Dale, Laila Nawar, Ezzeldin Osman Hassan, Hala Youssef, and Nahla Abdel-Tawab. 1998. "A descriptive study of the postabortion caseload in Egyptian hospitals," paper presented at the Global Meeting on Postabortion Care: Advances and Challenges in Operations Research. Population Council, New York, 19–21 January.

Johnson, Brooke, Michael T. Mbizvo, Tsunzai Chipato, and Felicity Zawaira. 1998. "Conducting follow-up with postabortion women in Zimbabwe: Some preliminary descriptive findings," paper presented at the Global Meeting on Postabortion Care: Advances and Challenges in Operations Research. Population Council, New York, 19–21 January.

Lema, V., S. Kamau, and Khama Rogo. 1989. *Epidemiology of Abortion in Kenya.* Nairobi: Centre for the Study of Adolescence.

Ministry of Health (MOH), Government of Kenya. 1997a. *A Question of Survival? Review of Safe Motherhood.* Report prepared by Wendy J. Graham and Susan F. Muray, Options Consultancy Services. Nairobi: MOH.

Ministry of Health (MOH), Division of Primary Health Care, Government of Kenya. 1997b. *Reproductive Health/Family Planning Policy Guidelines and Standards for Service Providers.* Nairobi: MOH.

Ndhlovu, Lewis, Julie Solo, Robert Miller, Kate Miller, and Achola Ominde. 1997. *An Assessment of Clinic-based Family Planning Services in Kenya: Results from the 1995 Situation Analysis Study.* Nairobi: The Population Council.

Rogo, Khama. 1993. "Induced abortion in Kenya," paper prepared for the International Planned Parenthood Federation. Nairobi: Centre for the Study of Adolescence.

World Health Organization (WHO). 1993. *The Prevention and Management of Unsafe Abortion.* Report of a Technical Working Group. Geneva: WHO.

———. 1994. *Abortion: Tabulation of Available Data on the Frequency and Mortality of Unsafe Abortion,* 2nd ed. Geneva: WHO.

4

Improving the Quality of Services and Contraceptive Acceptance in the Postabortion Period in Three Public-Sector Hospitals in Bolivia

Juan Díaz, Máriel Loayza,
Yamile Torres de Yépez, Oscar Lora,
Fernando Alvarez, and Virginia Camacho

Maternal mortality is one of the most important public health problems in Bolivia; although the Ministry of Health (MOH) has declared that maternal mortality is one of its first priorities and several campaigns aimed at reducing it have been implemented, the rate is 390 maternal deaths per 100,000 live births, one of the highest in the region. Based on the latest available data it is estimated that 27–35 percent of maternal deaths are due to complications from abortion (Encuesta Nacional de Demografía y Salud 1994; UNICEF 1992). In 1994 the Ministry of Health (MOH) declared that maternal mortality was one of the most important women's health problems and instituted a plan for its accelerated reduction. This included the goal of reducing induced abortions and their complications.

Analysis of abortion in Bolivia is difficult because, as in other countries of Latin America and the Caribbean (LAC), statistical information is scant and estimates of its incidence are not reliable. There is evidence, however, that due to very restrictive legislation, most women try to solve problems resulting from unwanted pregnancy and induced abortion without consulting public-sector medical services. This explains why 95 percent of deaths due to induced abortion occur at the woman's home

(Ministerio de Relaciones Exteriores y Culto 1994). Women usually present for services only after they have suffered long periods of pain and bleeding; frequently complications are severe and lead to serious sequelae or even to death (Rance 1993). In addition, women do not admit to inducing their abortions because of the risk of being mistreated, denounced, or sued.

Between 1966 and 1976, abortion complications represented 46 percent of all obstetric hospitalizations; in the next decade they made up 51 percent of all such hospitalizations (Rance 1990; UNFPA 1990). A report published by USAID in 1990 stated that, in the Bolivian social security system, by far the most important cause of hospitalization of women of reproductive age was complications of illegal abortions (USAID 1990).

The Caja Nacional de Salud (Social Security Institute) found that the unit cost of treating induced abortion is several times higher than that for deliveries because most women present with complications at more than one time after the induction of their abortion, which, in most cases, has been done by a person without formal training in gynecology or even in medicine. The most frequently used methods to induce abortion are introducing objects, curettage, oral abortifacients, and injections.

Women presenting to hospitals with postabortion complications are intensively interrogated to discover whether the abortion was illegally induced. It is a common practice to charge a higher fee to women presenting clear evidence of induced abortion. In some cases the fee charged is so high that it prevents hospitalization or leads to a significant negative impact on the family budget.

The rationale given by providers for this excessive fee is that it might discourage repeated abortions. Sometimes women are mistreated or simply not accepted in the hospital. On the other hand, women who supposedly have spontaneous abortions and are unable to pay the entire fee are interviewed by a social worker who is then authorized to lower or even waive the fee.

It is worth noting that a small proportion of women (17 percent) who resort to abortion had at one time used a modern contraceptive method (Bailey et al. 1988). The same study showed that most women declared that either they did not believe in the efficacy of contraceptive methods or they were not informed about them.

Data from an unpublished survey of women with abortion complications, conducted by the Bolivian Society of Obstetrics and Gynecology (Taborga, Pooley, and Rada 1988), showed that lack of information was the main reason women did not use contraception (48 percent). Eighteen percent said that they thought they would not get pregnant or that they were not able to get pregnant. Almost 10 percent gave religious reasons for not using contraception. Only 2 percent mentioned lack of access as the reason for not using contraceptive methods. The remaining 22 percent did not use contraception because they wanted to get pregnant, were already pregnant, or were lactating. The study also showed that most women did not receive contraceptive counseling after resolution of the abortion, confirming that postabortion contraceptive services have not received priority.

A qualitative assessment conducted by the MOH in collaboration with the World Health Organization showed that access to abortion services is limited. Some hospitals, mainly Catholic ones, do not accept women if they are suspected of having induced their abortions. In addition, counseling during the postabortion period is not given, and contraceptive methods are not offered. As a consequence, many women get pregnant soon after their abortions and resort to another induced abortion, again placing their lives at risk (Camacho et al. 1996).

Based on that assessment, the MOH decided to implement a strategy to improve women's access to and the quality of postabortion services, including postabortion contraception as a means of decreasing mortality due to repeated abortions. Moreover, postabortion contraception is considered the best means to break the vicious cycle of unwanted pregnancy followed by induced abortion, lack of counseling, and new unwanted pregnancy (Benson 1996).

The MOH requested technical assistance from the Population Council in order to implement a pilot project aimed at assessing the feasibility of carrying out a program to improve the quality of services for postabortion complications, including contraceptive counseling and services, and the impact on client satisfaction and contraceptive acceptance. This chapter presents the results of the pilot project undertaken in three public-sector hospitals from October 1995 through December 1997.

Materials and Methods

Study Sites

The study was undertaken in three maternity hospitals in three cities: Hospital de la Mujer, La Paz; Instituto de Maternidad Percy Boland Rodríguez, Santa Cruz de la Sierra; and the Hospital Gineco-Obstétrico, Jaime Sánchez Porcel, Sucre. The three hospitals are the most important of their respective departments and are women's health referral centers. They attend primarily people from middle and low socioeconomic levels.

The largest, with 165 beds for obstetrics and gynecology, is in Santa Cruz, the largest of the three cities in our study, with approximately 870,000 inhabitants. Before the initiation of the project, the hospital had already implemented some family planning activities. In addition, some physicians were implementing selected activities in the postabortion period, including providing contraceptive services. More than 1,400 cases of complicated abortions were attended in the hospital during the year before the initiation of the project. Two or three months after project initiation, the hospital opened an outpatient clinic specifically devoted to adolescents.

The hospital in La Paz has fewer beds devoted to gynecology (58), although the population of the city (830,000) is comparable to that of Santa Cruz. The social and economic status of the population attended is similar to that attended in the Santa Cruz hospital, but the proportion of indigens is higher. Indigens have a cultural resistance to seeking hospital-based care, which may explain why the number of abortions attended in the La Paz hospital the year before the project (253) was far lower than the number attended in Santa Cruz. During the first months of the project after the training course, hospital personnel, especially physicians, were reluctant to initiate project activities. They were apprehensive about possible negative reaction of the church, which exerts strong influence on the health authorities. This fact explains, at least in part, the lower contraceptive acceptance in La Paz, compared with Santa Cruz.

The third hospital is in Sucre, a smaller city with only 176,000 inhabitants. Sucre is the official capital of the country and the base of the Judiciary. It is home to a well-known university, with one of the best law schools in the country and several other highly regarded faculties. Because the university receives students from all over the country, Sucre has a greater percentage of adolescents, most of whom are living away from their families. Their abortion rate is high, and it is for this reason the abortion rate in the city is far higher than that in La Paz and Santa Cruz. During the year before the project, the hospital attended 414 abortions (2.4 per 1,000 inhabitants) compared to 1.6 per 1,000 in Santa Cruz and 0.3 per 1,000 in La Paz. Implementation of the project was difficult because the Judiciary insisted that all women who have induced abortions be denounced and prosecuted. In 1994 and 1995, judges had sued and condemned at least 10 women for having induced abortions. For this reason, physicians were reluctant to participate in a program designed to give greater attention to all women having abortions, induced or spontaneous. It was not easy to convince physicians to stop denouncing women, but agreement was obtained during the second year. In turn, judges began simply ignoring the fact that induced abortions were no longer denounced.

At the beginning of the project, the three hospitals improved their postabortion facilities and equipment significantly, making the hospitals appropriate for attending the demand for services. The technical level of the personnel was similar in the three hospitals. La Paz had more problems implementing good counseling, mainly because of the initial reluctance of physicians to authorize postabortion counseling and family planning services.

None of the three hospitals previously had a specific program for postabortion care. Women with postabortion complications were attended as emergencies and discharged from the hospital as soon as possible without receiving postabortion counseling. In addition, before the initiation of the project, women were frequently mistreated because physicians and most other health providers considered them to be criminals whom they should punish for having initiated abortion. The situation was worse in Sucre where, due to the legal situation, physicians acted more as prosecutors than as physicians.

For all these reasons, women with postabortion complications tried to avoid attending these hospitals. When they finally consulted, it was usually with severe complications, after long periods of suffering at home. The situation was somewhat better in the hospital in Santa Cruz, where some physicians had been trained in the technique of manual vacuum aspiration (MVA) and some actions aimed at improving the quality of care had been implemented previously.

Training and Monitoring

Physicians and counselors at the three participating hospitals attended a training course on elements of postabortion care, including contraceptive technology. The course emphasized the importance of appropriate counseling during the postabortion period, related both to contraception and to other health issues, such as resumption of sexual activity and infection prevention. The main objective of the training was to change the attitude of health providers, emphasizing the need to treat women as human beings in need of health care rather than as criminals. Training also emphasized that the staff should use all opportunities available during the women's stay at the hospital to provide information and counseling on postabortion care. Particular emphasis was given to avoiding another abortion.

The initial assessment of conditions at the three hospitals showed that physicians and other personnel involved in the treatment of abortion complications were technically well prepared and did not need training on technical issues.

At each of the hospitals one of the trainees acted as coordinator of the activities, trained the rest of the personnel, and supervised them in order to maintain high-quality services. In addition, the general coordinator of the project maintained continuous contact with the hospitals and visited them at several times after training. Monitoring and supervision visits showed that the quality of care, specifically counseling, improved significantly after training. These visits were useful in reinforcing the training and providing opportunities to retrain some health workers who still were not providing considerate treatment to women.

Improvement of Facilities and Equipment

Two rooms, one to perform curettage and another for individual counseling, were equipped and placed in service in each of the three hospitals. This allowed the hospitals to give priority and privacy to women presenting with postabortion complications. It also served to define a patient flow for these cases that was independent of and not interrupted by the other activities of the hospitals.

Clinical Activities and Data Processing

After the training course, the participating hospitals implemented a counseling program that included activities at admission, in the surgical room, and after curettage. At each point, women were offered the opportunity to decide to use contraception and to choose a method. Those who did not reach a decision had an additional opportunity during the postabortion follow-up visit scheduled one month after discharge from the hospital. All data were registered in a logbook and also in the clinical records of the hospitals.

After discharge, the women received a card with instructions and an appointment for the postabortion follow-up visit. After this visit, women were then scheduled for a six-month visit.

The project evaluation consisted of a pre- and postintervention assessment of the quality of postabortion services and the level of contraceptive acceptance over the duration of the study. Qualitative analysis was performed through structured questionnaires and in-depth interviews with women and health providers. Quantitative analysis was based on service statistics.

Results

Evaluation of Training and Quality of Services

Evaluation of the pre- and posttraining questionnaires showed an important improvement in the level of providers' knowledge of postabortion care, including contraception. In addition, monitoring visits showed that providers changed the way they treated women with postabortion complications. They became more considerate and compassionate, treating women as patients in need of assistance rather than as criminals who should be punished for their actions. Counseling was implemented and offered over the course of women's hospital stays.

Interviews with women in the three hospitals showed that a great majority mentioned that they had been well treated and emphasized the supportive attitudes of the nurses and auxiliaries. Most women stated that the counseling they had received had been very appropriate and useful. Several women mentioned spontaneously that the quality of the counseling was perhaps the most important reason they had evaluated the attention they received as good.

The changes in provider attitudes and improvement of quality of services became apparent in Santa Cruz soon after training. In Sucre, it took longer but changes were also very positive. In La Paz, however, improvements in quality, especially in counseling, were very slow and did not reach the same level as at the other hospitals.

Quantitative Results

Table 4.1 shows that the monthly average number of women coming to the three hospitals for postabortion complications remained fairly stable during the study period, maintaining levels comparable with the prestudy period. With the exception of the hospital in Sucre, a slight increase was observed in 1997. During the study period, all three participating hospitals attended a population very similar to the one attended during the five years before project initiation. Therefore the changes in the number or characteristics of women coming to the hospitals for treatment of abortion complications may be due to the intervention.

TABLE 4.1
Monthly average number of women with postabortion complications

	Before training	After training		
Hospital	Jul–Dec 1995	Jan–Jun 1996	Jul–Dec 1996	Jan–Jun 1997
La Paz	35	36	38	47
Santa Cruz	136	138	135	146
Sucre	38	32	33	33

TABLE 4.2
Percent distribution of women with postabortion complications, by age

	La Paz		Santa Cruz		Sucre	
Age (years)	1996	1997	1996	1997	1996	1997
≤19	15.9	15.6	15.5	30.1	11.9	29.6
20–34	65.8	63.9	73.5	57.0	72.4	63.6
≥35	18.4	20.6	11.1	12.9	15.8	6.8
N	441	379	1,635	1,300	387	294

The rate of moderate to severe complications (e.g., severe anemia, infection, and uterine perforation) in women admitted to the hospitals varied from 3.4 percent to 8.4 percent in different periods (data not shown). The rate of complications was somewhat higher in La Paz, due to higher rates of infection. Four women, two in Santa Cruz and one in each of the other hospitals, died as a consequence of their abortions. The four cases arrived at the hospital in very bad condition, after a long period of illness at home or in another health facility.

Table 4.2 shows the age distribution of women over the two years of the project. In Santa Cruz and Sucre, the percentage of adolescents with postabortion complications sharply increased in the second year. In 1997 roughly 30 percent of all women in both hospitals were less than 20 years old. In La Paz, the proportion of women less than 20 years old remained fairly stable during the study period.

Other characteristics of women coming to the three hospitals remained the same during the study period and were very similar to the ones observed in the prestudy period. Most women were poor, and between 60 and 70 percent were married or in a consensual union (data not shown).

The history of previous abortions among women in the three hospitals is shown in Table 4.3. The percentage of women who had no previ-

TABLE 4.3
Percent distribution of women with postabortion complications, by number of previous abortions

	La Paz		Santa Cruz		Sucre	
Previous abortions	**1996**	**1997**	**1996**	**1997**	**1996**	**1997**
None	51.3	52.3	65.9	54.3	73.7	73.8
One	30.6	31.9	22.2	26.2	17.8	18.0
Two or more	18.1	15.8	11.9	19.5	8.5	8.2
N	441	379	1,635	1,300	387	294

TABLE 4.4
Percentage of women receiving contraceptive counseling

	Before training	After training		
Hospital	**Jul–Dec 1995**	**Jan–Jun 1996**	**Jul–Dec 1996**	**Jan–Jun 1997**
La Paz	2.8	77.3	74.7	84.6
Santa Cruz	12.2	90.1	100.0	100.0
Sucre	3.6	73.2	92.4	97.0

ous abortions was higher in Sucre, while the percentage of women who had two or more abortions was lower. The proportion of women with a history of previous abortions remained fairly stable during the study period in La Paz and Sucre. In Santa Cruz, the proportion of women with two or more abortions was higher in 1997.

Contraceptive counseling was almost nonexistent in two of the three hospitals before the study. Nevertheless, interviews with women during the six months before the study showed that some counseling activities had been developed, mainly in Santa Cruz. Table 4.4 shows that counseling sharply increased after training of personnel. The increase was very rapid in Santa Cruz, where all women received counseling on contraception starting with the second half of 1996. Sucre saw a substantial increase in counseling as well, reaching almost 100 percent.

In La Paz the percentage was somewhat lower because some physicians refused to participate and influenced personnel during the periods they were in charge of the emergency room. Although the general coordinator of the study made several monitoring visits to this hospital, by July 1997 some physicians still remained reluctant to participate.

TABLE 4.5
Percentage of women accepting contraception following treatment for postabortion complications, by method

Hospital and method	Before training Jul–Dec 1995	After training Jan–Jun 1996	Jul–Dec 1996	Jan–Jun 1997
La Paz				
IUD	2.9	25.0	13.2	25.5
Hormonal	5.7	5.6	10.5	10.6
Other	5.7	30.6	28.9	27.7
None	85.7	38.9	47.4	36.2
Santa Cruz				
IUD	2.9	31.2	41.5	36.3
Hormonal	4.4	37.7	39.3	39.0
Other	2.9	4.3	7.4	12.3
None	89.7	26.8	11.9	12.3
Sucre				
IUD	0.0	12.5	27.3	27.3
Hormonal	2.6	6.3	9.1	18.2
Other	10.5	28.1	27.3	36.4
None	86.8	53.1	36.4	18.2

All women who received counseling declared that counselors were very friendly, gave complete information about methods, and left the decision on method choice up to the woman. In addition, counselors also gave good and complete information on when and where to return for postabortion follow-up.

Table 4.5 shows total contraceptive acceptance. As expected, contraceptive acceptance in the first period (before training of personnel) was low, between 10 and 15 percent. Women who accepted contraception in this period were mostly those who initiated a follow-up visit and requested a contraceptive method.

Contraceptive acceptance in the three hospitals increased soon after training and the implementation of the counseling program. In La Paz, contraceptive acceptance in the first six-month period after training was 61.2 percent. Acceptance decreased to 52.6 percent in the next period and then increased to 63.8 percent in the last period. The acceptance of IUDs followed the same pattern, with a sharp initial increase, a decrease in the next period, and a recovery in the third period.

In Sucre the process was slower; however, a steady increase was observed during the period evaluated. At the end of the study period total acceptance reached a higher level than it did in La Paz.

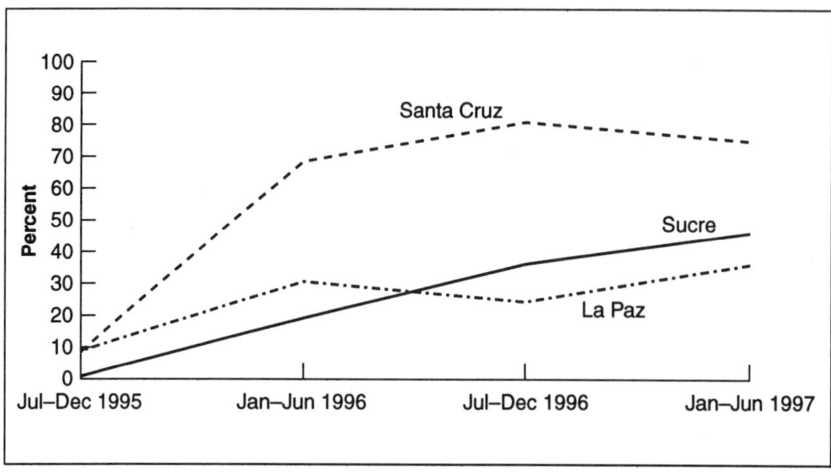

FIGURE 4.1 Percentage of women accepting modern contraception

Contraceptive acceptance in Santa Cruz was the highest, 73.2 percent in the first six-month period after training and 87.6 percent in the last period evaluated. In the last period observed, acceptance of hormonal methods stood at 39.0 percent and IUDs at 36.3 percent. It is also worth highlighting that in La Paz and Sucre a substantial increase was observed in the acceptance of other methods such as condoms (condom data included as part of other methods).

Figure 4.1 illustrates the rise in acceptance of modern contraception (IUDs and hormonal methods) in the three hospitals during the periods evaluated. Santa Cruz exhibited the highest rates and the steepest increase after training.

Sucre had a slower takeoff but showed a steady increase, attaining moderately high rates of acceptance. In third place, La Paz had a fairly quick response, but the acceptance rate presented great variability over time due to several changes in the composition of the staff during the project. Surprisingly, hormonal methods had high acceptance, mainly in Santa Cruz. The services at all three hospitals had a reputation of being IUD clinics, and it was expected that this method would be favored by providers. However, the increase in acceptance of pills and injectables clearly demonstrates that the concept of free informed choice truly was incorporated by counselors and physicians.

TABLE 4.6
Percentage of women attending postabortion follow-up visit

	Before training	After training		
	Jul–Dec 1995	Jan–Jun 1996	Jul–Dec 1996	Jan–Jun 1997
La Paz	2.0	25.1	29.5	48.8
Santa Cruz	3.6	17.1	29.8	20.8
Sucre	2.3	14.0	22.2	28.4

All women, whether or not they accepted a contraceptive method, were scheduled for a follow-up visit approximately one month after discharge. Before the initiation of the project this was not standard procedure, which explains why the percentage of women attending a follow-up visit in the pretraining period was very low in the three hospitals (Table 4.6).

After training, the percentage increased in the three hospitals, with La Paz showing the highest return rates, reaching 48.8 percent during the first half of 1997. Sucre presented a lower but steady increase, reaching 28.4 percent in the same period. In Santa Cruz the rate also increased but was variable. During the first half of 1997 the percentage was lower than it was in the second half of 1996.

Discussion

It is widely accepted that successful family planning programs that increase contraceptive prevalence are effective in preventing unwanted pregnancies and, consequently, induced abortions. The impressive increase of contraceptive prevalence observed worldwide in the last three decades has had an important effect on maternal mortality, but there is still room for improvement. This was clearly demonstrated in Chile where the introduction of family planning led to a significant drop in hospitalizations due to abortions and in maternal mortality attributed to abortion (Barzelatto 1986; Viel 1986). Conversely, in countries where access to contraception is difficult and antiabortion policies are actively implemented, maternal mortality due to abortion increased (Hord et al. 1991).

It has also been demonstrated that targeting family planning to groups at high risk for unwanted pregnancy can decrease maternal mortality (Ickis 1987; Ross, Rich, and Molzan 1989). Unfortunately, although it is widely recognized that women in the postabortion period constitute a high-risk group, only a few programs have focused on them.

There are many reasons for the lack of focus on postabortion counseling and contraception acceptance. Hospitals and health providers spend minimal time on counseling, and women often do not return for follow-up. In addition, postabortion care is usually given in wards where family planning is not routinely offered, and the approach to care is usually strictly curative. From the clinical point of view, sometimes a woman's health is precarious after an abortion, and she is not in a situation conducive to receiving counseling about contraception; usually her only concern is recovering and going back home. From the psychosocial and cultural perspective, the main difficulties are lack of adequate support in the postabortion period and little knowledge about contraceptive use after abortion. Clinics are also not prepared to talk about sexuality, and there is commonly a lack of knowledge about the return of fertility after an abortion.

For these and other reasons, postabortion family planning is a service almost nonexistent in the LAC region, although in the 1970s some authors showed that it was feasible to provide postabortion family planning and that this service was widely accepted by women (Goldsmith et al. 1972; Hardy and Hend 1975). In 1990 Profamilia and the Instituto Peruano del Seguro Social published the results of a program of postabortion contraception, coordinated by the Population Council, that showed training and motivation of personnel was critical for the success of the program (Profamilia and Instituto Peruano del Seguro Social 1990).

These successful experiences with postabortion contraception, showing that modern contraceptive methods are perfectly suitable for use during this period, suggest that the lack of effective implementation of these programs derives mostly from social and political rather than technical reasons. The main problems stem from three overarching factors that have contributed to isolating abortion from family planning and other reproductive health services.

First, the legal and administrative constraints to abortion force many women to seek care in clandestine environments, where family planning is usually not available. In addition, women's low socioeconomic status and the taboos regarding abortion combine to make the health needs of women who have abortions a very low priority. Finally, the United States government's Mexico City Policy (promulgated at the 1984 International Conference on Population and rescinded in 1993) prohibited foreign nongovernmental organizations that receive US funds from engaging in most abortion-related activities.

Improving access to services for women with postabortion complications is the first step to improving the quality of services. Services offering compassionate, humanized, and technically adequate care will attract women who will seek care before serious complications arise. It is also clear that quality of services, including better interpersonal communication, is the main factor that will create a favorable environment for effective counseling and acceptance of contraceptive methods.

The results of this study show that it is feasible to increase quality of services with very modest material input and an emphasis on training, oriented mainly to obtaining a change in providers' attitudes. The results also show that hospitals where staff were highly motivated and remained in their positions after training showed more improvement than those where personnel left the hospital soon after they were trained. In addition, the commitment and support of authorities, program monitoring, and active supervision are crucial in order to obtain and maintain improvements in quality.

In Santa Cruz, where almost all the personnel trained remained in their jobs through the entire study period, eventually 100 percent of women were discharged from the hospital having received counseling on contraception. Conversely in La Paz, where most of the trained professionals were replaced at various times after training, the percentage of women receiving counseling increased less than in Santa Cruz and varied over time.

The importance of motivating personnel was also clearly illustrated in Santa Cruz. At the initiation of the study, counseling activities were performed by the registered nurse trained for that activity. She was a highly qualified professional, but she was not motivated to implement the project because she had several other responsibilities and counseling was an additional burden. As a consequence, counseling rates were very low in the first two months. The supervisor detected the situation and replaced her with a nurse auxiliary, who was trained by the nurse and was highly motivated. The results were impressive and immediate: Counseling rates increased to 100 percent in a short period. This person was such a good counselor and so popular in the hospital that women in the postpartum period also began to attend the postabortion counseling sessions.

From the point of view of users, counseling is the key issue in quality of services. Users' evaluation of quality showed a clear positive relationship with the quality of counseling and with providers' attitudes. Warm and compassionate providers were almost always evaluated as excellent providers.

Contraceptive acceptance increased dramatically in the three hospitals soon after initiation of the project. In the first six-month period after training, contraceptive acceptance reached 73.2 percent in Santa Cruz, 61.2 percent in La Paz, and 46.9 percent in Sucre. With the exception of La Paz, where various trained professionals were replaced, contraceptive acceptance continued increasing, reaching 87.6 percent in Santa Cruz and 81.9 percent in Sucre. It is clear that contraceptive acceptance depends more on the quality of services, particularly counseling, than on the characteristics of the population, as demonstrated by the negative impact on acceptance of the replacement of trained personnel observed in La Paz.

The differences between the three hospitals were due more to the influence of external factors. In La Paz, the turnover of hospital authorities, in addition to high staff turnover, led to changes in the policy of service delivery. One of the directors of the hospital, who was in charge for only a short period of time, attempted to suspend the program and removed the trained staff.

In Sucre, the difficulties were mainly with members of the Judiciary, who insisted that physicians denounce women inducing abortion. It was not an easy process, but physicians gradually stopped denouncing women and adopted a caring attitude, which was stimulated by training and continuous supervision. This translated to a slow but steady increase in contraceptive acceptance.

Those who oppose the promotion of postabortion contraception argue that in this period women are extremely vulnerable and will accept whatever is offered, without making an informed choice. Coercion to accept a method may occur, as has been demonstrated in selected case studies. However, our data show that, when training is adequate and counseling is properly given, women can indeed freely choose the method that best fits their current needs, or choose not to use contraception at all.

This is evident in Santa Cruz, where IUDs are traditionally the most prevalent method, in part because it is the method strongly promoted by the hospital. We expected that IUDs would be by far the method most widely accepted. To our surprise, in the last period evaluated, hormonal methods had a higher acceptance than IUDs. Condoms also had a significant acceptance (condom data included as part of other methods).

It has also been argued that there is no need to offer contraception immediately after abortion. Rather, women can come to a follow-up visit one month later, at which point they can arrive at a decision on method choice and initiate its use. This can be risky for women for two reasons, however. First, it has been demonstrated that ovulation frequently occurs during the first four weeks after an abortion, and most women resume sexual activities before the first menses. This places them at risk of becoming pregnant. Offering contraception one month after abortion is effective only if women do not resume sexual activities for 30 days. Also, despite improvement in the quality of counseling, the percentage of women who returned for a scheduled follow-up visit was not very high in our study. In the hospital in La Paz, which had the highest return rate, it was only in the third period evaluated that the return rate came close to 30 percent. In the other two hospitals the return rate remained under 30 percent throughout the study period, confirming the fact that it is very difficult to reach high levels of return. It is still more difficult to maintain high levels of return in routine work, when the stimulus of the research project has ended. Moreover, a great proportion of women live far from the hospital and do not have access to services designed to deliver IUDs and other clinic-based methods to them. While women are provided information on what they should do and where they should go if they experience complications, the health facilities located closer to their homes often are not able to provide contraceptive methods; therefore, it is important to provide contraceptive services while these women are in the hospital.

In summary, our findings indicate that it is feasible to implement a postabortion program that significantly improves the quality of care, including contraception acceptance, in the postabortion period with scarce material inputs, even in resource-constrained facilities.

The key elements for obtaining these results are:

- training providers on technical issues but, more importantly, on how to give considerate and compassionate care;
- improving providers' communications skills;
- encouraging continuous support from the administrative and technical authorities; and
- providing refresher training and continuous active supervision.

The best indicator of the success of this project has been the request from the MOH and the directors of the women's health division, who are not those who authorized and initiated the project, to maintain the activities in the hospitals already involved and to replicate the project in other regions of the country.

The current challenge for the three hospitals is to maintain and improve the quality of services they now provide after the resources of the project have been exhausted and the service activities become part of the normal routine.

References

Bailey, P.E., L. Llanos, L. Kushner, M. Welsh, and B. Janowitz. 1988. "A hospital study of illegal abortion in Bolivia," *PAHO Bulletin* 22(1): 27–41.

Barzelatto, J. 1986. "Abortion and its related problems," in *Infertility Male and Female,* eds. S.S. Ratnam, Eng-Soon Teoh, and C. Anandakumar. Carnforth, United Kingdom: The Parthenon Publishing Group, pp. 1–6.

Benson, J.V. 1996. "Meeting women's needs for post-abortion family planning. Framing the questions," *Issues in Abortion Care,* no. 2. Carrboro, N.C.: Ipas.

Camacho, V., A. Galvez Murillo, M. Paz, R. Simmons, A. Young, X. Machicao, L. Bahamondes, M.Y. Mackuch, M.D. Castro, J. Diaz, and J. Skibiak. 1996. *Expandiendo opciones de Planificación Familiar: Diagnóstico cualitativo de la Atención en Salud Reproductiva en Bolivia* [Expanding family planning options: qualitative diagnosis of reproductive health care in Bolivia]. Geneva: WHO.

Encuesta Nacional de Demografía y Salud (ENDSA). 1994. *Demographic and Health National Survey, Bolivia.* La Paz, Bolivia: National Institute of Statistics.

Goldsmith, A., R. Goldberg, H. Eyzaguirre, and C. Lizana. 1972. "Immediate post-abortal intrauterine contraceptive device insertion: A double-blind study," *American Journal of Obstetrics and Gynecology* 112(7): 957–962.

Hardy, E. and K. Hend. 1975. "Effectiveness of a contraceptive education program for post-abortion patients in Chile," *Studies in Family Planning* 6(7): 188–191.

Hord, C., H.P. David, F. Donnay, and M. Wolf. 1991. "Reproductive health in Romania: Reversing the Ceausescu legacy," *Studies in Family Planning* 22(4): 231–140.

Ickis, J. 1987. "Structural issues related to delivery systems" in *Organizing for Effective Family Planning Programs,* R.J. Lapham and G.B. Simmons, eds. Washington, D.C.: National Academy Press, pp. 145–159.

Ministerio de Relaciones Exteriores y Culto (MREC). 1994. *Informe Sobre el Avance de las Mujeres en Bolivia* [Report on the advancement of women in Bolivia]. La Paz, Bolivia: Ministerio de Desarrollo Humano.

Profamilia and Instituto Peruano del Seguro Social. 1990. *Immediate Post-partum and Post-abortion Family Planning Program.* New York: Population Council.

Rance, Susanna. 1990. *Planificación Familiar: Se Abre el Debate* [Family planning: opening the debate]. La Paz, Bolivia: Consejo Nacional de Población.

———. 1993. "Necesidades de información sobre el aborto: Reflexiones a partir de un estudio hospitalario" [Information needs on abortion: reflections based on a hospital study], presented at a seminar sponsored by UMSA, Ipas, and the faculty of medicine of La Paz.

Ross, J.A., M. Rich, and J. Molzan. 1989. *Management Strategies for Family Planning Program.* New York: Center for Population and Family Health, School of Public Health, Columbia University.

Taborga, Celia, Bertha Pooley, and Luisa Rada. 1988. "El aborto en Bolivia" [Abortion in Bolivia], Discussion Document no 2. La Paz: Centro de Investigacion, Educacion y Servicios.

UNFPA. 1990. *Programme Review and Strategy Development Report, Bolivia.* New York: UNFPA.

UNICEF. 1992. *Analysis of the Situation of Children and Women in Bolivia.* La Paz: UNICEF.

USAID. 1990. Bolivia project paper, reproductive health services. AID/LAC/P-540. Washington, D.C.: USAID.

Viel, B. 1986. "Induced abortion in Latin America: Impact on health," in *Prevention and Treatment of Contraceptive Failure,* U. Landy and S.S. Ratnam, eds. New York: Plenum Press, pp. 67–72.

5

Improving Postabortion Care with Limited Resources in a Public Hospital in Oaxaca, Mexico

Ana Langer, Cecilia García-Barrios, Angela Heimburger, Lourdes Campero, Karen Stein, Beverly Winikoff, and Vilma Barahona

Aside from spontaneous miscarriages, an estimated 3.4 million abortions are performed each year in 19 Latin American countries, even though throughout the region abortion is legally restricted, clandestine, and unsafe (except in Cuba) (Alan Guttmacher Institute 1994). In Mexico, the Alan Guttmacher Institute has calculated the frequency of induced abortion to be 533,100 cases per year, the overwhelming majority of which are performed unsafely, as abortion is generally legal only when pregnancy puts the woman's life in danger or is the result of a proven rape, or when the fetus presents anomalies that are incompatible with life. Even under these limited conditions, it is difficult for a woman to gain access to services to terminate her pregnancy legally.

Complications from unsafe or incomplete abortion occur frequently, the most serious being sepsis, hemorrhage, genital damage, and intra-abdominal injury. In addition to the physical trauma, women also bear a psychological burden that is seldom mentioned. Worse, the physical complications often lead to death. Pregnancy termination at the hands of untrained and inexperienced providers and its resulting complications are the third leading cause of maternal mortality in Latin America and Mexico (CONAPO 1996). These statistics are certainly underestimated, as unsafe abortion is also responsible for a considerable but unquantified number of deaths attributed to hemorrhage or infection. On the other hand, treatment for the complications of clandestine abortion consumes the largest amount of reproductive health care resources in Mexico outside of normal childbirth. Nearly all of these complications and deaths could be prevented through more widespread and correct use of contraceptive methods, legalization of abortion, provision of safe pregnancy termination services, and adequate care for complications of spontaneous or induced abortions in a hygienic setting by a qualified practitioner (WHO 1994).

Research on Abortion in Mexico

Research on abortion in Mexico, undertaken by diverse national and international organizations, has concentrated on determining its prevalence, the characterization of women who have abortions, conditions associated with the decision to terminate or continue a pregnancy, abortion as a cause of maternal death, opinions and views of health personnel about women who have abortions, and the experience of abortion from women's perspectives (Rivas Zivy and Amuchastegui Herrera 1996; Romero 1994). This previous research has contributed to the understanding of abortion as a public health problem in Mexico and has documented the discriminatory treatment and low-quality health care women receive from health institutions when receiving emergency medical care and the considerable burden of physical and emotional suffering that results from unsafe abortion.

Drawing upon this information, priority strategies for programs and activism in Mexico have been developed, such as the extension and improvement of the quality of family planning services and improving the quality of postabortion care. In the research field, on the other hand, it is imperative to move from descriptive studies to the design and evaluation of models and dissemination of strategies that will diminish the negative impact of abortion on women's lives.

Improving the Quality of Postabortion Care in Mexico

In Mexico, unsafe abortion and its complications have only recently been publicly acknowledged by the government as serious public health problems. In response, health institutions are seeking to improve the quality of the postabortion care they provide. One of the most direct means of reducing the suffering and death caused by unsafe abortion is to strengthen the capacity of health care institutions to provide high-quality postabortion care services that are cost-effective, accessible, and sustainable. The three principal elements of this strategy are: (1) emergency treatment for complications of spontaneous abortion and abortions performed under unsafe conditions; (2) postabortion contraceptive counseling and services to prevent future unwanted pregnancies; and (3) establishment of links between emergency care of postabortion complications and other reproductive health services (Greenslade et al. 1994).

In response to these concerns, a project was set up to assess the quality of postabortion care in a public hospital in Oaxaca, Mexico, in order to design and implement a comprehensive strategy to improve such care. Evaluation of the project's effectiveness was undertaken by comparing the quality of care before and after the program was carried out. At no time was any attempt made to distinguish between cases of spontaneous and induced abortion. This hospital was chosen as the study site because of the number of postabortion admissions, the interest of the hospital authorities in improving the quality of care, and the willingness of the professional staff to participate. Although no formal survey was carried out, this hospital is considered reasonably representative of other public health institutions in Mexico as it is part of the Ministry of Health hospital system. The project was carried out from June 1995 through December 1997 by the Population Council and the Dr. Aurelio Valdivieso General Hospital in Oaxaca in collaboration with Ipas and with the financial support of the European Union.

The project's main objective was to test a model to improve the quality of postabortion care in Mexico's public services. In order to improve the clinical management of incomplete abortion, physicians were trained to replace the traditional technique of sharp curettage (also known as dilation and curettage, or D&C) with manual vacuum aspiration (MVA). Additional steps were taken to improve the content and quality of postabortion family planning counseling, increase the choice of available contraceptive methods, and foster more humane treatment of patients by all medical personnel (physicians, nurses, and social workers).

Project Site

Oaxaca is the capital of one of the poorest and most rural states in Mexico, with a large indigenous population that has had little or no schooling. The state of Oaxaca has a relatively high percentage of women who do not speak Spanish, but rather one of over 20 indigenous languages. The study was conducted at the Dr. Aurelio Valdivieso General Hospital, the largest public hospital in the city of Oaxaca. It receives uninsured patients with scarce economic resources and is also a teaching hospital for the local university. The hospital serves patients from the capital city as well as indigenous patients referred from rural areas that lack the medical infrastructure to attend to their problems. Up to four women daily arrive at the emergency room seeking treatment for incomplete abortion and related complications. In some cases, women who present with extreme pain and hemorrhaging are transported to the hospital by ambulance; otherwise, they must provide their own transportation, often by public bus, and may travel for three to eight hours.

The constant, large volume of patients in general who arrive at the hospital tends to saturate services that already suffer from a lack of adequate supplies and a shortage of personnel. Frequently, priority medical attention is accorded to women in labor or those about to undergo a cesarean section, while postabortion patients are made to wait standing in the hallway of the emergency room. Once admitted for the initial medical appraisal, women are seen by medical interns and occasionally residents but are seldom attended by staff physicians. The typical evaluation consists of cursory questioning about the patient's signs and symptoms; annotation of her reproductive history, including date of last menstrual period to gauge gestational age; and a brief physical examination. Prior to the intervention, women undress and undergo examination in front of various hospital personnel; often they have no robe or sheet to cover them. Once women are admitted to the obstetric ward, they are usually treated with some form of D&C under general anesthesia and discharged within 48 hours (Langer et al. 1997).

Methodology

Research Design

We used a quasi-experimental design to measure changes in the quality of postabortion services associated with the implementation of the intervention. This approach allows for the evaluation of the effects of an intervention by comparing relevant variables before its implementation (baseline evaluation) and after its completion (follow-up evaluation), using independent samples from the study population, but without a comparable assessment in a similar control population (Fisher et al. 1991).

Data Collection

The specific sources of information for this study included:

Structured interviews with postabortion clients. After obtaining informed consent, trained interviewers administered questionnaires to 339 postabortion patients who were willing to participate (132 at baseline and 207 postintervention). The 45-minute interviews were conducted on the hospital premises in a room separate from the treatment ward to ensure privacy and unrestricted participation. The results of the baseline interviews were used to adapt the intervention to the needs of this specific population.

Observation of clinical procedures, contact between providers and patients, and characterization of the hospital environment. Using a standard guideline, trained personnel conducted 16 observations of patients arriving with incomplete or complicated abortion during the study period. Patients were followed from hospital admission in the emergency room through discharge; observation included initial medical evaluation, confinement in the OB/GYN ward, second medical evaluation by the resident OB/GYN on call, preparation and execution of the uterine evacuation procedure (MVA or D&C), postprocedure recovery, and family planning counseling and method provision.

In-depth interviews with members of the hospital staff (physicians, nurses, and social workers) who provide postabortion services. Using a predetermined list of questions, 23 interviews were conducted with members of the hospital OB/GYN staff (five physicians and five nurses preintervention, and eight physicians and five nurses postintervention). Trained interviewers explored the providers' technical knowledge as well as their attitudes and self-reports of diagnosis and treatment of incomplete and complicated abortions, interpersonal relations between provider and patient, appropriate counseling for patients, and contraceptive method provision.

In-depth interviews with postabortion patients. A subsample of 16 postabortion clients in the study were interviewed after their surgical procedure prior to hospital discharge (six preintervention and ten postintervention). The guided interviews were 30–45 minutes long and took place on the hospital premises but outside the OB/GYN ward. Patients were questioned about their perceptions of the abortion experience and choice of a contraceptive method. The interviews were recorded, transcribed, and analyzed using the software package *Ethnograph*.

Review of medical records. The hospital records of all women who received treatment during the study period were reviewed to obtain information on their reproductive history, medical complications, procedures employed to complete uterine evacuation, family planning, and length of hospital stay.

The baseline results were used to design a training program for the providers, while the evaluation data were used to assess the impact of the program.

The preintervention data collection period was seven months long, and the postintervention period was six months in duration. A one-year period elapsed between the pre- and postintervention data collection activities, during which the project became operational.

Population: Comparison Between Pre- and Postintervention Groups

The population of women under study is not representative of all women who experience an abortion, whether induced or spontaneous. Rather, the women recruited for participation in this study represent only those women who managed to arrive at an appropriate health facility to seek emergency care. Women who experienced uncomplicated abortions, those who attended private hospitals, and those who experienced complications but had no access to medical attention or died before they could get to a hospital were not included in this study. All women who were asked to participate in the study accepted; therefore, no selection bias occurred on the basis of refusal to participate.

Women in the pre- and postintervention groups had very similar sociodemographic characteristics. The average age was approximately 26 years for both groups. In both groups, slightly more than three-fifths of the women came from semirural or urban areas. Most (70 percent) were housewives, and roughly equal percentages of women lived permanently with their spouses; very few no longer maintained any type of relationship with their partners when the abortion occurred. About three-fourths of the women were economically dependent on their partners, and approximately two-thirds of the spouses who provided the household income had no fixed employment.

The only characteristic that differed before and after the program was the level of schooling, which was significantly higher for the postintervention group (77 percent of the women had completed at least primary school, as compared to 62 percent for the preintervention group).

Reproductive History

While other factors remained the same, the women surveyed in the postintervention group had fewer former pregnancies and fewer living children (Table 5.1). There were fewer women with five or more pregnancies and with five or more living children in the postintervention group. Furthermore, significantly more women wanted to get pregnant again in the postintervention group (69 percent postintervention vs. 55 percent preintervention). To control for the differences found in the number of pregnancies, number of living children, and desire to have more children, we adjusted for these variables during analysis.

Conditions under which pregnancy occurred. The percentage of women who described their pregnancy as wanted (Table 5.2) proved to be the same in the pre- and postintervention groups (62–63 percent). Fewer than 20 percent of women in both groups reported using a contraceptive when the pregnancy occurred. Among all women who termed the pregnancy "unwanted," fewer than one-third reported having used a contraceptive

TABLE 5.1
Reproductive history, pre- and postintervention

Characteristic	Preintervention (N=132)	Postintervention (N=207)
Mean number of pregnancies	3.7	2.8*
Number of pregnancies (%)		
1	25.8	28.5
2–4	41.7	53.1
≥5	32.6	18.4
Mean number of living children	2.25	1.52**
Number of living children (%)		
None	30.3	35.7
1	20.5	23.7
2–4	32.6	34.3
≥5	16.7	6.3
Desires future pregnancy (%)	54.6	68.5*
Number of children who have died (%)		
None	82.6	88.4
1	12.1	10.6
≥2	5.3	1.0
History of previous abortion (%)	15.9	10.6
Number of previous abortions (%)		
None	84.1	89.4
1	12.9	9.2
≥2	3.0	1.4
Ever used a contraceptive method (%)	45.5	46.3

Note: Sample sizes correspond to most variables presented in this table, although denominators may change for some due to missing values.

* $p \leq 0.01$. ** $p < 0.05$.

method when the pregnancy occurred. The most commonly utilized methods were the "modern" ones, such as the intrauterine device (IUD), oral contraceptives, hormonal injections, and condoms.

The large majority of women in both groups had a uterine height of 12 cm or less on presentation for treatment. Most women presented with retained products of conception. Fewer than 10 percent of women in both groups sought attention due to other complications: among them, the most frequent was hemorrhage (4 percent preintervention vs. 2 percent postintervention) followed by sepsis (3 percent vs. 2 percent) (Table 5.3).

Hospital Arrival

Almost half of the women in both groups mentioned that they had been very apprehensive upon arrival at the hospital. The main causes were fear

TABLE 5.2
Contraceptive history, pre- and postintervention

Characteristic	Preintervention (%) (N=132)	Postintervention (%) (N=207)
Current pregnancy wanted	62.9	62.3
Contraceptive method used when pregnancy occurred	18.9	15.8
Reported correct use of method (among those who used a method)	28.0	43.8
Among those with unwanted pregnancy:		
Method use at time of pregnancy	32.7	31.1
Reported correct use of method	26.7	34.8
Use of modern contraceptives at time of pregnancy	62.5	60.9
Use of natural contraception at time of pregnancy	43.8	39.1

Note: None of the results are statistically significant. Sample sizes correspond to most variables presented in this table, although denominators may change for some due to missing values.

of bleeding, physical pain, surgery, and possible death. Other less frequent causes were fear of becoming infertile, receiving poor-quality attention, and not knowing what was going to happen to them. No significant differences were found in either numbers or reasons for fear between the pre- and postintervention groups.

While women were examined quickly upon hospital admission, the majority of them had to wait for six hours or more before receiving emergency treatment. Service providers said that the hospital's emergency and obstetric services were often overcrowded and understaffed; therefore, priority was often given to other obstetric events, especially cesarean sections. Although many women reported having felt great pain, fewer than one in 10 received pain medication prior to the procedure. Respect for women's privacy was virtually ignored, and many women were examined in the presence of three or more staff members and medical students. Very little information was given to the women about the procedure itself, the subsequent self-care regimen, or the importance of contraception. Partly as a result, three out of four women left the hospital without a contraceptive method (Langer et al. 1997).

Intervention

Based on the seven salient elements of the postabortion quality of care framework adapted for this study and the findings of the baseline evalua-

TABLE 5.3
Postabortion patients' clinical conditions and uterine evacuation procedure, pre- and postintervention

Characteristic	Preintervention (N=136)	Postintervention (N=207)
Mean uterine height (cm)	10.4	10.3
Uterine height (%)		
0–12 cm	83.8	85.2
>12 cm	10.3	12.9
Not recorded	5.9	1.9
Complication (%)	8.8	5.7
Hemorrhage	4.4	2.4
Sepsis	2.9	1.9
Uterine evacuation technology (%)		
D&C	89.6	20.8*
D&C with MVA	10.4	1.1
MVA	0.0	78.1*

Note: Sample sizes correspond to most variables presented in this table, although denominators may change for some due to missing values.

* $p<0.05$.

tion (see Results section), we designed an intervention in collaboration with the hospital staff. The essential steps were to: (1) modify hospital procedures to reduce waiting time, improve pain management, and ensure patient privacy; (2) instruct all attending medical personnel in the MVA technique as a substitute for D&C; (3) train staff members on the importance of provider–patient relations, such as delivering relevant information throughout the period of diagnosis, treatment, and recovery; providing support; and counseling the patient for appropriate postabortion contraception; and (4) design printed materials to reinforce the messages of the intervention. Although public health service personnel are often pressed for time and short on resources, several of the physicians and nurses in the Oaxaca hospital expressed concern and offered suggestions for improving services when they were confronted with our baseline findings.

The following activities were implemented as part of the intervention:

Modification of hospital procedures. As a result of the workshops held with the OB/GYN service staff, hospital physicians and administrators prepared a new protocol for postabortion patient treatment. The main modification stipulated that all patients with a uterine height of less than 12 cm would undergo MVA with local anesthesia and would be provided with analgesics before and after the procedure. It was also determined that all operating rooms would function 24 hours a day, seven days a week, to provide more timely attention to postabortion patients arriving at the hospital at night and during the weekends. Finally, shaving of pubic hair was eliminated from the preoperative procedures.

Whereas limited family planning counseling had been offered on a sporadic basis, as part of the intervention contraceptive counseling became a standard component of postabortion care. While the method mix did not change, family planning services were stocked with a more readily available supply of hormonal contraceptives and condoms, in addition to the steady supply of IUDs already available in all public-sector hospitals, in order to offer these temporary methods as an option for every woman prior to hospital discharge.

MVA training. Changes in the clinical management of postabortion patients were introduced through a one-week intensive training program on MVA that included demonstrations followed by supervised practice and monitoring. A "training of trainers" strategy focused on developing a core of master trainers who would then instruct their junior colleagues and residents individually, providing supervision as well as follow-up training. In the intervening months, several supervision and follow-up visits were carried out by Ipas personnel to discuss with staff the difficulties they were facing with routine use of MVA.

Training in family planning counseling. Upon request of the hospital staff, a theoretical/practical course was held to train physicians and nurses in the provision of postabortion family planning counseling. During this course, it was emphasized that, at a minimum, all women should be provided information during the postabortion period about: (1) the possibility of getting pregnant before their next menstrual period; (2) safe methods to use to avoid or postpone pregnancy; and (3) immediate and future family planning services (Leonard and Ladipo 1994).

Interpersonal relations workshop to promote humane postabortion care and enhance the provision of information and counseling. All participating physicians, nurses, and social workers in the hospital's OB/GYN services were invited to attend a two-day workshop on interpersonal relations in order to sensitize them to the circumstances of the abortion experience and modify the often negative attitudes demonstrated by providers toward women in need of postabortion care.

Printed materials to reinforce the intervention. Informative posters entitled "Quality and Warmth in the Care of Postabortion Patients" were distributed in areas visible to the medical staff as a reminder of the information that should be provided to all postabortion patients. Brochures containing crucial information about potential complications, family planning, and sexuality, as well as the date of the patient's scheduled follow-up appointment were handed out to patients as a take-home reminder and to provide a written guideline for nurses or other members of the hospital staff.

Results

The effects of the program on the quality of postabortion care were estimated by comparing indicators of the care provided to women in the hospital before and after the implementation of the program.

Technology Used for Uterine Evacuation

One of the main objectives of the program was the introduction of MVA to handle incomplete abortion, and in this the success of the intervention was evident. Before the study, most of the postabortion patients with a uterine height of 12 cm or less underwent D&C (90 percent) or a combination of D&C and MVA (10 percent). After the program, the tendency was reversed: 78 percent of patients were treated with MVA alone. Additionally, only 1 percent were treated with a combination of D&C and MVA (Table 5.3). These results reflect the confidence and promptness with which the providers adopted MVA as the preferred procedure for incomplete abortion, despite the fact that, during the preintervention phase, some providers were skeptical about the introduction of this technique at the hospital.

Immediate Complications Related to the Uterine Evacuation Procedure

This project did not evaluate the efficacy and safety of MVA as compared to D&C in terms of postoperative complications, because it has been

TABLE 5.4
Mean waiting time and length of hospital stay, pre- and postintervention

Characteristic	Preintervention	Postintervention	Difference
Waiting time to receive first medical attention	25.3 min	24.7 min	0.6 min (2.4%)
Waiting time for uterine evacuation	13.3 hrs	10.5 hrs	2.8 hrs* (21.1%)
Postprocedure time	18.2 hrs	11.6 hrs	6.6 hrs** (36.3%)
Total length of hospital stay	29.5 hrs	18.9 hrs	10.6 hrs** (35.9%)

* p<0.05. ** p<0.01.

tested before by Ipas and others (Greenslade et al. 1993). Moreover, in both phases of the intervention, very few immediate complications were associated with either MVA or D&C; in fact, the only complication that could be directly attributed to D&C was a uterine perforation in the preintervention phase. Furthermore, the sample size was too small to detect any significant differences between the baseline and postintervention groups (Table 5.3).

Waiting Time and Length of Hospital Stay

The time patients spent waiting before receiving initial medical attention in the emergency room did not diminish as a result of the intervention. However, the majority of patients in both groups (71 percent) were attended to in less than 30 minutes, which we consider reasonable for emergency services (Table 5.4).

The time spent between hospital admission and surgery was significantly reduced, by an average of three hours (a 21 percent decrease, from 13.3 hours to 10.5 hours) in the postintervention group, due to changes in the hospital routine and in the providers' attitudes. This was the most significant time reduction in relative terms because it meant that women in pain received care sooner.

Another substantial effect of the intervention was the decrease in postprocedure time, which was reduced by nearly seven hours (a 36 percent decrease; from 18.2 hours to 11.6 hours) on average. This reduction was largely due to the fact that MVA, as opposed to D&C, does not

TABLE 5.5
Pain management, pre- and postintervention

Characteristic	Preintervention (%) (N=136)	Postintervention (%) (N=207)
Patient was asked about pain before procedure	90.2	86.1
Analgesics given to women reporting moderate to intense pain before procedure	26.7	25.7
Pain control during procedure		
General anesthesia	91.2	29.7*
Cervical block	0.7	58.9**
Epidural block	2.2	2.4
Patient was asked about pain after procedure	89.3	88.1
Patient had moderate to intense pain after procedure	9.8	19.8*
Analgesics given for pain after procedure	97.7	96.0

Note: Sample sizes correspond to most variables presented in this table, although denominators may change for some due to missing values.

* $p<0.01$. ** $p<0.05$.

require general anesthesia. With MVA, women recovered faster and were ready to be discharged sooner.

As a whole, the intervention achieved an average 11-hour decrease in the total length of hospital stay. Two factors that contributed to this decrease were the utilization of all OB/GYN operating rooms 24 hours a day (so that women who arrived at night no longer had to wait until the next morning for treatment) and the type of anesthesia used (administration of a cervical block does not require the presence of an anesthesiologist). This statistically significant 36 percent time reduction was considered beneficial for the hospital in terms of savings (the most expensive cost element was bed-time use; see Chapter 6 in this volume for more information) and for the women, as the amount of time they spent in this painful situation was reduced.

Pain Management Prior to the Procedure

One of the objectives of the intervention was to ensure adequate pain management before, during, and after the uterine evacuation procedure (Table 5.5). The large majority of women reported being asked whether they were experiencing pain prior to the procedure. However, only about one-fourth of the 45 women in the initial period who reported having moderate to intense pain were given some type of analgesic. Frequently, a doctor would ask, "Are you in pain?" only to write down the patient's response in her medical file without prescribing medication or giving her an explanation or even a comforting word.

In spite of the emphasis on pain management during the professional workshops, and the fact that a specific protocol was designed as part of the intervention, physicians did not change their before-procedure pain management practices.

Pain Management During and After the Procedure

Before the intervention, general anesthesia was routinely used during D&C (Table 5.5). After the program was implemented, and as a consequence of the introduction of MVA, a substantial change took place: The use of general anesthesia decreased significantly from 91 percent to 30 percent, and was replaced with a paracervical block. The use of this local anesthesia increased from less than 1 percent to 59 percent. Doctors were initially reluctant to give up the practice of putting their patients to sleep because of their lack of experience in administering cervical blocks and their general resistance to change. In the end, however, both the patients and the hospital benefited: There was a lower risk of complications, both the recovery time and the hospital stay were shorter, and the costs were significantly reduced—all of which represent important achievements of the intervention.

There were no changes in postprocedure pain management, as almost all patients (more than 95 percent) were already given a postoperative analgesic as a matter of course. The proportion of women who reported intense pain after MVA (20 percent) was significantly greater than the number of women who reported intense pain after D&C (10 percent).

We suggest several hypotheses to explain the intervention's limited effect on altering pain management practices, especially before uterine evacuation. First, many physicians view pain as a warning sign; thus, masking it with analgesics prior to treatment might be considered dangerous. Second, analgesics may be in short supply at the hospital and may not be available in sufficient quantity to offer them preoperatively to everyone. Some physicians may prefer to restrict the use of pain medication for the most severe cases or for postprocedure administration. Third, women experience more pain during an MVA procedure because they do not receive general anesthesia and are alert throughout, with full recall of the experience afterward. Fourth, physicians may not be adequately skilled in providing local anesthesia for cervical dilation. Fifth, some physicians may wrongly interpret women's stoicism as an absence of pain, and we were unable to modify their perception. Finally, not alleviating women's pain may be a conscious or unconscious response by providers as a woman's "just reward" for possibly inducing an abortion. In-depth interviews with providers about these issues are needed to explore these questions further.

In light of these findings, however, we suggest that future interventions place more emphasis on safe pain management, training of providers in pain-control techniques, and the procurement of a reliable and adequate supply of analgesics to offer to all postabortion patients. As such, the hospital protocol and practice could be modified so that women would automatically be offered analgesics prior to the procedure. Not only would this alleviate pain while waiting for treatment, it also might reduce the pain experienced during MVA, depending on the time elapsed.

Information Provided to the Patient About Diagnosis and Treatment

The intervention achieved a significant improvement in the provision of information to patients, although this was not uniform throughout the care process. While there was a significant increase in the proportion of women who received information about their diagnosis before entering the operating room (from 68 percent preintervention to 87 percent postintervention), there was scant change regarding information about the ensuing treatment. After the intervention, a relatively large proportion of patients (13 percent) still did not receive any explanation about the procedure that was to be performed.

Before the program was implemented, the explanations given to the patient were brief and sketchy:

> Madam, you have an abortion and we're going to perform a sharp curettage.

Furthermore, most of the patients did not understand either their diagnosis or treatment.

The qualitative study revealed some favorable comments about the quality of the information provided to the patient in the postintervention phase. In general, physicians gave women more detailed and clearer information:

> You're going to stay in the hospital because you have an incomplete abortion. What we're going to do now is to clean your womb. It is a small surgical procedure, which is not dangerous but requires hospitalization. You will possibly be ready to go by 8 p.m., but probably you won't leave until tomorrow.

However, attending physicians gave few women the opportunity to voice any questions or doubts they had concerning their diagnosis or treatment prior to entering the operating room either before or after the intervention (11 percent vs. 18 percent), with no significant difference between groups. There was a small but insignificant increment in the proportion of women who had their questions answered about diagnosis and treatment (36 percent preintervention vs. 43 percent postintervention). The following statements may exemplify the main reasons why the women did not attempt to ask for clarification:

> They're going to say that I'm nosy.
>
> I just assumed they were not going to tell me anything.
>
> They kept going in and out [of the recovery room], so I couldn't ask them.
>
> I didn't want to ask, because the doctors only say a couple of words and then leave.
>
> No, I was too embarrassed, I couldn't.
>
> If I do ask, [the doctor's] going to scold me.
>
> I didn't feel confident enough.

Before the intervention, providers said they were aware of the importance of offering the patient information about her diagnosis and treatment, but they blamed lack of time and the hospital routines for the poor information they provided. However, partly through the interpersonal

TABLE 5.6
Provider–patient relations, pre- and postintervention

Characteristic	Preintervention (%) (N=136)	Postintervention (%) (N=207)
Patient knew which physician performed the procedure	17.4	74.4*
Physician introduced self by name	26.1	51.0*
Physician addressed patient by name	59.1	84.8*
Provider gave patient explanation prior to the procedure	45.5	92.4*
Patient received information about her recovery	19.8	62.6*
Words used by provider were easy to understand	91.7	91.3
Patient felt great confidence in physician	52.4	73.6*

Note: Sample sizes correspond to most variables presented in this table, although denominators may change for some due to missing values.

* $p<0.05$.

relations workshops and posters on display at the hospital, the providers became more sensitized to the concept of the quality rather than the quantity of information. Consequently, in-depth interviews revealed that providers began to accept more personal responsibility for their actions and sought fewer excuses (e.g., excessive workload) to explain the lack of communication and deficient information provided to patients.

Provider-Patient Relationship During the Uterine Evacuation Procedure

Before the intervention, the surgeon generally did not introduce him/herself to the patient, or address the patient by name (Table 5.6). Fewer than one-fifth of the women (17 percent) even knew which doctor had performed the procedure. In only ten of these cases did the doctor explain what s/he was going to do prior to the procedure. However, these findings are not altogether surprising in light of the fact that D&C patients received general anesthesia—in some cases even before the performing physician had entered the operating room. Preintervention shadow observations[1] revealed that the nurse would usually talk to the woman only while placing her on the stretcher or operating table to ask her whether she was allergic to some medication and to check her vital signs. Afterward, the nurse would direct her attention to whatever the surgeon requested.

Once the program was implemented, the care and information provided to the woman during MVA improved. Observers noted that after entering the operating room, the surgeon would stay with the patient, at times even accompanying and talking to her from the waiting area to the operating room. Consequently, the percentage of women who knew which doctor performed the procedure increased fourfold in the postintervention group. Among this subgroup of women, there were some other significant improvements among the postintervention group: The doctor introduced him/herself more frequently and more often addressed the patient by name. In general, doctors and nurses used this contact to explain parts of the procedure to the patient before beginning. After the intervention, nurses approached the patient more often to comfort her, sometimes of their own accord and at other times following the resident's lead.

In the postintervention phase, the doctor or nurse was three times more likely to explain the outcome of the MVA procedure and give some indication of the patient's health status than s/he was preintervention. However, we should take into consideration the fact that women in the postintervention group were also less likely to have received general anesthesia, a circumstance that may improve short-term recall.

During the postintervention observations and interviews, we found that aside from giving more information, doctors, nurses, and even medical students had more caring attitudes and maintained longer visual contact with the patient during the uterine evacuation procedure. Qualitative results suggest that improvements in both the provider–patient relationship and the quality of information provided to the patient might have had a positive effect on reducing patient anxiety levels by enabling them to feel they had attained more control over the postabortion experience.

Information About Postabortion Complications and Care

More information was provided to postintervention patients regarding possible postabortion complications, as well as requisite follow-up care (Table 5.7). In the preintervention period, only 3 percent of the women received some information and 6 percent were told to return to the hospi-

TABLE 5.7
Patient information and care recommendations, pre- and postintervention

Characteristic	Preintervention (%) (N=132)	Postintervention (%) (N=207)
Patient received information about:		
Use of medication at home	3.8	15.0*
When to resume normal work activities	7.6	27.1*
When to resume sexual relations	14.4	38.8*
Return of fertility	19.1	54.4*
Warning signs of possible complications	3.0	50.7*
What to do in case a complication occurs	6.1	50.7*
Patient satisfied with information received	17.6	72.5*

Note: Sample sizes correspond to most variables presented in this table, although denominators may change for some due to missing values.

* $p<0.05$.

tal immediately or call the nearest physician should any problem arise. Postintervention, these percentages increased significantly.

The preintervention study also showed very poor provision of information on follow-up care: Few women received information about the use of subsequent medication (analgesics or antibiotics) at home; when they could resume normal work activities; when they could safely have sexual relations again; and the almost immediate return of fertility. Of the women in the preintervention group, only 18 percent declared that they were satisfied with the explanations they received.

Follow-up information was emphasized during training sessions. In addition, informational flyers that covered each topic with written and graphic instructions were distributed as a guide for onsite counseling by providers and as a written reminder for patients to take home and share with family members if desired. This two-pronged approach was intended to facilitate direct questioning and serve as a future reference. The postintervention evaluation consequently showed significant increases in information provided to patients (Table 5.7).

Privacy

While patient privacy is a key component in the quality of reproductive health care, observations showed that the privacy offered for various services by public hospitals is very limited. During the preintervention stage, consultations were often interrupted when staff members opened up the curtain dividing the consultation room from the rest of the emergency room, exposing the patient to anyone passing by.

The intervention had a positive effect on some practices associated with the modesty and privacy of the patient. For example, a door was installed to replace the curtain on the outside of the examining room, allowing for greater privacy during consultations. In the preintervention interviews, all patients mentioned having changed clothes in the presence of several people or having been examined without being covered by a sheet. As a result of the intervention, all postabortion patients at the hospital were covered with a robe or sheet during the initial medical exam. While this simple practice had seldom been adopted before, it was not associated with significant changes in the variables used to measure privacy. The reason doctors gave for the lack of privacy is that the Dr. Aurelio Valdivieso Hospital is a teaching facility for the state-run medical school and that medical students are required to observe and practice all procedures as part of their curriculum.

Counseling in Family Planning

Although international quality-of-care guidelines and the official Reproductive Health and Family Planning Program in Mexico both indicate that family planning services should be included in postabortion care, the baseline results showed that integration at this hospital was very limited, a situation common to many other health centers in the country. In preintervention interviews, only 42 percent of the postabortion patients received some counseling on family planning (Table 5.8).

As a result of the training sessions and the information transmitted during the interpersonal relations workshops, the percentage of postintervention patients who received counseling doubled. Furthermore, almost half of the women were counseled directly by the attending physician. These data, together with qualitative indicators from observations and in-depth interviews, point to the program's positive effect on provid-

TABLE 5.8
Postabortion family planning counseling, pre- and postintervention

Characteristic	Preintervention (%) (N=136)	Postintervention (%) (N=207)
Patient received family planning counseling	42.4	85.5*
Among those who received counseling:		
Counseling provided by physician who performed procedure	8.9	45.8*
Person who gave counseling introduced self by name	18.2	36.2*
Patient addressed by name	55.4	72.7*
Counseling included explanation about:		
Family planning benefits	37.5	67.2*
Existing methods	19.6	50.9*
Advantages and disadvantages of each method	3.6	8.5
Method preference	57.1	81.7*
Patient felt enough confidence to ask questions	18.2	28.4
Doubts or concerns about methods were answered	44.7	70.4*
Patient felt time dedicated to counseling was sufficient	25.0	58.0*
Patient felt satisfied with counseling information	74.5	94.2*
Patient felt satisfied with manner of treatment by counselor	89.1	97.1*

Note: Sample sizes correspond to most variables presented in this table, although denominators may change for some due to missing values.

* $p<0.05$.

ers' attitudes about the importance of offering family planning counseling to their patients.

In spite of the failure to fully explain the advantages and disadvantages of each method, there was a significant improvement in the discussion about the patient's method preference, which is essential for correct and continuous contraceptive use. These results support the findings of previous studies mostly carried out in the 1970s and early 1980s: Not only do the majority of women who are offered contraception following an abortion accept it, but many women also begin using more effective methods after abortion (Benson et al. 1992). It is therefore very important that postabortion programs take into account individual needs, rather than hospital targets, and satisfy those needs with adequate information, empowered choice, and informed consent in the event of method acceptance (Faúndes 1991).

TABLE 5.9
Acceptance of postabortion contraception, pre- and postintervention

Characteristic	Preintervention (%) (N=132)	Postintervention (%) (N=207)
Patient accepted a contraceptive method	29.5	59.7*
Among those patients who accepted a contraceptive method:		
Patient received method prior to discharge	29.5	56.0*
Method preferred**		
Injections	35.9	58.5
IUD	30.8	26.0
Tubal ligation	28.2	8.9
Oral contraceptives	5.1	5.7
Condoms	0.0	0.8
Method received†		
Injections	48.7	51.2
IUD	33.3	16.3
Tubal ligation	17.9	10.6
Oral contraceptives	0.0	13.0
None	0.0	8.9
Patient received method of her choice	78.4	78.9
IUD inserted or tubal ligation performed without authorization	4.5	1.9

Note: Sample sizes correspond to most variables presented in this table, although denominators may change for some due to missing values.

* $p<0.05$. ** $p=0.02$. † $p=0.01$.

The intervention successfully encouraged interactive counseling sessions. Consequently, more women stated they felt confident enough to ask questions, and the fraction of patients whose concerns were resolved during counseling increased. Moreover, twice as many patients felt that the amount of time devoted to counseling was sufficient, and significantly more patients were satisfied with the information they received.

Use of Family Planning Methods

Analysis of the acceptance and delivery of postabortion contraception was based on data registered in women's clinical records and interviews with patients. Table 5.9 shows that before the intervention 30 percent of the patients declared having accepted a postabortion contraceptive method, and 30 percent of all the women reported having received the method at the hospital. Among the patients who did accept a method, the methods chosen were hormonal injectables, followed by the IUD, tubal ligation, and oral contraceptives.

The postintervention study showed a marked, statistically significant increase in the percentage of women who accepted a postabortion contraceptive method (from 30 percent to 60 percent), and in the percentage who received the method at the hospital before discharge (from 34 percent to 56 percent). While preference for the IUD and the pill remained unchanged, there were significant differences noted in other type of methods preferred among patients who received counseling: Requests for hormonal injections increased from 36 percent to 59 percent, while the percentage of patients who wanted a tubal ligation decreased from 28 percent to 9 percent. About three-fourths of patients in both groups indicated that they received their method of choice, but they were still given a limited array of choices. This finding suggests that contraceptive choice may have been based more on method availability and other factors than on the patient's informed selection.

Alarmingly, the results of this study showed that 5 percent of patients in the preintervention period either had an IUD inserted or a tubal ligation performed without their knowledge or approval. This proportion decreased to 2 percent in the postintervention period, but the practice still occurred. It is imperative to maintain an active surveillance of possible cases of violations of informed consent and reproductive rights and to ensure that such violations are eventually eliminated from hospital procedures.

Conclusions

Our intervention was successful in part because the design was comprehensive and because we emphasized an exchange of information: listening to patients and, in turn, providing good counseling. In addition to offering training in technical skills, a special focus was placed on improving interpersonal relationships and on the more humane aspects of postabortion care. These quality dimensions are frequently neglected but have a measurable influence on the effectiveness of a service or program.

The favorable economic effect on hospital savings documented by the complementary cost evaluation study, which demonstrated significantly lower costs of this program as compared to routine attention, fully justifies the recommendation of adoption of the program by public hospitals in Mexico (see Chapter 6 in this volume). Additionally, it can be seriously considered a viable alternative for other public health centers.

However, there are still challenges to be met regarding postabortion care. First, it is important to know what happens to women some time after an abortion experience: Do they still use contraception? Are they facing a new unwanted pregnancy? Do they make more frequent use of the whole range of reproductive health services? Second, it is necessary to follow up the program at the hospital: Are the changes that were implemented still in full force? Are trained professionals transferring their skills to new health personnel? Are there any difficulties in replacing equipment or purchasing more materials? What should be done to ensure the correct operation of the program? For those quality-of-care elements that the project did not succeed in modifying, such as providing ambulatory outpatient care for postabortion patients, we need to examine in greater depth the underlying reasons for the failure and advocate solutions for change.

This study in Oaxaca, as well as other studies in Latin America and disparate regions of the developing world aimed at improving postabortion care (Benson et al. 1998; Chambers and Saldaña-Rivera 1996; Fuentes Velazquez, Billings, and Cardona Perez 1998; Huntington and Nawar 1998; Solo et al. 1998; see also Chapter 4 in this volume), show that it is possible to improve the quality, effectiveness, and efficiency of postabortion care programs in public hospitals that are often underfunded, understaffed, and short on medical supplies. Our work, using both quantitative and qualitative methods to assess the impact of the program, also shows that the attitudes and practices of clinicians can be favorably modified, even with respect to sensitive matters like abortion. Likewise, it is evident that women appreciate good-quality care and welcome a greater constellation of services when the attention provided is more humane and adapted not only to their physical needs, but also to their emotional needs.

Those of us who work in health-related areas cannot elude the responsibility for the deaths of thousands of women in the world every year as a result of abortions performed under inadequate conditions. Because this procedure is largely clandestine and is a very sensitive subject in many cultures, many turn a blind eye and prefer to ignore the problem. However, the severe restrictions placed on safe services and the subsequently widespread practice of unsafe abortion are realities in many parts of the world and have reached the level of a "clandestine epidemic" in Latin America (Paxman et al. 1993). Acknowledging and understanding barriers to improved treatment of the victims of this epidemic will enable us to develop more humane programs for women suffering postabortion complications. In summary, action is required now to help accomplish the universal objective of improving the reproductive health of women. To achieve this goal requires a personal and institutional commitment from all who work in this field.

Acknowledgments

The authors wish to acknowledge the generous funding for this project provided by the European Union and the technical assistance provided by Ipas colleagues. We are very grateful for the hard work and steady participation of our colleagues, Dr. Francisca Ramirez and Beatriz Casas, and the support and participation of the patients and OB/GYN staff at the Dr. Aurelio Valdivieso General Hospital. We would like to extend a special thanks to hospital director Dr. Arturo Molina, chief of the hospital's OB/GYN ward Dr. Victor Morales, and onsite physician coordinator Dr. Felipe Sainoz.

Note

1 Shadow observations are nonparticipatory but direct observations in which highly skilled analysts note all characteristics of the circumstances, surroundings, and interactions involved at the study site during prolonged, usually uninterrupted, periods of observation. It is the chief method of ethnographers and is useful for observation of clinic operations and administrative procedures (Fisher et al. 1991).

References

Alan Guttmacher Institute. 1994. *Clandestine Abortion: A Latin American Reality.* New York: Alan Guttmacher Institute.

Benson, J., V. Huapaya, M. Abernathy, and J. Naghata. 1998. "Provider practices and patient perspectives in an integrated postabortion care model in Peru," paper presented at Global Meeting on Postabortion Care Operations Research, The Population Council, New York, 19–21 January.

Benson, J., A.H. Leonard, J. Winkler, M. Wolf, and K.E. McLaurin. 1992. *Meeting Women's Needs for Post-Abortion Family Planning: Framing the Questions,* Issues in Abortion Care monograph 2. Carrboro, N.C.: Ipas.

Chambers, M.V. and A. Saldaña-Rivera. 1996. "Resumen de experiencias programáticas con la atención postaborto en México" [Summary of programmatic experiences with postabortion care in Mexico]. Bulletin. Carrboro, N.C.: Ipas.

Consejo Nacional de Población [National Council on Population] (CONAPO). 1996. "Indicadores basicos de salud reproductiva y planificación familiar" [Basic indicators of reproductive health and family planning]. Mexico City, Mexico: CONAPO, p. 26.

Faúndes, Aníbal. 1991. "Calidad de la atención en la anticoncepción postparto" [Quality of care in postpartum contraception], presented at the Family Health International Postpartum Conference, September. Family Health International (FHI) Translation Series, no. 7S (unpublished).

Fisher, A.A., J.E. Laing, J.E. Stoeckel, and J.W. Townsend. 1991. *Handbook for Family Planning Operations Research Design,* 2nd ed. New York: Population Council.

Fuentes Velazquez, J.A., D.L. Billings, and J.A. Cardona Perez. 1998. "Women's experience of pain during postabortion care in Mexico," paper presented at Global Meeting on Postabortion Care Operations Research, The Population Council, New York, 19–21 January.

Greenslade, F.C., A.H. Leonard, J. Benson, J. Winkler, and V.L. Henderson. 1993. "Manual vacuum aspiration: A summary of clinical and programmatic experience worldwide," monograph. Carrboro, N.C.: Ipas, pp. ix–xi.

Greenslade, F.C., H. McKay, M. Wolf, and K. McLaurin. 1994. "Atención postaborto: Iniciativa de salud femenina" [Postabortion care: a women's health initiative], *Adelantos en el Tratamiento del Aborto* [Advances in Abortion Care] 4(1). Carrboro, N.C.: Ipas.

Huntington, D. and L. Nawar. 1998. "Introducing improved postabortion care in Egypt: Moving from a pilot study to large-scale expansion," paper presented at Global Meeting on Postabortion Care Operations Research, The Population Council, New York, 19–21 January.

Langer, A., C. García-Barrios, A. Heimburger, K. Stein, B. Winikoff, V. Barahona, B. Casas, and F. Ramirez. 1997. "Improving postabortion care in a public hospital in Oaxaca, Mexico," *Reproductive Health Matters* 9: 20–28.

Leonard, A.H. and O.A. Ladipo. 1994. "Planificación familiar post-aborto: Factores que influyen en la elección individual de métodos anticonceptivos" [Postabortion family planning: factors in individual choice of contraceptive methods], *Adelantos en el Tratamiento del Aborto* [Advances in Abortion Care] 4(2). Carrboro, N.C.: Ipas.

Paxman, J., A. Rizo, L. Brown, and J. Benson. 1993. "La epidemia clandestina: La práctica del aborto illegal en America Latina" [The clandestine epidemic: the practice of illegal abortion in Latin America], *Perspectivas Internacionales en Planificación Familiar* [International Family Planning Perspectives] special issue, pp. 9–15.

Rivas Zivy, M. and A. Amuchastegui Herrera. 1996. *Voces e Historias Sobre el Aborto* [Voices and stories about abortion]. Mexico City, Mexico: Edamex and Population Council.

Romero, M. 1994. "El aborto entre las adolescentes" [Abortion among adolescents] in *Razones y Pasiones en Torno al Aborto* [Reasons and passions related to abortion], ed. Adriana Ortega Ortiz. Mexico City, Mexico: Edamex and Population Council, pp. 242–245.

Solo, J., A. Ominde, M. Makumi, D. Billings, and C. Aloo-Obunga. 1998. "Creating linkages between incomplete abortion treatment and family planning services in Kenya: What works best?" report. The Africa Operations Research and Technical Assistance Project II, New York: Population Council.

World Health Organization (WHO). 1994. *Abortion: A Tabulation of Available Data on the Frequency and Mortality of Unsafe Abortion*, 2nd ed. Geneva: WHO/OMS Maternal and Safe Motherhood Programme.

6

Estimating Costs of Postabortion Services at Dr. Aurelio Valdivieso General Hospital, Oaxaca, Mexico

Carlos Brambila, Ana Langer,
Cecilia García-Barrios,
and Angela Heimburger

Health care systems around the world are facing problems associated with providing high-quality care with increasingly constrained resources. Out of an estimated 40–60 million induced abortions each year worldwide, approximately 200,000 women in developing countries die from abortion-related complications (Germain 1989). Some health care systems spend close to 60 percent of their OB/GYN budgets treating this problem (von Allmen et al. 1977). The standard of care requires that unsafe abortion be treated in a hospital/medical facility with adequately trained personnel. Studies done at Kenyatta National Hospital in Nairobi, Kenya, showed that 25 percent of all OB/GYN hospital admissions were for cases of incomplete abortion (Aggarwal and Matti 1980). Given the high percentage of resources devoted to treating this condition, it is imperative to evaluate and develop cost-effective methodologies to provide high-quality care.

Unsafe abortion performed by untrained and inexperienced providers, and its resulting complications, is the fourth leading cause of maternal mortality in Mexico (SSA 1992). The Alan Guttmacher Institute has calculated that at the beginning of the 1990s there were over half a million cases of induced abortion per year in Mexico alone. Many authorities feel that these statistics underestimate the true picture, as many abortion-related deaths are attributed to nonspecific hemorrhage or infection. For these reasons, incomplete and unsafe abortion is a serious public health problem in Mexico.

As in other developing countries, the costs associated with incomplete abortion in Mexico are extremely high, and treatment of this condition consumes the greatest amount of reproductive health care resources other than those devoted to normal births. Therefore, strengthening the capacity of health care institutions to provide high-quality postabortion care services that are cost-effective, accessible, and sustainable is a major public health objective.

Although evacuation by dilation and curettage (D&C) is still the standard of care for managing incomplete abortion in many developing countries (McLaurin, Hord, and Wolf 1991), efforts to control costs and improve quality of care have led to the development of manual vacuum aspiration (MVA). Research in Colombia, Kenya, Mexico, and Tanzania has shown that MVA is more cost-effective than D&C (Caceres, Gomez, and Vega 1981; Johnson et al. 1993; Magotti et al. 1995). These studies also found that outpatient management using either MVA or D&C resulted in shorter patient stays and hence lesser resource utilization, leading to decreased overall costs. On the other hand, these studies did not overtly address the issue of quality of care received by patients undergoing either D&C or MVA.

To improve its service-delivery model, the Dr. Aurelio Valdivieso General Hospital in Oaxaca implemented a redesigned service-delivery model for women seeking care for incomplete abortion. A full description of this intervention is found in the chapter by Ana Langer and colleagues in this volume.

Prior to the implementation of this intervention, the hospital most often performed D&C and did not routinely offer family planning counseling and contraceptive education to its patients. The goal was to provide high-quality care in a cost-efficient manner for cases of incomplete abortion. Integral components of this service-delivery model included:

- preferential use of MVA;
- provision of family planning counseling;
- easy availability of contraceptive methods; and
- availability of patient educational material focused on postabortion

care recommendations, warning signs of possible complications, and contraception.

The model was developed in consultation with various service providers and was introduced in meetings, seminars, and discussion groups so that all OB/GYN and hospital personnel were fully conversant with it. The improved service-delivery model was expected to improve quality of care and general patient satisfaction, leading to increased postabortion contraceptive use and decreased expenditures.

This study assesses the cost and quality implications of the new model, with the explicit aim of quantifying the savings (if any) resulting from the use of MVA. This study is unique because it is an attempt to understand the complete costs of a postabortion service-delivery model, identifying areas where maximum gains accrue in the care delivery process, while addressing simultaneously the quality of patient care.

Methods

Study Site

The Dr. Aurelio Valdivieso General Hospital is the largest public hospital in the state of Oaxaca, one of the poorest and most rural states in the south of Mexico. This civil hospital, situated in the capital city of Oaxaca, is managed by the Ministry of Health and serves the general public, the majority of whom come from poor socioeconomic backgrounds.[1] It also serves as a teaching hospital for the local medical school. Most patients come either from the surrounding urban areas or are referred from health centers in the largely indigenous, rural areas of the Oaxaca valley. In many cases, women must travel between three and eight hours to reach the hospital; approximately four women arrive each day to seek emergency treatment for incomplete or complicated abortions. Demand for services has grown sharply in the last few years.

In February 1996, with advice and support from the Population Council and funds from the European Union, Valdivieso Hospital initiated improvement of its postabortion services. Prior to the intervention, women who arrived at the hospital emergency ward in need of uterine evacuation were usually treated with D&C under general anesthesia and discharged within 48 hours. Family planning counseling was rare, and contraceptive methods were practically unavailable for the majority of postabortion patients upon hospital discharge.

Technique of Uterine Evacuation and Service Model

Routine Hospital Care Prior to the Intervention

Patients usually presented to the emergency room and were evaluated by the resident physician on call. Waiting time depended on the severity of the woman's condition; in general, deliveries were given higher priority than postabortion cases.

Patients had no privacy during the initial medical exam, as the front of the small consulting area was protected by only a thin curtain, and the back was open, allowing visual access to hospital personnel passing by. The attending resident took the medical history, examined the patient, and recorded observations in the clinical register. There was little interaction with the patient during this routine questioning, and often the physician addressed the patient only to request that she undress and lie on the examining table, with the result that patients received only minimal explanation of their medical situation.

Patients were then admitted and assigned to a bed in the OB/GYN ward. Postabortion patients were supposed to be roomed with women requiring hysterectomies or tubal ligations; however, because of space shortages they were often put with new mothers and their babies. Because Valdivieso is a teaching hospital, the medical residents and interns are generally responsible for the patient's diagnosis, surgical treatment, and monitoring. Although interns were usually responsible for taking the patient's medical history, this vital step would often occur after the uterine evacuation procedure had been carried out. D&C was performed in the operating room under general anesthesia.

During the postoperative recovery period, nurses would monitor the patient's vital signs, but there was little further interaction. Nurses did not counsel patients about postprocedure precautions or contraceptive method use. Prior to discharge, nurses would instruct patients in a perfunctory manner about diet, medications, and follow-up appointments.

Refined Service-Delivery Model

The objective of the service-delivery model was to improve postabortion quality of care while conserving resources. This was done by: (1) modifying hospital procedures to reduce waiting time, improve pain management, and ensure patient privacy; (2) using the MVA technique when indicated (instead of D&C); and (3) providing postabortion contraceptive counseling, educational materials, and contraceptives to patients.

Modification of hospital procedures. Workshops held with the gynecological service staff, hospital physicians, and administrators resulted in implementation of an improved protocol for treatment and care of patients with incomplete abortions: All patients with a fundal height of less than 12 cm would undergo uterine evacuation using MVA. All surgical operating rooms would function 24 hours a day, seven days a week, to enable postabortion patients arriving at night or during weekends to undergo MVA without undue delay. Family planning counseling would become a mandatory component of postabortion care services, and the family planning service was to be well-stocked with hormonal contraceptives, condoms, and IUDs, in order to provide a broad range of options for users. Contraceptives were to be given to the patient prior to hospital discharge.

The curtain in the consulting room of the emergency ward was replaced with a door. In addition, the back of the consulting room was sealed off to provide greater privacy. No attempt was made to reduce patient length of stay; however, use of MVA, which may be safely performed with local anesthesia, enabled hospital managers to reduce the length of stay to the minimum necessary.

Improvement of patient treatment, information, and counseling. Workshops were conducted to (1) sensitize providers to the circumstances facing women who experience an abortion, with the intent to modify their often negative attitudes toward these women; and (2) educate physicians and nurses in the provision of postabortion counseling, including family planning information.

These sessions emphasized the need to provide all women with information during the postabortion period about their almost immediate return to fertility and the possibility and risk of pregnancy before their next menstrual period; safe methods they could use to avoid or postpone pregnancy for at least six months; and where they could receive family planning services and methods on a regular basis. Furthermore, providers were taught how to support a woman's decision to use a contraceptive method, help identify which method was best suited for her, and train her (and her partner, if present) to use the method correctly. It was emphasized repeatedly that the patient be given the opportunity to ask questions and express her concerns.

In order to reinforce the points made during discussions and workshops, posters outlining salient points were displayed throughout the hospital, and patient brochures were printed and made available in waiting and consulting rooms.

Data Collection and Analysis

Cost Analysis

Cost analysis was based on the approach developed by Ipas (Abernathy et al. 1993). Fixed direct costs were estimated from information provided by hospital administrators, who furnished information on the salaries and average costs of hospital resource use.

Variable costs were estimated by following individual cases of incomplete or complicated abortion from the time of admission to hospital discharge. This shadow observation consisted of nonparticipant follow-up of patients during their entire hospital stay, with observers taking turns in three consecutive shifts. Nurses with prior experience in postabortion services at the hospital but not presently working in the OB/GYN area were trained over three days to conduct these observations. Patients included those with incomplete abortion, abortion in progress, and those with a case of dead and retained fetus who were admitted to the OB/GYN ward through the emergency ward. Cases of dysfunctional bleeding, threatened abortion, and abortion with complications such as uterine perforation and sepsis, as well as cases referred to the hospital from medical offices or other referral sources, were excluded.[2] To allow for normal variations in staffing and caseload, observations were made over a minimum ten-day period. Trained nurses used checklists to note material resources (medical instruments, drugs, disposable supplies, and so forth) used; data were collected on time spent by patients in each department or section and time devoted by hospital personnel to providing direct patient care. Indirect costs were not included in the analysis.[3]

To estimate preintervention costs, 11 cases were observed in this manner during a 20-day period in January 1996. Postintervention costs were estimated by shadow-observing 25 patients in July 1997. Costs were noted in Mexican pesos; however, in order to adjust for inflation, all costs are reported in constant January 1997 US dollars.[4] Cost categories reported in the analysis are listed below.

Hospitalization. Total yearly hospital expenditures for 1995 and 1996 were abstracted from the hospital's accounting system to ascertain hospitalization costs. Budget items included salaries of medical and administrative staff, medical supplies, instruments, food services, maintenance, and general services. These costs were prorated and adjusted for available beds and occupancy rate, to estimate the cost per bed per day of use.

Staff. Staff costs were estimated by prorating average salaries and benefits of specific providers for the time spent (in minutes) providing direct care to the patient. Time spent by providers (physicians, nurses, and administrative/support staff) at each station was explicitly noted in the shadow observations. For analytical purposes, this category excludes costs of family planning counseling, which is considered under family planning services.

Instruments and supplies. Specific quantities of each resource consumed were noted in the shadow observations. Consumable resources noted included medical instruments, other equipment and supplies, medicines, sterilization materials, and contraceptives. Costs of consumables are calculated on the basis of unit purchase price for the hospital. Transportation costs are included, but storage costs are excluded in this calculation.[5]

Family planning services. Since provision of family planning services was an important element of the service-delivery model, this cost was estimated separately. Observers registered the times of initiation and termination of all family planning information or counseling and noted the number and type of contraceptive materials provided to each patient. Costs were then estimated by prorating the average salary and benefits of the provider (physician or nurse) for the time spent per patient, and determining the purchase price of the contraceptive from the hospital administration records.

Intervention costs. It is vital for policymakers to know beforehand what a proposed intervention will cost, so that it can be included in a cost–benefit analysis of the proposed intervention. Keeping this in mind, we estimated the start-up costs for the service-delivery model separately. Intervention costs included direct project costs (project management, training sessions, travel, and so forth), supplies provided by Ipas (MVA syringes, printed materials, and so forth), and hospital costs (personnel training time, follow-up meetings, and supervision and monitoring). These intervention start-up costs were amortized over 10 years.

Quality of Care

In addition to using shadow observation to estimate costs, surveys were conducted to assess the service-delivery model's impact on quality of care. A baseline (preintervention) survey was conducted from July 1995 to January 1996. Data were collected on all patients admitted for incomplete abortion during this period. Included were those patients with incomplete abortion, abortion in progress, or those with a case of dead and retained fetus who were admitted to the gynecology floor through the emergency ward. The survey excluded cases of dysfunctional bleeding, threatened abortion, and abortion with complications such as uterine perforation and sepsis, as well as cases that were referred to the hospital from medical offices or other referral sources. A total of 132 patients were included in the survey.

The survey questionnaire, administered by three trained interviewers, ascertained basic sociodemographic information, surgical procedure received, details of pain management, degree of information provided to patient, level of provider–patient interaction, and details about the family planning counseling session. This questionnaire was supplemented with clinical information obtained from patients' medical records.

The postintervention survey of 207 patients was conducted from January to June 1997, using the same instrument.

Results

Sample Characteristics

Women in the pre- and postintervention groups shared similar sociodemographic characteristics. The average age was 26 years in both groups, and nearly 75 percent lived permanently with their spouses. Slightly more than three-fifths came from urban areas. Most women were housewives and economically dependent on their partners.

Length of Stay

Figure 6.1 delineates the mean length of patient stay per station in the pre- and postintervention period. Preintervention, the average wait was approximately 8.7 hours to undergo D&C, while the mean wait to undergo MVA was 5.8 hours postintervention. Once patients were released from the operating room, they waited approximately 17.9 hours to be discharged. This was reduced to 11.1 hours in the postintervention period. There was not a significant change in the operative time (26.6 minutes preintervention vs. 30.7 minutes postintervention). Overall, there was a 36 percent reduction in the average total length of stay per patient. The mean time spent in direct patient care by type of provider in the preintervention and postintervention phases is shown in Table 6.1. Presurgery nursing time (time from admission to procedure) decreased by 29 minutes (92.8 minutes preintervention vs. 63.8 minutes postinterven-

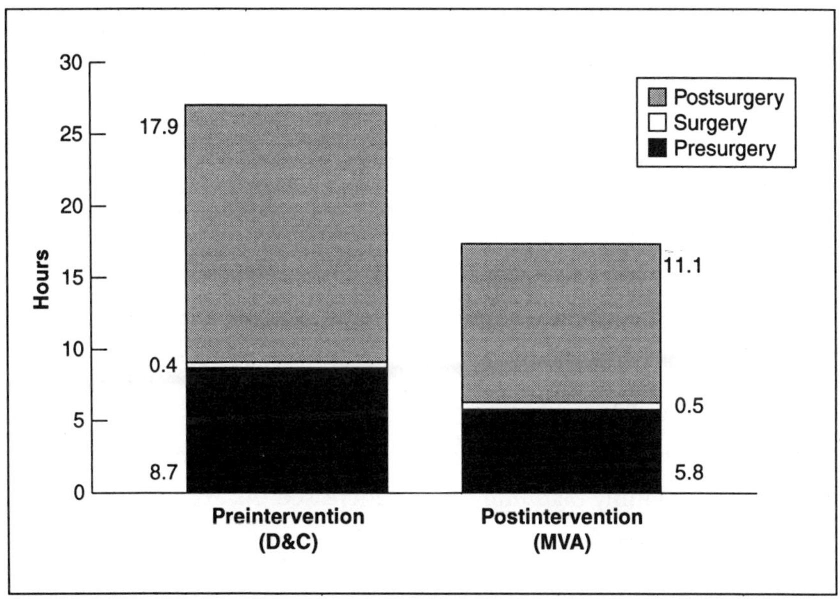

FIGURE 6.1 Mean length of patient stay per station, pre- and postintervention

tion), while physician time decreased by 13 minutes. In the operating room, physician time decreased by approximately 24 minutes, while nursing time increased by approximately ten minutes in the postintervention period. Postsurgery nursing time (time from procedure to hospital discharge) decreased by nearly 30 minutes, and physician time decreased by about seven minutes, compared to the preintervention period.

Changes in the total length of stay are not attributable exclusively to use of MVA; as noted earlier, however, use of MVA allowed hospital managers to reduce the length of stay to the minimum necessary. Reorganization of attention to postabortion patients resulted in less waiting time before surgical intervention, less direct intervention by physicians, more nursing time during surgery, and less recovery time. These results may be interpreted as a more efficient use of service provider time.

Cost of Treating Patients

Figure 6.2 shows the average cost of treating a postabortion patient in the pre- and postintervention phases. The average total cost in the preintervention phase (using D&C as the procedure of choice) was US$264.47.

TABLE 6.1
Mean per-patient time in minutes spent by service provider, pre- and postintervention

	Nurse		Physician	
	Preintervention (D&C)	Postintervention (MVA)	Preintervention (D&C)	Postintervention (MVA)
Presurgery	92.8	63.8	88.1	75.1
Surgery	22.2	32.1	80.3	56.2
Postsurgery	74.8	45.1	25.6	18.2

This decreased by almost 32 percent to $180.22 when the improved service-delivery model was implemented. Substantial reductions took place in the categories of hospitalization, staff, and instrument/supply costs, while costs for family planning services increased. As expected, there was substantial intervention cost in the postintervention period. Table 6.2 describes these changes in greater detail.

Hospitalization. On a dollar basis, the largest reduction occurred in the costs associated with hospitalization. Preintervention hospitalization costs were $150.77, and these decreased by nearly $65.00 (43 percent) in the postintervention period to $85.89.

Staff. Staffing costs decreased by 33 percent, from $21.70 in the preintervention period to $14.50 postintervention. In both periods, nursing costs account for most of the cost of personnel; there was, however, a reduction in this expenditure, from $12.70 to $9.30.

Instruments and supplies. Costs of instruments and supplies decreased from $91.80 in the preintervention phase to $32.50 in the postintervention phase, a reduction of almost 65 percent ($59.30). Reductions occurred across all categories: instruments (89 percent), supplies (52 percent), medicines (68 percent), and sterilization materials (60 percent).

Family planning services. Costs of family planning services increased from $0.20 to $2.90, with increases in both staff ($0.20 preintervention to $1.60 postintervention) and contraceptives ($0.00 preintervention to $1.30 postintervention).

Intervention costs. The amortized intervention cost per patient was $44.43, which includes project costs ($266,532), supplies (including syringes)

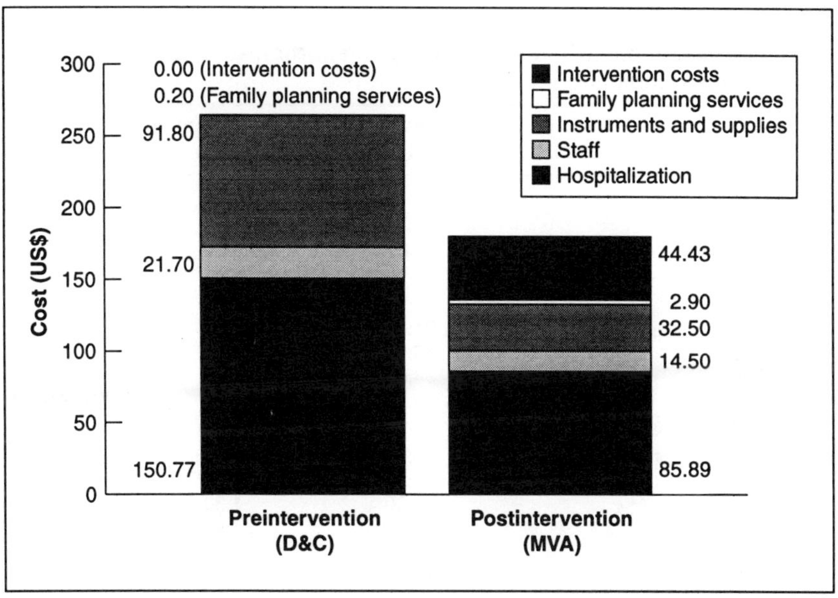

FIGURE 6.2 Cost summary of postabortion services, pre- and postintervention

provided by Ipas ($3,000), and hospital expenses (personnel training time, follow-up meetings, and supervision and monitoring, totaling $7,641).[6]

Quality of Care

Quality of care results are shown in Table 6.3. There was no difference between the pre- and postintervention groups with regard to pain management. Nearly equal percentages of women were given analgesics pre- and postsurgery in the two groups.

There were significant differences in the two groups with regard to information provided to patients, physician–patient interaction, and family planning counseling. Patients were more likely to be informed about their diagnostic results, surgical procedures, and postoperative progress in the postintervention phase, and patients were more satisfied with the information provided. Physicians were more likely to introduce themselves and address the patient by her name in the postintervention period, thus increasing the patient's confidence in her treating physician.

TABLE 6.2
Mean per-patient costs in US dollars of postabortion services, pre- and postintervention

	Preintervention (D&C)	Postintervention (MVA)	Change
Hospitalization	150.77	85.89	–64.88
Staff	21.70	14.50	–7.20
Physicians	7.60	4.80	–2.80
Nurses	12.70	9.30	–3.40
Other	1.40	0.40	–1.00
Instruments and supplies	91.80	32.50	–59.30
Instruments	13.50	1.50	–12.00
Supplies	34.60	16.70	–17.90
Medicines	40.70	13.10	–27.60
Sterilization materials	3.00	1.20	–1.80
Family planning services	0.20	2.90	+2.70
Staff	0.20	1.60	+1.40
Contraceptives	0.00	1.30	+1.30
Intervention costs	0.00	44.43	+44.43
Total costs	264.47	180.22	–84.25

TABLE 6.3
Quality of postabortion care provided, pre- and postintervention

Care provided	Preintervention (%) (D&C) (n=132)	Postintervention (%) (MVA) (n=207)
Pain management		
Patient received presurgery pain treatment	26.7	25.7
Patient received postsurgery pain treatment	97.7	96.0
Information provided		
Patient informed about diagnostic result	68.3	87.3*
Patient informed about surgical procedure	83.2	87.3*
Patient informed about postsurgical progress	19.8	62.6*
Patient satisfied with information received	17.6	72.5*
Physician–patient interaction		
Physician introduced self to patient	26.1	51.0*
Physician addressed patient by name	59.1	84.8*
Patient felt confidence in her physician	52.4	73.6*
Family planning counseling		
Patient received family planning counseling	42.4	85.5*
Patient discussed preferred method	57.1	81.7*
Patient accepted method prior to discharge	28.8	57.0*

* $p<0.05$

Patients were also more likely to receive family planning counseling in the postintervention phase. Providers were more likely to discuss patient preferences with them, and patients had a higher likelihood of accepting a method of their choice prior to hospital discharge.

Discussion

The results of this study show that the improved service-delivery model achieved significant cost savings and simultaneously improved quality of care for patients undergoing postabortion treatment. There was a 36 percent reduction in the length of stay in the hospital from (27.0 to 17.4 hours), with the lower figure comparable to that reported in the literature. Johnson and colleagues (1993) found that the average duration of stay in Kenyan hospitals for patients undergoing D&C ranged from 40.9 to 100.7 hours, while the average stay for MVA patients ranged from 18.8 to 23.9 hours. In the same multicenter study, the average stay for D&C patients in Mexico ranged from 11.7 to 29.9 hours, and the stay for MVA patients for the lone hospital performing MVA in their sample was 11.4 hours. In a report from Tanzania, hospital stay for MVA patients was 41 percent shorter than that for D&C patients (Magotti et al. 1995).

It is imperative to understand the factors behind this significant reduction, for it is easy to be misled into thinking that it is due to the introduction of MVA alone. While MVA reduces postsurgical recovery time, as the procedure does not require general anesthesia, the service-delivery model also saw a reduction in preoperative waiting time, due largely to the policy of keeping the surgical ward operating 24 hours a day, thus eliminating the wait many postabortion cases had to endure in the past.

The other notable change was the increase in the time spent in ultrasound diagnostics, from eight minutes preintervention to nearly 39 minutes postintervention, an indication perhaps of the increased attention being paid to improving the quality of patient care (data not shown).

Reporting their results in May 1991 US dollars, Johnson and colleagues (1993) found that the average per-patient cost of D&C in Mexican hospitals varied from \$79 to \$235, while the cost of MVA was \$65.73, a difference of 17–72 percent. They reported that hospitalization accounted for the largest proportion of average cost per patient, with personnel costs the second greatest contributors. In our study, the cost (in January 1997 US dollars) of treating patients with D&C was \$264.47, and we achieved a 32 percent reduction with the introduction of the improved service-delivery model to $180.22, even though the intervention itself was assigned a cost of $44.43 per patient. Assuming an annual caseload of 600 postabortion cases, these costs translate to potential cost savings of $50,550 per year.

The bulk of these dollar savings arise from decreased length of hospital stay. Substantial savings were also achieved through reductions across all categories of instruments and supplies used in the service-delivery model. The cost of supplies decreased because fewer glucose solutions, surgical gloves, and elastic bandages were used in the MVA procedure. While the reduction in medicines was essentially due to decreased use of Xylocaine tablets, there was a significant increase in the use of thiopental sodium. These changes reflect the different anesthetic requirements of MVA as compared to D&C. The reduction in the cost of instruments was due to the fact that the cost of MVA syringes was considered part of the intervention costs, and was subsumed under that category. Studies have shown that the average proportion of total patient cost attributable to MVA instruments and their resterilization is 1 percent in Mexico and 9–16 percent in Kenya (Johnson et al. 1993). This difference may be explained by the more expensive cost of labor in Mexico compared with Kenya, and not by the cost of instruments per se.

Staffing costs decreased postintervention; however, they do not constitute a major portion of total cost. While nursing costs were higher than those for physicians, they did not equal more than 6 percent of the total costs pre- and postintervention. This finding was also reported from research in Tanzania (Magotti et al. 1995).

As expected, costs for family planning services increased. This was due in equal measure to the time spent by the provider counseling the patient and providing contraceptives, but the cost of these services accounted for only 1.6 percent of total costs.

This study explicitly quantified the costs of intervention, because policymakers need this information to make cost-effectiveness judgments when introducing similar programs in their health care facilities. While Ipas provided supplies free or at low cost (such as MVA syringes, training materials, pamphlets, leaflets, and posters) we attempted to quantify these and include them in our calculations. We also included direct project costs (salaries of training personnel, training expenses, and so forth) and costs of hospital personnel involved in various workshops. Many studies do not explicitly address these costs. We feel it is important to discuss them up front, as they constitute a major portion ($44.43 per patient or nearly 25 percent) of the average per-patient cost for the MVA service-delivery model.

In addition to significant cost savings, the service-delivery model improved the quality of postabortion care for patients at Valdivieso Hospital. Significant improvements were noted in physician–patient interaction and information exchange, leading to greater trust between the provider and patient and increased compliance with provider recommendations. These improvements were reflected in part by the significantly increased acceptance of family planning methods by patients prior to discharge.

Conclusion

Our results demonstrate that it is feasible to achieve cost savings without compromising quality of care for postabortion patients. Future research will determine whether these findings can stand the test of time and can be successfully implemented in other facilities in Latin America. Furthermore, this service-delivery model might be used as a template for similar programs in other medical specialties. The success of such a model depends not only on the introduction of the improved surgical procedure, but also on concurrent refinement of patient management protocols. In addition, wholehearted support from health facility management and providers is a crucial, but oft-neglected, ingredient.

Notes

1 In Mexico, almost one-third of the population has no health insurance (private or social) and thus receives care in public institutions similar to Valdivieso Hospital.

2 These patients were excluded because they were not the "typical" patients seen by the hospital on a routine basis; these few cases would have biased the mean costs greatly. Moreover, the resources used to treat complications would have been nearly identical irrespective of the evacuation procedure used (D&C or MVA).

3 Indirect costs include the depreciation of infrastructure and capital goods such as vehicles, medical and nonmedical equipment, instruments, and so forth, as well as

state- and central-level administrative costs. These were not included because there is no reliable accounting information available at the state or central levels to ascertain them and because, from the policy perspective, these costs are outside the control of hospital directors and administrators. Moreover, they would have been, in all probability, equal in the pre- and postintervention periods.

4 Inflation in Mexico was 52.0 percent in 1995, 27.0 percent in 1996, and 8.7 percent in 1997.

5 Storage costs are subsumed under yearly hospital expenditures, and thus are included under hospitalization costs.

6 Further details can be obtained from the authors. Briefly, the cost ($277,173) was amortized over a ten-year period, and costs for the 15-month intervention were calculated. These were then divided by the total number of postabortion cases treated in the 15-month period. A ten-year period was chosen as an amortization considering the average working period of basic service personnel, excluding students and residents. This statement means that we may expect trainees to use their knowledge and skills at the hospital for an average of ten years.

References

Abernathy, M., C. Hord, L.A. Nicholson, J. Benson, and B.R. Johnson. 1993. *A Guide to Assessing Resource Use for the Treatment of Incomplete Abortion.* Carrboro, N.C.: Ipas.

Aggarwal, V.P. and J.K. Matti. 1980. "Review of abortions at Kenyatta National Hospital, Nairobi," *East African Medical Journal* 57(2): 138–143.

Caceres, G.H., F. Gomez, and A. Vega. 1981. *Manejo Hospitalario del Aborto Incompleto: Estudio Comparativo del Curetaje Uterino versus la Aspiración por Vacío* [Hospital management of incomplete abortion: comparative study of uterine curettage versus vacuum aspiration], monograph series 16. Bogotá, Colombia: Corporación Centro Regional del Población, pp. 45–81.

Germain, A. 1989. "The Christopher Tietze International Symposium: An overview," *International Journal of Gynaecology and Obstetrics* 3(suppl): 1–8.

Johnson, B.R., J. Benson, J. Bradley, and A. Rabago Ordonez. 1993. "Costs and resource utilization for the treatment of incomplete abortion in Kenya and Mexico," *Social Science and Medicine* 36(11): 1443–1453.

Magotti, R.F., P.G. Munjinja, R.S. Lema, and E.K. Ngwalle. 1995. "Cost-effectiveness of managing abortions: Manual vacuum aspiration (MVA) compared to evacuation by curettage in Tanzania," *East African Medical Journal* 72(4): 248–251.

McLaurin, K.E., C.E. Hord, and M. Wolf. 1991. "Health system's role in abortion care: The need for a pro-active approach." *Issues in Abortion Care* no. 1. Carrboro, N.C.: Ipas.

Secretaría de Salud (SSA). 1992. *La Mujer Adolescente, Adulta y Anciana y su Salud* [The adolescent, adult and elderly woman and her health]. Mexico City, Mexico: SSA, Dirección General de Salud Materno Infantil.

von Allmen, S.D., W. Cates Jr., K.F. Schulz, D.A. Grimes, and C.W. Tyler. 1977. "Costs of treating abortion-related complications," *Family Planning Perspectives* 9(6): 273–276.

7

Cost Analysis of Postabortion Services in Egypt

Laila Nawar, Dale Huntington,
and Mohammed Naguib Abdel Fattah

Complications resulting from induced abortion are an important health problem for women in many countries, especially those that are less-developed. In countries where induced abortion is illegal or allowed only on narrow grounds (e.g., in cases of rape, incest, or to protect a woman's health) the practice is generally undocumented and frequently dangerous; nevertheless, it is obtained by millions of women.

In Egypt abortion is permitted only in cases of life-threatening maternal health considerations. In addition, it is surrounded by many religious and social sanctions. These circumstances have constrained the provision of high-quality emergency health care services to postabortion patients, including the discussion and provision of family planning. The standard treatment of incomplete abortion is dilation and curettage (D&C), which is usually performed in the operation theater under general anesthesia.

Introducing Improved Postabortion Care in Egypt

In 1994 a small-scale pilot study was conducted by the Egyptian Fertility Care Centre and the Population Council's Asia and Near East Operations Research and Technical Assistance (ANE OR/TA) Project (Huntington et al. 1995) to improve postabortion care in Egypt. The study, conducted in two hospitals, introduced improvements in postabortion care through an intensive training program and follow-up monitoring that centered on the use of manual vacuum aspiration (MVA) under local anesthesia. Infection control practices and counseling procedures were also substantially strengthened, including referral for family planning. Results from the pilot study showed significant improvement in the care of postabortion patients.

The success of this pilot study led the ANE OR/TA Project to develop a comprehensive "Introduction Program for Improved Postabortion Care in Egypt," which was approved by the government of Egypt. A major component of this program was a small-scale expansion of improved postabortion care services in ten hospitals, both medical universities and public-sector hospitals (Nawar and Huntington 1997). This chapter presents results from a cost analysis, conducted as part of the 1996–97 expansion program, of the medical procedures associated with adopting MVA within a package of improved quality of care.

Study Sites

Two types of government health facilities were selected to illustrate the costs associated with improving postabortion care and to establish a cost-effective basis for guiding future hospital management practices and protocols related to postabortion care.

Abou Korkas District Hospital is a small district hospital in rural Upper Egypt with 210 beds and an occupancy rate of 34 percent. It admits 0–2 incomplete abortion cases per day. Menia General Hospital is a larger hospital situated in the capital city of the Menia governorate. It has 358 beds and an occupancy rate of 68 percent. It admits 2–3 incomplete abortion cases per day. Both are fairly representative of district and general hospitals within the Ministry of Health and Population (MOHP) sector.

Study Methodology

The study compared costs associated with the treatment protocols of the two surgical methods (D&C and MVA) used to treat postabortion patients, through pre- and postintervention surveys in the two hospitals. Between the surveys the expansion program introduced comprehensive improvements in the medical care and counseling of postabortion patients (described in Nawar and Huntington 1997). A standard methodology (Abernathy et al. 1993) for assessing treatment costs of patients with incomplete abortion was adapted for use in Egypt. The hospitals' overhead costs were estimated in collaboration with the Data for Decision Making team of the MOHP and the Harvard School of Public Health. A brief description of these two cost components is given below.

Treatment Costs

On-site assessment and designation of all patient treatment areas was completed at each of the two hospitals. Treatment areas are those stations in the hospital that correspond to different hospitalization stages (e.g., reception, operation theater, recuperation). In addition, the study team observed all transfers between treatment areas and noted waiting times from admission through discharge. Four nurses in each hospital were trained and closely supervised to collect (through shadow observation) the following information in each treatment area and at patient transfer from one area to the next:

- time spent (in minutes) by each member of the hospital staff interacting with the patient, by category of staff; and
- detailed listing of all medications and materials used in patient treatment.

Collection of treatment cost data was completed over two shifts daily from 7:00 a.m. to 11:00 p.m. during a continuous 30-day period in both the pre- and postintervention phases. Each enrolled patient was closely followed through all treatment areas by two observers per shift; one noted staff time and the other medications and materials used. This intensive observation allowed for only one patient to be tracked at a time. It was therefore not possible to observe all postabortion patients, especially when admissions were narrowly spaced; however, a majority of cases were observed in each hospital (90 percent in Menia Hospital and 94 percent in Abou Korkas Hospital). The number of patients observed at the different treatment areas varied, as not every patient followed the same treatment path in the course of her hospitalization. In addition, women with major presenting complications were not included in this study (i.e., cases requiring intensive monitoring before concluding the operations); only routine cases were eligible for cost analysis.

TABLE 7.1
Number of patients observed, pre- and postintervention: Menia General and Abou Korkas District Hospitals

	Preintervention[a]	Postintervention			
Hospital	**D&C**	**D&C**	**MVA**	**MVA + D&C**	**Total**
Abou Korkas District Hospital	15	6	12	0	18
Menia General Hospital	35	8	23	4	35

[a] In the preintervention period no patients were treated with MVA.

Hospital Overhead Costs

Five staff members from each hospital were trained to collect data on all categories of hospital overhead costs during the last fiscal year for which data were available (1994–95). Total costs for each of the two hospitals during the year were assigned to the hospital departments according to the proportion of support provided by each department through a standard step-down method: Overhead departments provide support to intermediate service and direct service departments, and intermediate service departments provide procedures and services to patients in direct service departments.[1]

Findings

Number of Patients Observed

The numbers of patients shown in Table 7.1 reflect differences in the daily caseload received by each site, which explains the higher number of patients observed in Menia General Hospital. In total, 35 patients were observed in Menia General Hospital in the pre- and postintervention periods, while 15 and 18 patients were observed in Abou Korkas Hospital pre- and postintervention, respectively. During the preintervention period all patients received D&C, whereas after the study intervention was introduced the majority of patients received MVA (some patients received D&C, depending on how the attending physician felt about using D&C and MVA). In addition, four patients in Menia Hospital were treated by both MVA and D&C. Observers reported that for these cases, physicians began the procedure using MVA and then switched to D&C to be certain

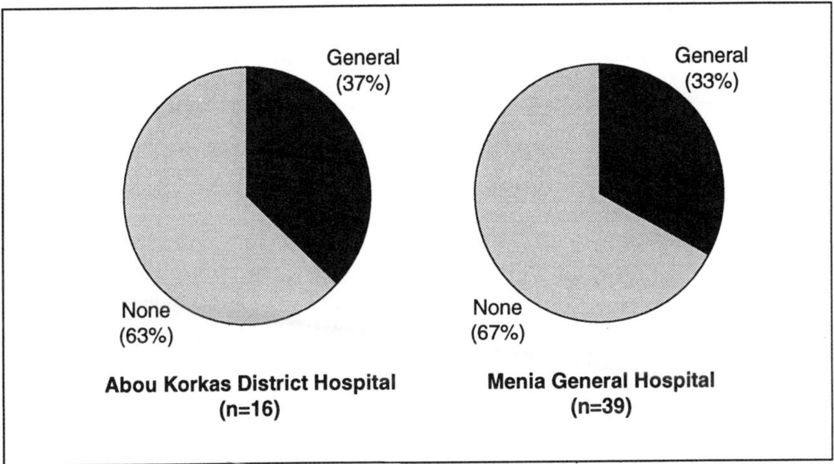

FIGURE 7.1 Type of anesthesia used in treating postabortion patients undergoing D&C, preintervention
Source: Medical records.

uterine contents were completely evacuated. In the preintervention period, most postabortion cases were treated without any anesthesia (Figure 7.1), which has implications for costs associated with improving services.

Patient Treatment Time Through Service Stations

Table 7.2 presents a summary of patient time (in minutes) spent in treatment at Menia Hospital, using only observations related to cases treated with MVA in the postintervention period.[2] According to observations conducted in the preintervention, the average time spent by the patient between admission and discharge was 1,109 minutes (18.5 hours) ranging from 100 to 2,600 minutes. The average patient time spent at the hospital declined in the postintervention, when MVA was used (771 minutes [12.9 hours]). The decline in patient time occurred mostly in the postoperative phase.

The average time spent in presurgery represents only 13 percent of the overall average patient treatment time in the preintervention period, and 16 percent in the postintervention period. Both before and after improvements in care were introduced, the time for surgical interventions averaged about 24 minutes, representing only 2–3 percent of average patient time. To explain why average surgery time is equal in the pre- and

TABLE 7.2
Summary of patient time in minutes, pre- and postintervention, by treatment phase: Menia General Hospital

Treatment phase	Preintervention (D&C) (n=35)	Postintervention (MVA) (n=23)
Total preoperative time	3,474	2,920
Average preoperative time	146	127
Total operative time	837	544
Average operative time	24	24
Total postoperative time	32,621	14,257
Average postoperative time	939	621
Total time	36,932	17,721
Average time	1,109	771
Maximum time	2,600	2,322
Minimum time	100	149

postintervention periods, it is worth noting that many physicians were just learning how to perform MVA at the time of the study; therefore, they were not carrying out the procedure as efficiently as they would have if they knew it better. Both pre- and postintervention, patients spent the largest amount of time (81–85 percent, on average) in the postoperative phase.

Table 7.3 presents comparable data on patient time at Abou Korkas Hospital. While average preoperative time remained nearly unchanged or increased slightly in the postintervention compared to the preintervention period (21 minutes vs. 19 minutes), average operative time declined (13 minutes vs. 17 minutes). In addition, average postoperative patient time substantially declined, from 527 minutes in the preintervention to only 140 minutes in the postintervention period. On average, the patient stayed at the hospital in the preintervention between admission and discharge for 564 minutes (9.4 hours) compared with 174 minutes (2.9 hours) in the postintervention, representing a 69 percent reduction in total time spent in the district hospital.

Interviews with Menia General Hospital senior staff indicated that the hospital's patient management protocols do not allow for patient discharge to occur before the next day's morning rounds, when the physician-in-charge signs the necessary papers that allow the patient to leave

TABLE 7.3
Summary of patient time in minutes, pre- and postintervention, by treatment phase: Abou Korkas District Hospital

Treatment phase	Preintervention (D&C) (n=15)	Postintervention (MVA) (n=12)
Total preoperative time	256	178
Average preoperative time	19	21
Total operative time	262	158
Average operative time	17	13
Total postoperative time	7,871	1,685
Average postoperative time	527	140
Total time	8,389	2,021
Average time	564	174
Maximum time	1,053	373
Minimum time	97	102

the hospital. In some cases, however, a patient's relatives may exert pressure to allow patient discharge directly after treatment, and the attending physician may ask the physician-in-charge to sign discharge paperwork before the next morning. This is not the case, however, at Abou Korkas Hospital, where physicians sign discharge paperwork as soon as patient treatment is complete. Patients are therefore free to leave the hospital when they feel able or when their relatives are available to pick them up, which results in some cost savings. The improvements in the quality of postabortion services did not include modifying the discharge procedures, hence there was no change in this policy at either site between the pre- and postintervention surveys.

In addition, preoperative waiting time may be affected by a number of factors that were not addressed by the program to improve quality of services. For example, incomplete abortion cases may be assigned relatively low priority compared with other life-threatening or urgent cases (e.g., emergency cesarean sections). Providers' attitudes are another factor that can influence the amount of nontreatment time a patient spends in the hospital. For example, physicians who do not consider postabortion care a priority may not attend postabortion patients immediately.

Figure 7.2 illustrates the average amount of time spent in the three major service stages at each hospital.

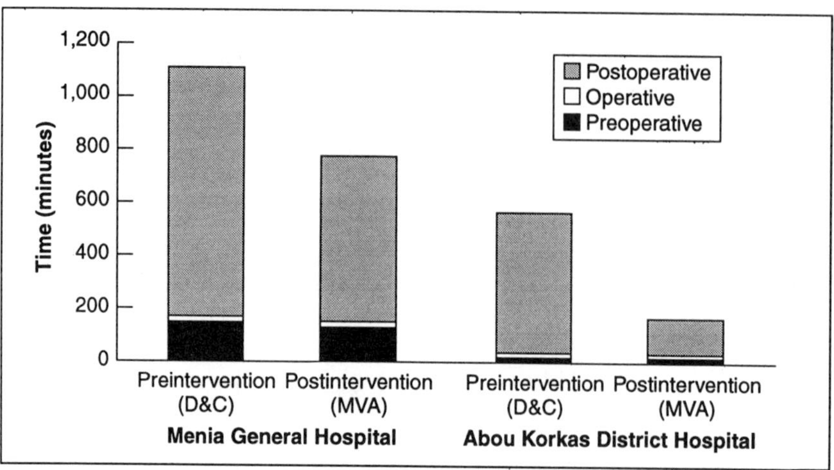

FIGURE 7.2 Average patient time in minutes, by treatment phase: Menia General and Abou Korkas District Hospitals

Hospital Overhead Costs

Hospital costs for the 1994–95 fiscal year estimated for the two hospitals indicated an overhead cost of LE27.00 (US$7.96)[3] per day for Menia General Hospital and LE31.27 ($9.22) for Abou Korkas District Hospital. Table 7.4 shows the distribution of these costs per day for the two hospitals. The hospitals devoted most of their financial resources to operation theaters and utilities.

Human Resources Time

Table 7.5 summarizes the average time (in minutes) that staff at the two hospitals spent interacting directly with patients pre- and postintervention. Residents are clearly major providers of service to postabortion patients in both hospitals. They are responsible for examination/diagnosis, preoperative patient care and preparation, and performing the operation, but are not heavily involved in postoperative monitoring.

According to the observations made, nurses also play an important role in service provision during all treatment phases. In addition to preparing patients for examination, caring for them during the preoperative phase, and assisting residents during the operation, they are responsible

TABLE 7.4
Percent distribution of per-day overhead components: Menia General and Abou Korkas District Hospitals

Item	Menia General Hospital	Abou Korkas District Hospital
Per-day overhead	LE27.00 $7.96	LE31.27 $9.22
Building	3.5	4.7
Equipment	1.8	0.7
Utilities	15.8	12.5
Overhead support	8.9	5.1
Kitchen	2.6	1.2
Ambulance	1.3	—
Inpatient laboratory	4.1	0.8
Inpatient pharmacy	2.0	2.2
Operation theaters	52.0	61.2
Inpatient radiology	3.4	3.3
Blood bank	4.5	7.9
Postmortem	0.1	0.4
Total	100.0	100.0

for postoperative routine check-up and patient monitoring, including giving medicine. They also provide family planning counseling to patients before discharge. In addition to residents and nurses, janitors were also observed to play an important role in service provision to postabortion patients. They transfer patients to main service stations, clean service sites, and assist nurses in patient preparation and cleaning.

In the preintervention period, each patient at Menia General Hospital was given, on average, 45 minutes of direct attention by the resident, and 50 and 31 minutes by the nurse and janitor, respectively. Specialists devoted only five minutes of their time, on average, to each patient. In the postintervention, the total time spent by each of these providers on patient care declined. In contrast, in Abou Korkas Hospital residents and nurses devoted less time to each patient in the preintervention (each an average of 18 minutes), but more time in the postintervention (20 and 23 minutes, respectively) as a result of improving the quality of care (e.g., providing counseling).

TABLE 7.5
Summary of average time in minutes spent per patient by service providers: Menia General and Abou Korkas District Hospitals

Service provider	Menia		Abou Korkas	
	Preintervention (n=35)	Postintervention (n=23)	Preintervention (n=15)	Postintervention (n=12)
House officer	3.6	7.8	—	—
Resident	45.0	25.4	18.0	20.0
Specialist	5.2	3.0	0.8	0.0
Consultant	0.1	0.0	—	—
Nurse	50.1	36.8	18.1	23.0
Janitor	31.2	19.0	19.0	15.0
Registrar	—	—	0.3	0.9

Human Resources Cost

Tables 7.6 and 7.7 present data on total cost, in Egyptian pounds, of labor time by type of provider in the two study sites in the pre- and postintervention phases. The total cost of labor is estimated on the basis of salary per minute and the total time spent by each service provider at all service stations.

Although residents and nurses are the main service providers, their participation in patient treatment is inexpensive due to their low salary levels. In general for the two study sites the participation of residents and nurses represents each about one-third of total labor cost (somewhat more in the postintervention period).

Tables 7.6 and 7.7 also show average cost of labor per patient at the two study sites in pre- and postintervention phases. In Menia General Hospital average labor cost per patient was LE2.41 ($0.71) in the preintervention using D&C and LE2.24 ($0.66) in the postintervention using MVA. In Abou Korkas District Hospital average labor cost per patient was even lower, LE1.22 ($0.36) in the preintervention using D&C, and LE1.41 ($0.42) in the postintervention using MVA. These data indicate that the savings in staff time in Menia General Hospital associated with the use of MVA in the postintervention (or even the relative increase in staff time in Abou Korkas District Hospital in the postintervention)

TABLE 7.6
Total cost of labor in Egyptian pounds (LE), by service provider, and average cost of labor per patient: Menia General Hospital

Service provider	Cost per minute	Preintervention (D&C) (n=35)	Postintervention (MVA) (n=23)
House officer	.020	2.52	3.60
Resident	.030	24.70	15.55
Specialist	.034	6.27	2.34
Consultant	.055	0.22	0.00
Nurse	.026	32.90	22.25
Janitor	.020	17.70	7.66
Total		84.31	51.40
Average cost (LE)		2.41	2.24
($)		0.71	0.66

TABLE 7.7
Total cost of labor in Egyptian pounds (LE), by service provider, and average cost of labor per patient: Abou Korkas District Hospital

Service provider	Cost per minute	Preintervention (D&C) (n=15)	Postintervention (MVA) (n=12)
Resident	.030	6.70	6.80
Specialist	.034	0.24	0.00
Nurse	.026	6.53	7.13
Janitor	.020	4.80	2.81
Registrar	.020	0.00	0.20
Total cost		18.38	16.94
Average cost (LE)		1.22	1.41
($)		0.36	0.42

are not reflected in substantial changes in labor cost due to the low salary levels of the principal service providers.

Costs of Supplies, Materials, and Medicines

During the introduction of improved postabortion care through the pilot study (Huntington et al. 1995), hospital staff opposed the reuse of MVA cannulas because of concerns about proper sterilization; all cannulas were discarded after a single use. This treatment protocol has continued to date in Egypt. In addition, observers documented use of more than one cannula in treating some patients: Some newly trained residents started the operation with a cannula of one size, which was then changed to one of more appropriate size in the course of conducting the operation. This practice was a factor in elevating the cost of supplies during the postintervention when MVA was used.

On average, the cost of supplies, materials, and medicines per patient increased substantially in the postintervention (MVA) compared with the preintervention (D&C).[4] This cost is estimated at LE25.57 ($7.54) in the preintervention and LE32.40 ($9.56) in the postintervention for Menia General Hospital. Comparable costs at Abou Korkas District Hospital are LE12.80 ($3.78) in the preintervention and LE25.23 ($7.44) in the postintervention (data not shown). These increases are due to the relatively insufficient use of medical supplies and pain control medication in the preintervention, and the improvements in the quality of care during the postintervention that required a more intensive use of medical supplies.

Final Per-Patient Cost Items

Tables 7.8 and 7.9 show summary totals of the combined costs (grouped in three categories) per patient in the two study sites for the preintervention (D&C) and postintervention (MVA).

The data indicate an 8 percent increase in the total per-patient cost in Menia General Hospital and a 32 percent increase in the total cost per patient in Abou Korkas District Hospital after improvements in the quality of services were introduced.

Cost increases are due mainly to the increase in the costs of supplies and medicines associated with use of MVA. These costs are not offset by reductions in length of hospital stay. In both pre- and postintervention phases, supplies, materials, and medicines made up the major portion of postabortion service costs, accounting for about one-half of the total cost per patient in the preintervention and from two-thirds to more than four-fifths of total cost per patient in the postintervention at both study sites. This differs from comparable findings from other countries that indicate the major source of postabortion service costs is bed time use (Johnson et al. 1993; see also Chapter 6 in this volume). However, a study in Ecuador

TABLE 7.8
Summary of cost items per patient in Egyptian pounds (LE): Menia General Hospital

		Postintervention (MVA)	
	Preintervention (D&C)	Actual cost per single use of MVA cannula	Estimated cost per MVA cannula reuse
Per-bed time use	20.8	14.5	14.5
Labor cost	2.4	2.4[a]	2.4[a]
Supplies and medicines	25.6	36[a]	28.7[a]
Total cost (LE)	48.8	52.9	45.6
Total cost ($)	14.40	15.60	13.45

a Includes additional costs for MVA syringe sterilization, LE0.21 for nurse salaries, and LE3.6 for drugs.

TABLE 7.9
Summary of cost items per patient in Egyptian pounds (LE): Abou Korkas District Hospital

		Postintervention (MVA)	
	Preintervention (D&C)	Actual cost per single use of MVA cannula	Estimated cost per MVA cannula reuse
Per-bed time use	12.2	3.8	3.8
Labor cost	1.2	1.6[a]	1.6[a]
Supplies and medicines	12.8	29.3[a]	22.4[a]
Total cost (LE)	26.2	34.7	27.8
Total cost ($)	7.73	10.24	8.20

a Includes additional costs for MVA syringe sterilization, LE0.20 for nurse salaries, and LE4.1 for drugs.

(Johnson et al. 1992) found that the major source of postabortion service costs was supplies, materials, and medicines.

The next most significant source of cost is per-bed time use for both study sites. However, because MVA use in the postintervention resulted in a shorter recovery period, its relative contribution to total per-patient cost declined in the postintervention from 43 percent to 27 percent in Menia General Hospital and from 47 percent to only 11 percent in Abou Korkas District Hospital. Because Abou Korkas patient management protocols allow patients to be discharged after treatment when they feel able, savings in both patient time spent at the hospital and cost-per-bed time use are quite substantial.

In order to estimate the cost savings of multiple use of MVA cannulas, an assumption was made that each cannula would be used for 10 procedures. This was determined to be an appropriate estimate of reuse, given that in countries allowing multiple use of cannulas, a single cannula may be used for 40 procedures, while Egypt has placed restrictions on multiple use. Estimated costs of materials and medicines declined substantially in the two study sites (see last column of Tables 7.8 and 7.9) when this assumption was carried out; consequently, the final cost estimate per patient in the postintervention was close to the per-patient total cost in the preintervention (and even lower in the case of Menia General Hospital). However, these estimates do not include the cost of sterilizing cannulas for reuse, which is difficult to estimate since this was never attempted in Egyptian hospitals.

A final observation drawn from Tables 7.8 and 7.9 is that labor cost constitutes only a small proportion of total cost per postabortion patient in both pre- and postintervention phases (about 5 percent). This conforms to other studies that estimate the direct contribution of labor cost in postabortion service at 7 percent of the total cost (see Chapter 6 in this volume).

Discussion

This study relied on the direct observation of all elements contributing to treatment costs, and it collected hospital overhead costs using a rigorous methodology developed and implemented by a Harvard University team within the MOHP. Within the Egyptian setting it is a pioneering attempt to analyze the costs of postabortion treatment service, for both the traditional technique and the innovative technique that involves multiple aspects of improved quality of care.

Study findings indicate that the cost of materials and medicines is by and large the major component of total per-patient cost. These costs increased substantially with adoption of MVA in the postintervention. A major source of this increase is the cost of cannulas, which were not reused. Moreover, newly trained physicians were inefficient both in the use of cannulas and in the time they spent in the operating room. This implies that in order to achieve the full benefit of MVA, its adoption should be accompanied by changes in hospital protocol that allow sterilization and reuse of cannulas. In addition, effective training of staff on the use of the new technique is necessary, and future cost studies should be undertaken after staff members are well versed in the new procedures and can avoid using unnecessary additional medical supplies.

Another source of costs is the length of time patients stayed in the hospital during the postoperative period. This declined somewhat in the postintervention with use of MVA, particularly in the district hospital, which allows patient discharge directly after treatment. Clearly modifications in hospital discharge protocols are needed to eliminate unnecessary patient waiting time, which can also help bring costs down.

Furthermore, use of MVA requires neither heavy sedation nor extended postoperative patient monitoring. Therefore, it could be performed in a treatment room rather than in an operation theater. If successfully adopted in Egypt's hospitals, use of MVA will alleviate pressure on operation theater space and will result in more cost savings.

Conclusions

The effective introduction of MVA within a package to improve postabortion care requires commitment at top policy and program levels to change some patient management practices. In addition, physicians need to be permitted the flexibility to adapt some procedures according to patient needs. Patient discharge protocols need to be reviewed, efficacy of conducting the procedure in treatment rooms needs to be considered, and effective training of medical staff needs to be carefully planned and implemented. Internationally accepted protocols for MVA use should be applied. Sterilization and reuse of cannulas will certainly prove to be a cost-effective clinical practice that at the same time maintains safety of the new technique.

The implementation of the above alterations, though seemingly difficult and time consuming, can facilitate efforts to reduce costs of improved postabortion service while achieving important gains in the quality of care provided.

Notes

1 There are three functional departments in the hospital: overhead, intermediate service, and direct service. The direct service department includes inpatient, outpatient, emergency unit, dental unit, and renal dialysis unit.

2 Detailed information regarding numbers of patients and providers who participated in various stages of treatment is available from the authors (e.g., table averages were calculated from detailed data set; the reader will not be able to calculate table averages based on summarized information provided in tables).

3 US$1=LE3.39 as of mid-1996.

4 The per-patient costs of materials and medicines do not include costs of drugs needed to sterilize the MVA syringe, which, on average, was reused for 20 patients. Nurses were instructed to estimate both the costs of drugs needed for sterilizing the syringes and the time they devoted to this infection control procedure. These estimates are shown in the final per-patient cost items.

References

Abernathy, M., C. Hord, L.A. Nicholson, J. Benson, and B.R. Johnson. 1993. *A Guide to Assessing Resource Use for the Treatment of Incomplete Abortion.* Carrboro, N.C.: Ipas.

Huntington, Dale, Ezzeldin Osman Hassan, Nabil Attallah, Nahid Toubia, Mohamed Naguib, and Laila Nawar. 1995. "Improving the medical care and counseling of postabortion patients in Egypt," *Studies in Family Planning* 26(6): 350–362.

Johnson, B.R., J. Benson, J. Bradley, and A. Rabago Ordonez. 1993. "Costs and resource utilization for the treatment of incomplete abortion in Kenya and Mexico," *Social Science and Medicine* 36(11): 1443–1453.

Johnson, B.R., J. Benson, J. Bradley, A. Rabago, C. Zambrano, L. Okoko, L. Vasquez, P. Quiroz, and K. Rogo. 1992. "Costs and resource utilization for the treatment of incomplete abortion with dilation and curettage and manual vacuum aspiration in Kenya, Mexico, and Ecuador," report. Carrboro, N.C.: Ipas.

Nawar, Laila and Dale Huntington. 1997. "Expanding improved postabortion care is underway," paper presented at the XXIIIrd IUSSP General Population Conference, Beijing, China, 11–17 October.

8

Midwives and Comprehensive Postabortion Care in Ghana

Deborah L. Billings, Victor Ankrah,
Traci L. Baird, Joseph E. Taylor,
Kathlyn P. P. Ababio, and Stephen Ntow

Since the global launching of the Safe Motherhood Initiative in 1987, research and programmatic evidence has shown that prompt treatment of obstetric emergencies is one of the keys to reducing maternal mortality (Maine 1991, 1997). Each year an estimated 585,000 women worldwide die from complications related to pregnancy and childbirth, including unsafe abortion, hemorrhage, obstructed labor, sepsis, and hypertensive disorders (WHO 1996).[1] Unsafe abortion accounts for 13–14 percent (75,000–80,000 women) of all maternal deaths throughout the world each year, and women living in developing countries, particularly throughout sub-Saharan Africa, experience the greatest risk of death as well as short- and long-term morbidity (WHO 1993, 1994, 1997). Despite the central role that unsafe abortion plays in maternal mortality, few countries have recognized it as a public health problem and incorporated strategies to address it in their safe motherhood programs.

Whether women receive prompt care for complications due to unsafe abortion depends upon a variety of individual, social, economic, and political factors, including women's economic and educational status, gender-power relations, perceptions of illness, distance between women's homes and the closest facility with providers trained and equipped to provide emergency care, availability of transport, cost of services, and availability and quality of care. According to the "three delays model," developed by

Thaddeus and Maine (1990), these factors influence three key moments in the process of seeking and providing care, when delays may occur in:

- making the decision to seek care;
- reaching a health care facility with providers trained and equipped to offer services; and
- receiving adequate treatment upon arrival at the facility.

The operations research project presented in this chapter tested one strategy for minimizing these three delays in relation to emergency treatment for incomplete abortion in Ghana. The purpose of the project was to train and equip registered midwives[2] working in primary-level public health centers and private maternity homes,[3] as well as first referral-level district hospitals, to deliver postabortion care (PAC) services. Such services have been endorsed by organizations such as the World Health Organization (WHO) and the International Confederation of Midwives (ICM), yet few attempts have been made to decentralize the provision of postabortion care, both by type of health care provider and by health care facility (Hord and Delano 1996; Taylor et al. 1997).

Unsafe Abortion in Ghana

The Ghana Ministry of Health (MOH) recognizes unsafe abortion as one of the primary causes of maternal mortality in the country. It is considered a major public health issue that needs to be addressed in order to improve the lives of women. Unsafe abortion and its complications contribute to the high maternal mortality ratio in Ghana, which has been estimated to be between 214 and 740 deaths per 100,000 live births (GSS and MI 1994; Ghana MOH 1996). Hospital-based studies report that about 22 percent of all maternal deaths in Ghana are the result of unsafe abortion (Deganus-Amorin 1993), and a 1994 communiqué issued by the Ghana Medical Association (GMA) states that unsafe abortions are "presently the single highest contributor to our high maternal mortality rate" (GMA 1994).

Decentralizing Postabortion Care in Ghana

In Ghana, where approximately 70 percent of the population resides in rural areas, access to emergency treatment for abortion complications has been limited. Hospital-based physicians have been the only providers authorized and trained to offer such care. Figures from the GMA (1996) indicate that 40–50 percent of all physicians practicing in Ghana are located in urban teaching hospitals and medical schools. Only 2 percent are stationed in health facilities located closer to the communities where most women reside. In contrast, registered midwives practice in a wide range of facilities in Ghana, including primary-level public health centers and private maternity homes. Midwives often are the only trained health care providers readily available to most women.

During the past decade, midwives in Ghana have embraced the concept of reproductive health and have expanded their roles as health care providers for women (Ababio and Baird 1998). Many have been trained to provide family planning counseling and services. More recently they have participated in the Life Saving Skills (LSS) program developed by the American College of Nurse Midwives.[4] The skills they develop through the program have enabled midwives to stabilize and treat women experiencing a variety of obstetric emergencies. The Ghana Registered Midwives Association (GRMA), an association of private and public registered midwives, has been central to these efforts as well, as it provides continuing education. Thus, midwives have come to perceive themselves as providers who should offer a full range of services in order to address women's reproductive health needs.

Ghana's MOH policy explicitly recognizes the important role of midwives in reducing maternal mortality. In its groundbreaking 1996 National Reproductive Health Service Policy and Standards, midwives at all levels of the health care system are defined as appropriate providers of PAC services, including: (1) emergency treatment for incomplete abortion with manual vacuum aspiration (MVA);[5] (2) postabortion family planning counseling and methods; and (3) information to help link women with other reproductive health services.

In a bid to test the strategy outlined by the MOH's reproductive health policy, an operations research project was implemented by the MOH, GRMA, and Ipas to determine the feasibility, acceptability, benefits, and challenges of decentralizing the provision of PAC services such that they would be provided by midwives working in primary-level facilities. The objectives of this project were to demonstrate whether postabortion care provided by trained midwives working in health centers and maternity homes:

- was feasible given the existing health infrastructure;
- was acceptable to women, health care providers, community leaders, and policymakers;
- improved access to PAC services; and
- improved linkages between the emergency treatment of incomplete abortion and the provision of postabortion family planning services.

Methodology

The project staff used a quasi-experimental preintervention, postintervention design with nonrandomized intervention and control groups. Four districts in the Eastern Region were chosen as study areas: East Akim, Kwahu South, Manya Krobo, and Birim South. East Akim and Kwahu South served as training districts while Manya Krobo and Birim South were control sites. The four districts have comparable health service resources and similar religious, ethnic, and economic profiles. Control sites share no common borders with the training sites.

The operations research process was divided into three phases:

Phase One: Baseline Assessment of PAC Services

The baseline assessment was conducted from January through June 1996 in district hospitals and in selected health centers and maternity homes that refer patients to district hospitals in each of the four study areas. Table 8.1 outlines the interviews that were conducted during this phase. The sample included all women who were treated for incomplete abortion in six district hospitals over a continuous two-week period; all physicians and midwives in district hospitals who participate in the care of women with abortion complications; all midwife supervisors in the four study districts; and a subsample of midwives working in health centers and maternity homes that refer women to the district hospitals.[6] The mid-

TABLE 8.1
Data collection conducted during baseline assessment of PAC services in four districts, Eastern Region

Data collection method	Number of interviews
Structured questionnaires	
Women treated for incomplete abortion in six district hospitals over a continuous two-week period; predischarge interview	29
Physicians based in six district hospitals who regularly provide care to women arriving with abortion complications	11
Midwives based in six district hospitals who regularly assist with care to women arriving with abortion complications	31
Midwives based in public health centers and private maternity homes	50
Midwife supervisors (of both private and public midwives in the sample)	13
Semistructured tape-recorded interviews	
Community leaders	20
National-level policymakers	9

wives from the two intervention districts later participated in the postabortion care training.

Phase Two: Intervention

The intervention consisted of training, monitoring and support visits, and community education activities. Forty midwives and four physicians from district hospitals, health centers, and maternity homes in East Akim and Kwahu South were trained in postabortion care. Training took place from May through August 1996, and monitoring was carried out from January 1997 through July 1998. The competency-based training incorporated information about Ghanaian law regarding abortion and utilized participatory methods to build midwives' skills in stabilizing and referring patients, using MVA for uterine evacuation in cases of incomplete abortion, preventing infection, maintaining instruments, managing pain, providing postabortion family planning, and recordkeeping. All trainees also had clinical practice in performing MVA during and, when necessary, after the training. They were certified to provide PAC services only after instructors observed that the midwife or physician was able to perform MVA safely and effectively.

Physicians and midwives participated in the same training sessions, which established trust among them and respect for each other's skills. Joint training also facilitated discussion about and development of stronger referral and counter-referral protocols between primary-level facilities and the district hospitals. Subsequent to the training, ongoing monitoring/support visits were made to trained midwives to assess their practice and address any problems they were encountering. Refresher training was given to all trained midwives and physicians in May 1997.

Phase Three: Postintervention Evaluation of PAC Services

Interviews conducted during the baseline assessment were repeated in the same sites following the intervention, and additional data collection instruments were added between February 1997 and July 1998. Table 8.2 outlines the data collection methods used in the postintervention evaluation of services.

In addition to the methods listed in Table 8.2, data were collected to assess the cost of PAC services for the patient by facility, and a skills assessment (modified from one developed by Winkler and Verbeist [1997]) of a randomly selected subsample of midwives was conducted by a physician–nurse team.

Baseline Findings

The following section highlights the major findings from the baseline assessment phase of the project.[7]

Feasibility and Acceptability of Training and Equipping Midwives to Provide Postabortion Care

Policymakers, community leaders, physicians, midwife supervisors, midwives, and women treated for incomplete abortion in district hospitals were asked their opinion of the feasibility and appropriateness of training midwives to provide PAC services to women with an incomplete abortion. In this evaluation, particular emphasis was placed on training midwives to use MVA. Overall, broad-based support was voiced, with many commenting that women's access to emergency services would be improved if midwives could treat women directly rather than referring them to the nearest hospital. Below we highlight some of the reasons most com-

TABLE 8.2
Data collection conducted during postintervention assessment of PAC services in four districts, Eastern Region

Data collection method	Number of interviews
Structured questionnaires	
Women treated for incomplete abortion in six district hospitals over a continuous two-week period; predischarge interview	59
Physicians based in six district hospitals who regularly provide care to women arriving with abortion complications	8
Midwives based in six district hospitals who regularly assist with care to women arriving with abortion complications	19
Midwives based in public health centers and private maternity homes	43
Midwife supervisors (of both private and public midwives in the sample)	14
Women treated for incomplete abortion by midwives in health centers and maternity homes	78
Semistructured tape-recorded interviews	
Community leaders	39
National-level policymakers	9
MVA logbook review	
Women treated with MVA in district hospitals, health centers, and maternity homes	323

monly cited by various categories of respondents for training midwives to provide PAC services:

- Women treated for incomplete abortion in district hospitals

> Because the midwife lives in the same community with me, I wouldn't have paid money on transport and my relatives would have been around to assist me.

> The services would be nearer [to me] and I know that if I don't receive immediate help I may die.

- Physicians in district hospitals

> Some of the patients come from far away, so if the midwife in their community can provide PAC services, this saves lives, money, and prevents complications.

- Midwives in primary-level facilities

> Some people are shy about confiding in people they are not familiar with. The midwife lives in their community and therefore the patients will confide in her.

- Midwife supervisors

> Lives will be saved, especially in communities and villages where women will utilize the health centers and will not have to travel to the hospital. This will also reduce transportation costs for the women.

- Policymakers

> It is important that emergency treatment be given to these women at the source and at the spot where they live. Doctors are not available for people to get emergency treatment, whereas there are enough midwives who can assist if these patients are aware that they can go to them for help.

Reservations were expressed by some of the interviewees, and the project team attempted to address these throughout the course of the study. The most prominent reservations concerned women's confidentiality when treated by someone known to other community members; midwives recognizing the limits of their practice and referring when necessary; and ensuring that midwives not use the MVA equipment to induce abortion.[8]

Potential to Improve Linkages Between Emergency Treatment and Postabortion Family Planning Services

Prior to the intervention postabortion family planning services were not being offered systematically at any of the district hospitals included in this study. During the baseline interviews, women were asked about family planning services. Their responses indicated weak services. For example, when asked whether anyone on the hospital staff had spoken with them about family planning, 90 percent of all women in the sample said no one had spoken to them; 97 percent were not told where to obtain family planning methods in their community; and no women interviewed actually chose a family planning method before leaving the hospital.

Nonetheless, 90 percent of all women thought that, in general, women who come to the hospital with abortion complications would like to receive family planning information before leaving the hospital, and 93 percent thought that their partners should also receive this information. Eighty-three percent thought that women with abortion complications would like to receive a method before leaving the hospital. The provision of family planning counseling and methods was most commonly suggested by women as a way to improve their hospital care.

The majority of providers in district hospitals (94 percent) agreed that patients with incomplete abortion should receive postabortion family planning counseling, although, as of the baseline assessment, this was not being carried out in district hospitals. Hospital-based midwives and physicians, as well as primary-level midwives and their supervisors, noted that family planning counseling and methods would be an important service that midwives in health centers and maternity homes could provide to women after treatment for incomplete abortion.

Because midwives working in primary-level facilities have LSS and family planning courses targeted to them, they are better prepared than midwives in district hospitals to offer family planning services. Figure 8.1 illustrates the type of training midwives in both the training and control districts had received prior to this project. Of the 50 midwives practicing in health centers and maternity homes, 80 percent had prior family planning training and 42 percent had LSS training. In contrast, only 15 percent of the 26 midwives working in district hospitals had prior training in family planning and 35 percent had received LSS training. Family planning training is correlated with membership in GRMA.

Intervention and Postintervention Findings

Feasibility and Acceptability of Training and Equipping Midwives to Provide Postabortion Care

Findings based on the training and supervisory experiences of the postabortion care trainers, as well as an inventory review of public health centers and private maternity homes, illustrate that midwives who were trained in postabortion care:

- had the requisite baseline skills necessary to provide safe uterine evacuation procedures, regardless of whether they had previous training in LSS, as well as the skills and supplies needed to offer postabortion family planning services;
- were equipped with most of the basic supplies, medications, and instruments needed to provide safe PAC services. Thus, substantial inputs were not required to properly equip midwives to offer uterine evacuation with MVA other than MVA kits, which were donated by Ipas. As was expected, no midwife had an MVA kit;

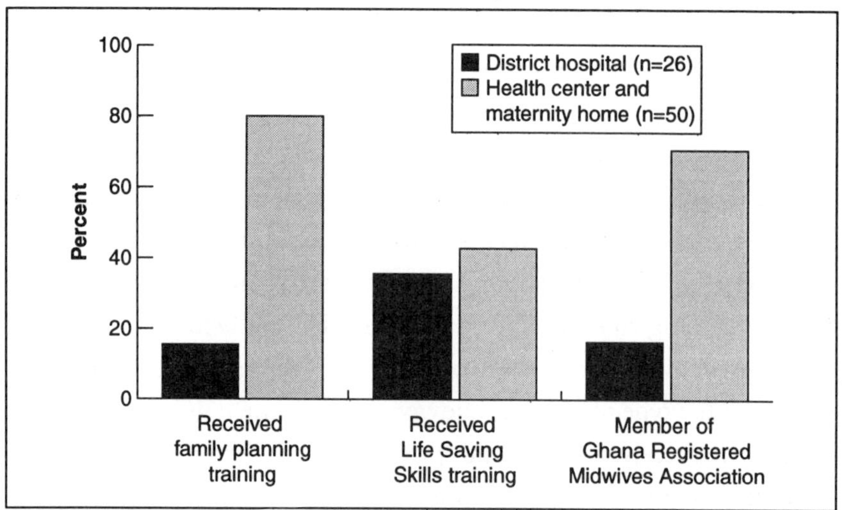

FIGURE 8.1 Training received prior to intervention by midwives based in district hospitals, health centers, and maternity homes

therefore, two double-valve syringes and multiple cannulas were provided to each midwife subsequent to her training;

- were enthusiastic about providing PAC services—both emergency treatment and family planning services—to women who came to them; and
- were enthusiastic about organizing and conducting community education activities with a variety of groups about unsafe abortion and the new services they were offering. This was particularly true of the private midwives, whose livelihoods depend on a solid client base.

Overall, implementation of PAC services by midwives was accomplished using existing resources within their health facilities, with the addition of donated MVA kits. Additional resources, such as fuel for the MOH vehicle, were needed for the training/monitoring team to conduct ongoing visits with the midwives; this input was invaluable to ensuring the quality of care delivered by the midwives. Looking to the future, a sustainable resupply system will need to be developed so that MVA replacement parts will not be difficult to find or expensive to purchase. A more sustainable system will also utilize Ghana's MOH Regional Resource Teams, referral hospital physicians, and midwife supervisors to provide support and feedback to trained providers.[9]

Overwhelming support for the provision of PAC services by midwives was expressed by all those interviewed during the postintervention phase. District hospital physicians emphasized their decrease in workload since midwives had been trained in postabortion care. Community leaders and policymakers evaluated the new services in a positive light, noting that enabling midwives to provide postabortion care was a sensible, even necessary use of existing resources. Midwives and their patients highlighted the various ways in which the new services had made an impact on their lives. Examples of the supportive comments made during the postintervention interviews include these:

- Midwives providing PAC services

> As a midwife and as a Ghanaian woman trained to provide services to women with incomplete abortion, I feel proud. I am now able to interact with women in my neighborhood about postabortion care . . . and they have confidence in me, as they come to me even at home.
>
> Postabortion care means a lot to me as a midwife. It has given me the experience to save lives, especially in the rural areas where there are no doctors. It has made me understand that, with courage, a midwife can perform well.
>
> Midwives in the community help a lot. Women don't have a lot of money. The last woman I treated with MVA could not even pay. But we save a life and we are helping the community.

- Women treated for incomplete abortion by midwives

> I felt comfortable with the midwife and more relaxed because the relationship was cordial, and less time and money were spent here than at the hospital. We are now friends and I am grateful.
>
> [The midwife] was going to her farm but came back and helped me out of my situation. If she hadn't helped me I would have died since there's no car plying the village. Thanks to the midwife.
>
> I welcomed the idea of family planning since I'm a divorced woman and caring for my children alone is a problem.

Improved Access to Services

Access is a multifaceted term that has sociocultural, economic, and geographic dimensions. We examined four of these dimensions: (1) distance from a woman's home; (2) cost of services and payment options; (3) waiting time for services/total length of stay; and (4) social proximity to the provider. Each dimension is related to one of the three types of delay defined above.

Overall, logbook data reveal that during a two-year posttraining period (July 1996–July 1998), 323 women were treated for incomplete abortion with MVA in East Akim and Kwahu South. Midwives working in maternity homes treated 139 of these women (43 percent); midwives in health centers treated 78 (24 percent); and of the 106 women (33 percent) treated in district hospitals, midwives alone performed MVA for 31 (29 percent) while 75 (71 percent) were treated by a physician–midwife team. Prior to the intervention, all 323 women would have had no option but to travel to the district hospital for emergency care by a physician.

Access to PAC services increased for women in the training districts, according to the four dimensions described above.

In general, health centers and maternity homes are located closer to women's communities than are district hospitals. Women who sought care at district hospitals tended to have easy access, in terms of distance and mode of transport, and indicated this as a reason for going directly to the district hospitals. Similarly, women treated in health centers and maternity homes noted their proximity as a major reason for seeking care at those facilities. Most noted that if midwives had not been prepared to offer emergency services, they would have had to travel a far greater distance in order to reach the nearest hospital.

The actual cost of MVA service varied from facility to facility (Table 8.3). On average, the services offered by private midwives (those in maternity homes) cost more than those offered by midwives in the public sector. Yet it is important to recognize that transportation costs are often lower or nil for women treated closer to home in maternity homes and health centers. In addition, private midwives often offer payment options, such as sliding-scale fees, credit, and in-kind payment. In general, these options are not available in public-sector facilities.

Estimates provided by incomplete abortion patients and midwives regarding waiting time/length of stay indicated that women at maternity homes and health centers spent an average of 1.5 hours from the time

TABLE 8.3
Cost to patient in cedis[a] of treatment for incomplete abortion: Training districts, March–May 1998

Cost	District hospital (n=3)	Health center (n=7)	Maternity home (n=12)
Mean	20,900	12,225	21,183
Range	15,400–25,700	10,000–15,700	9,700–33,900

a $US1.00=2,300 cedis.
Source: Cost-analysis forms.

they entered the facility until they were discharged. In contrast, women at district hospitals waited an average of 3.65 hours before being treated. Basing conclusions on women's estimates has limitations; however, the logistics of trying to follow women throughout the course of their care in the primary-level facilities was beyond the scope of this project.

Sociocultural access to emergency services for incomplete abortion improved by training midwives to provide PAC services. Women treated by midwives indicated their comfort in approaching the midwife with their problems and their relief when she was able to treat them. Some women emphasized the long-term relationships they developed with midwives since the time of their emergency care. Conclusions must be tempered, however, since only women who actually sought services from the midwives were interviewed. Further research should be conducted at the community level with a representative sample of women from different sectors to assess to what degree the midwife is viewed as a trusted member of the community, particularly in comparison with traditional birth attendants and other traditional practitioners.

Improved Linkages Between Emergency Treatment and Postabortion Family Planning Services

Compared to the preintervention phase of the project, and compared to control facilities during the postintervention phase, significantly more women received postabortion family planning services in the facilities located in the training districts in the two years following the training. Based on logbook reviews over the two-year posttraining period, comparable proportions of women received postabortion family planning counseling, regardless of facility (81 percent in district hospitals, 77 percent in health centers, and 92 percent in maternity homes). However, significantly more women left health centers and maternity homes with a method (70 percent and 55 percent, respectively) as compared to women treated in district hospitals (35 percent). The latter could be an underestimate if women actually received a method from the hospital's family planning clinic rather than on the ward where they were treated, as the logbook only recorded those women who accepted a method on the ward. Unfortunately, we were not able to refine the analysis to correlate women's reproductive intentions with whether or not they received a method, because midwives did not record this information in the logbooks. As noted earlier, fewer midwives working in district hospitals had prior family planning training and many requested intensive updates during the monitoring/support visits.

Conclusions

This project has demonstrated that postabortion care provided by trained midwives in primary-level facilities is feasible within the existing health care infrastructure in Ghana. Such care is acceptable to women, health care providers, community leaders, and policymakers. The training of primary-level midwives has also improved access to postabortion care and facilitated the provision of postabortion family planning services for women treated for incomplete abortion.

General Lessons Learned

- Operations research is a process that can be used to incorporate the perspectives of policymakers, physicians, midwives, and women into new policies, protocols, and training programs.
- Training midwives in postabortion care is a feasible and acceptable strategy for decentralizing PAC services, especially when supportive reproductive health policies and standards are in place.
- Joint training of midwives working at the primary level and physicians working at district hospitals strengthened referral mechanisms between the two levels of care.

- Collaborative links with district hospitals provided midwives with the opportunity to gain additional supervised clinical practice beyond the training sessions.
- Monitoring/support visits designed to encourage successes and address challenges provided participants with ongoing feedback about the services they offer and enabled them to express their needs for further training.

The unique experience of decentralizing PAC services in Ghana is one that needs to be shared, adapted, and adopted by providers, policymakers, international organizations, and women's health advocates throughout the world so that women have access to more prompt and comprehensive care when experiencing abortion complications (Billings 1998). In other settings, medical assistants, nurses, or other cadres of mid-level providers may be the most appropriate persons to be trained and equipped to provide PAC services.

In general, decentralizing the provision of postabortion care has decreased the three delays described by Maine and colleagues. Future studies should examine the impact of this strategy on maternal mortality and morbidity.

Acknowledgments

Ghana is one of the first countries in the world to address the problem of unsafe abortion by working to decentralize the provision of PAC services to midwives working at the primary level of the health care system. The operations research project presented in this chapter aimed to produce findings that would provide guidance to the MOH and GRMA as they work to implement Ghana's reproductive health policy. This project would not have been possible without the dedicated efforts of many active policymakers, health care providers, and patients. We would especially like to acknowledge the important contributions made by:

Ghana MOH: Dr. Eunice Brookman-Amissah, Minister of Health (at the time of the project), Mercy Abbey, M.Sc., Dr. Sam Adjei, Dr. A. Asamoah-Baah, Jane Cobbinah, Bechesani Demuyakor, Dr. Delanyo Dovlo, Dr. Henrietta Odoi-Agyarko, Dr. Aaron Offei, Dr. Kenneth Sagoe

GRMA: Florence Quarcoopome

Interviewers: Margaret Afoakwa, Kate Badoe, Rose Boateng, Happy Djokoto, Margaret Lartey, Pat Odoom, Wilhelmina Ofori, Evelyn Owusu-Acheaw

USAID: Dr. Benedicta Ababio, Lawrence Aduonum-Darko, Bob Haladay, Dr. Pamela Wolf

JSI/MotherCare: Ken Ames, Dr. Marge Koblinksy, Dr. Jeanne McDermott

Thanks also to all of the midwives, midwife supervisors, district hospital physicians, community leaders, and patients who graciously lent their time and energy to participate in this project.

Funding for this project was provided by John Snow, Inc./MotherCare Project and The Office of Health and Nutrition, Bureau for Global Field Programs, Field Support and Research, USAID, under the terms of contract number HRN-5966-C-00-3038-00.

Notes

1 Unsafe abortion refers to ". . . the termination of pregnancy performed or treated by untrained or unskilled persons. . . . Regardless of whether an abortion is spontaneous or induced, subsequent events and the care received determine whether the abortion is safe or unsafe" (WHO 1995: 13, 14). Unsafe abortion thus refers to both induced and spontaneous abortions (miscarriage) that are poorly performed or managed. However, data on spontaneous abortion are rarely reported in estimates of the impact of unsafe abortion on maternal mortality. The estimates cited in this chapter refer to unsafely induced abortion only.

2 A registered midwife is one who has certified medical or nursing training and works in a hospital, health center, or maternity home. It does not refer to a traditional midwife or birth attendant who has learned from experience and from other traditional midwives.

3 A maternity home is a facility owned and run by a private midwife in which she offers her services.

4 The Life Saving Skills program trains midwives in emergency obstetric care, including manual removal of placenta, vacuum extraction, partograph, rehydration therapy, infant and adult cardiopulmonary resuscitation, and suturing of the perineum (Marshall and Buffington 1991). In 1998, treatment of incomplete abortion was added to the LSS curriculum.

5 MVA is indicated as the most appropriate technique for the treatment of incomplete abortion, particularly given that it is safer than and as effective as sharp curettage during the first trimester (Baird, Gringle, and Greenslade 1995). In general, MVA is a low-cost procedure that does not depend on the availability of electricity or operating room facilities, thus making it accessible to providers working in lower-resource, primary care settings. WHO recommends that MVA be available at the primary care level as part of comprehensive care to reduce maternal mortality (WHO 1995).

6 Midwives were not randomly chosen within the districts. Instead, a comprehensive listing of all midwives in the districts was made, along with prior training they had received. Those who were previously trained in LSS and family planning, including IUD insertion and removal, were chosen first; midwives with family planning and IUD skills were in the second tier; midwives with family planning training in the third tier; and those without prior training in any of these skills were chosen last.

Concurrent with this, attention was given to ensuring even distribution throughout the districts.

7 For a full review of the baseline findings, see Ghana MOH, GRMA, and Ipas 1997.

8 Ghanaian law allows for legal abortion under a broad range of circumstances, including rape, incest, and risk to the physical or mental health of a woman. However, only registered physicians in government hospitals or in certified private hospitals or clinics can legally induce an abortion (Government of Ghana 1985).

9 Since October 1998, PRIME (a USAID contract administered by INTRAH that provides reproductive health training to primary-level providers) has been working with the MOH and GRMA to build these key components of sustainability, through a project entitled "Decentralizing and Integrating Life-Saving Skills and Postabortion Care Through the Safe Motherhood Program in Ghana."

References

Ababio, K. and T.L. Baird. 1998. "Working to reduce maternal mortality," *Midwifery Today (with International Midwife)* Spring (45): 47–49.

Baird, T.L., R.E. Gringle, and F.C. Greenslade. 1995. *MVA in the Treatment of Incomplete Abortion: Clinical and Programmatic Experience.* Carrboro, N.C.: Ipas.

Billings, D.L. 1998. *Training Midwives to Improve Postabortion Care: A Study Tour in Ghana, October 12–19, 1997.* Carrboro, N.C.: Research Triangle Institute and Ipas.

Deganus-Amorin, S. 1993. "Unsafe abortion and the Safe Motherhood Initiative in sub-Saharan Africa," presented at the Medical Women's International Association Congress, Nairobi, Kenya, 28 November–3 December.

Ghana Medical Association (GMA). 1994. *Communiqué: Resolved at the 36th Annual General Conference, Koforidua,* 15–18 June. Accra, Ghana: GMA.

———. 1996. *38th Annual General and Scientific Meeting Programme,* 18–20 June. Accra, Ghana: GMA.

Ghana Ministry of Health (MOH). 1996. *National Reproductive Health Service Policy and Standards.* Accra, Ghana: MOH

Ghana MOH, Ghana Registered Midwives Association (GRMA), and Ipas. 1997. *Training Non-Physician Providers to Improve Postabortion Care: Baseline Assessment of Postabortion Care Services in Four Districts of Eastern Region, Ghana.* Carrboro, N.C.: Ipas.

Ghana Statistical Service (GSS) and Macro International (MI). 1994. *Ghana Demographic and Health Survey 1993.* Calverton, Md.: GSS and MI.

Government of Ghana. 1985. *Criminal Code (Amendment) Law, 1985. P.N.D.C.L. 102., The Gazette.* Accra-Tema, Ghana: Ghana Publishing Corporation.

Hord, C.E and G. Delano. 1996. "Reducing maternal mortality from abortion: The midwife's role in abortion care," in *Midwives and Safer Motherhood,* ed. S.F. Murray. London: Mosby, pp. 63–78.

Maine, D. 1991. *Safe Motherhood Programs: Options and Issues.* New York: Center for Population and Family Health, School of Public Health, Columbia University.

———. 1997. "Lessons for program design from the PMM projects," *International Journal of Gynecology and Obstetrics* 59(suppl 2): S259–S266.

Marshall, M.A. and S.T. Buffington. 1991. *Life-Saving Skills Manual for Midwives, 2nd edition.* Washington, D.C.: American College of Nurse Midwives.

Taylor, J., T. Baird, D. Billings, and K. Ababio. 1997. "Training midwives in postabortion care: International support for policies and programs," in *The First World Congress on Maternal Mortality, Marrakesh (Morocco), March 8–14, 1997,* eds. D. Weinstein and F. Chervenak. Bologna: Monduzzi Editore.

Thaddeus, S. and D. Maine. 1990. *Too Far to Walk: Maternal Mortality in Context.* New York: Columbia University, Prevention of Maternal Mortality Program, Center for Population and Family Health, School of Public Health.

Winkler, J. and S. Verbeist. 1997. "Module 5: Postabortion care," in *PRIME: Reproductive Health Training for Primary Providers: A Sourcebook for Curriculum Development.* Chapel Hill, N.C.: INTRAH.

World Health Organization (WHO). 1993. *The Prevention and Management of Unsafe Abortion: Report of a Technical Working Group.* Geneva: WHO.

———. 1994. *Abortion: Tabulation of Available Data on the Frequency and Mortality of Unsafe Abortion,* 3rd ed. Geneva: WHO.

———. 1995. *Complications of Abortion: Technical and Managerial Guidelines for Prevention and Treatment.* Geneva: WHO.

———. 1996. *Revised 1990 Estimates of Maternal Mortality: A New Approach by WHO and UNICEF.* Geneva: WHO.

———. 1997. *Unsafe Abortion. Global and Regional Estimates of Incidence of and Mortality Due to Unsafe Abortion with a Listing of Available Country Data.* 3rd ed. Geneva: WHO.

9

Traditional Midwives and Postabortion Care Services in Morelos, Mexico

Deborah L. Billings, Xóchitl Castañeda Camey, Xóchitl Romero Guerrero, Julia Blanco Muñoz, Andrea Saldaña Rivera, M. Virginia Chambers, and Patricia Voorduin

Access to emergency obstetric services ensures the prompt treatment of complications and saves women's lives. This simple hypothesis, introduced by Allen Rosenfield and Deborah Maine in 1985 and supported by results from safe motherhood programs over the last decade, has advanced planning and action regarding the ways in which health systems can work to decrease levels of maternal mortality and morbidity (Rosenfield and Maine 1985; Maine 1997).

Complications from unsafe abortion, either induced or spontaneous, are one of the major causes of maternal mortality for women in the world today. Data from public-sector health institutions in Mexico indicate that unsafe abortion is the fourth most important cause of maternal mortality (Lezana 1999). As elsewhere in the world, Mexican women with the most difficult access to emergency care, including poor women, culturally marginalized women, and those living in rural areas, have a greater risk of dying than do women who can easily obtain services from the formal health care system (Langer, Hernández, and Lozano 1994).

This chapter describes one approach to improving access to emergency care for women living in rural areas of the state of Morelos, Mexico: incorporating traditional midwives into the process of emergency care so that postabortion care (PAC) services can be delivered promptly and safely.[1]

Following the recommendations of the World Health Organization (WHO), community-level providers have an important role to play in ensuring that women experiencing abortion complications reach emergency treatment services as quickly as possible (WHO 1995).

In rural Mexico, traditional midwives are often the only health care providers available to women. During the past two decades, Mexican health care systems have recognized the important role that traditional midwives play in the reproductive health of women and have conducted a variety of training programs for them. None, however, has addressed the ways in which traditional midwives could provide lifesaving services to women experiencing abortion complications; thus the project described in this chapter has broken new ground in Mexico.

The Role of Traditional Midwives in Women's Reproductive Health Care in Mexico

Traditional midwives play an important role in women's reproductive health in Mexico, in both rural and burgeoning urban areas. As noted by research conducted by the Secretaría de Salud (SSA) in 1994, "The coexistence of traditional and modern medical attention is a reality in Mexico. . . . Women do not separate themselves from traditional medical attention as they look for the warm and personalized care a midwife provides" (SSA 1994: 2). This holds true in Morelos, a predominantly urban and periurban state, where 24 percent of all births in cities with more than 20,000 inhabitants and 45–50 percent of all births in communities with less than 2,500 inhabitants are attended by midwives, despite a well-developed infrastructure of health centers and hospitals throughout the state (Marcos and Avilés 1996; SSA 1997).

That women continue to seek care from traditional midwives rather than from the formal health care system indicates that facilitating access to services is not simply an issue of geographic proximity. Economic and cultural factors that may inhibit women from seeking and obtaining care at a nearby clinic or hospital are also important dimensions of access. As Marcos and Avilés (1996) state:

> Many women who consult traditional midwives do not have any access to medical care. For these women the traditional midwife is the only existing resource. But even women who have access to medical services (through public health systems in Mexico) prefer to consult a midwife as well as the doctor. This can be explained by a cultural identification between the pregnant woman and the midwife. Both share the same classification system (cold and hot), and the same concept of health and illness. In addition, midwives provide therapies such as herbal medicines, baths, massage, and prayers. (p. 122)

During the last 20 years, the responsibilities accorded the traditional midwife have expanded as health care providers and institutions in Mexico recognize the potential role of midwives in providing health care services to community members in addition to prenatal, delivery, and postnatal care. The SSA, for example, has been active in training traditional midwives to provide vaccinations, oral rehydration therapy, and family planning in their communities. As an indication of its interest in improving coordination with midwives, in 1990–93 the SSA conducted a nationwide survey of over 11,000 midwives in order to improve its continued work with this cadre of providers, particularly in the areas of pre- and postnatal care, birthing practices, newborn care, and referral of women experiencing pregnancy complications.

Previous studies with midwives in Cuautla, a region of Morelos, indicate that few of them recognize risk factors related to women's prior gynecological history or current pregnancy condition (García Barrios et al. 1993).[2] These same studies show that conditions that may be related to abortion were recognized as danger signs by less than one-half of the midwives: bleeding during pregnancy (42 percent), premature contractions (36 percent), and desire not to be pregnant (33 percent). While training made a significant impact on midwives' knowledge of formal medicine, it did not alter their views on traditionally recognized risk factors for pregnant women, such as passing by a cemetery, watching a lunar eclipse, or ignoring the fetus's cravings (*antojos*), most often for a certain food.

In 1989, the SSA initiated the "Program for Traditional Midwives in Morelos," which provided additional training to 117 midwives; by 1990 the first "Birthing Centers" (*Posadas de Nacimiento*) were established; and in 1992 the Simplified Epidemiological System of Monitoring for the Midwife was designed so that both literate and nonliterate midwives could report their monthly activities. To date, 408 traditional midwives have taken part in training to improve their skills. The project described here, however, is the first in Mexico to explicitly address the issue of unsafe abortion with traditional midwives and to provide training that can improve their ability to stabilize and refer women who come to them with abortion complications.

Traditional Midwives Caring for Women with Abortion Complications

In 1995, the SSA for the state of Morelos, the Instituto Nacional de Salud Pública (INSP) in Morelos, and Ipas initiated a collaborative pilot project to improve women's access to postabortion care in Cuautla, Morelos. The 60-bed general hospital of Cuautla is one of the main hospitals in the state; it attends to women who need emergency care for abortion complications. Researchers and providers at the INSP and SSA have been conducting in-depth studies with traditional midwives in Yecapixtla, a municipality within Cuautla, since 1990. Past work has examined midwives' practices regarding pregnancy, birth, postnatal care, breastfeeding, and family planning (Castañeda, García, and Langer 1996; Castañeda, Guzmán, and Langer 1991; Castañeda Camey 1992; Castañeda Camey et al. 1996; Mellado, Zolla, and Castañeda 1989). The project described in this chapter, therefore, builds on a strong base of experience and collaboration among midwives, the SSA, and the INSP.

The primary goals of the demonstration project were to:

- improve emergency attention for abortion complications through the introduction of postabortion care in Cuautla Hospital. To this end, physician–nurse teams received comprehensive training in postabortion care, including uterine evacuation with manual vacuum aspiration (MVA); and
- incorporate midwives in Yecapixtla into the process of care by improving their skills in management of abortion complications. Most

importantly, midwives were trained to recognize the signs and symptoms of abortion complications and stabilize and refer women to Cuautla Hospital, roles that are in accordance with WHO's recommendations regarding the minimal components of emergency care that should be available at the community level so that women do not delay in seeking and finding the help they need (WHO 1995).

This chapter focuses on the second of these project goals.

Sources of Data

A variety of methods were employed to gather information on the concepts midwives use to understand and discuss abortion as well as the practices they undertake with women who come to them seeking care for abortion complications. Results from these different approaches complement one another and strengthen the overall findings.

Given the paucity of data regarding midwives' concepts of abortion and abortion care, the project team conducted ethnographic fieldwork with midwives before conducting the training. The information gathered through this work enabled the team to integrate midwives' concepts of and experiences with abortion into the training curriculum and to document and address barriers to incorporating midwives into the PAC process.

In-depth interviews with nine key midwives in Yecapixtla were conducted over a nine-month period by trained anthropologists from the INSP. Each of these midwives had participated in previous studies regarding their role in women's reproductive health care and were familiar with the researchers. Semistructured interviews of about four hours' duration moved from a general exploration of reproductive health to a specific examination of abortion beliefs and practices.

Additional data were collected from 64 midwives from the Jurisdicción Sanitaria No. III of the SSA, which includes Yecapixtla and Cuautla, during their bimonthly meeting in June 1996. A brief "quiz-like" questionnaire asked midwives about their knowledge of abortion complications and about their practices with women experiencing such complications. The 11 midwives who later participated in the training offered through this project were from this sample.

Lastly, pre- and posttraining evaluations of midwives' skills were conducted by hospital staff who served as trainers to midwives during a five-day training course in late January 1997. Trainers used a predefined checklist to evaluate midwives' knowledge and practice regarding the various types of abortion, signs and symptoms of complications, and their proper management. Much of the training consisted of one-on-one tutoring, as the number of trainers virtually equaled the number of midwives in the course. As such, participants were asked direct questions in addition to being asked to demonstrate certain procedures through dramatizations or role plays. Their evaluation scores were based on their performance using these two techniques.

Findings: Abortion Care Knowledge and Practices

The information obtained through the initial fieldwork provided valuable insights into the ways in which midwives understood, approached, and treated abortion and abortion patients; these insights aided in the development of appropriate training materials and strategies for working with midwives in the community.

Spontaneous Abortion

Midwives saw spontaneous abortion as a woman's failure to fulfill her primary gender role of reproduction. Women themselves were often blamed for their loss; as midwives noted, "These women don't know how to have children," or "They don't take care of themselves and because of this they abort."

Activities associated with the everyday lives of women were often mentioned by midwives in relation to spontaneous abortion. These included lifting heavy objects and engaging in excessive movement, both of which are common occurrences, as women plant and harvest tomatoes; carry children; and haul water, firewood, and laundry. In a previous study, midwives noted that during the first three months of pregnancy, "The fetus is still delicate, it hasn't adhered well and can easily separate itself [from the walls of the uterus] when the woman exerts a lot of force or carries heavy things" (INSP 1992: 12).

The shifting or displacement of internal organs that results in corporal disequilibrium is often invoked in rural areas of Morelos to describe the origins of illness or pain, including spontaneous abortion (Castañeda, Guzmán, and Langer 1991). Women were said to have an "open" or "loose" waist or hips or a "fallen" womb or ovaries (Castañeda, Guzmán, and Langer 1991). Both conditions are sometimes attributed to women engaging in heavy work, which can cause, as one traditional birth attendant (TBA) noted, the waist to "open" or the "ovaries, which are tied with threads, to break . . ." (INSP 1992). Midwives then turn to resources and practices that combine herbal remedies with physical therapy to reposition the organs and attempt to prevent the abortion from completing. These include administering sweat baths, massaging with herbal and alcohol mixtures, covering the woman with a heavy blanket, wrapping her waist tightly with a bandage, and hanging the woman by her feet in order to reestablish equilibrium within the woman's body.

Fright and anger, two conditions commonly experienced by women and perceived as important explanations for general illness and disease in Mexico, were also noted as causes of spontaneous abortion. Injury due to domestic violence was named numerous times as another significant cause of spontaneous abortion.

Midwives recognized malnutrition, resulting from the conditions of poverty in which many women live, and the fact that "women are the last to eat, after her husband and children, and eat the least nutritious foods" as causes of miscarriage (INSP 1992). They also indicated that when left unfulfilled, cravings for food (antojos) are an important cause of spontaneous abortion. Through the mother's womb the fetus itself experiences such cravings and "becomes very unsettled and begins to move around too much." Uterine contractions begin, as "the power of desire is very strong, enough so that the child may even come" (i.e., a spontaneous abortion ensues) (INSP 1992). The remedy lies in "feeding" cravings with the foods the woman so desires. When this is not possible, foods such as tortilla with salt, two grains of black corn, or cinnamon tea are said to counteract the effects of cravings.

Induced Abortion

Induced abortion was referred to by all of the midwives interviewed as "murder" or a "grave sin." Women who induce abortion are known by community members as *perras* (dogs/bitches) or *puercas* (pigs) and are accused of "eating" or "throwing away" the child. These labels were also given to women who abort repeatedly, whether the true cause is spontaneous or induced, because "people in the community suspect that if she is aborting time and time again it's because she must be doing or taking something that causes the child to be thrown away, or that she's not taking care to prevent the child from coming out." Thus, women whose health status causes them to abort numerous times are placed within the same punitive category as those who actively induce their abortions.

Midwives identified infection and hemorrhage as the most frequently seen short-term complications of abortion, while sterility was often mentioned as the most common long-term complication. Consequently, a woman who is infertile is suspected of having induced an abortion at some time during her life.

Whether complications result from spontaneous or induced abortion, midwives generally tell the woman to seek care from a health center or hospital. Few report stabilizing and formally referring women to another level of the health system. Only one of the midwives interviewed indicated that she had given intravenous glucose to stabilize a woman until she reached the attention of a specialist. Another noted that she rehydrated the woman, then gave her vitamins and an analgesic to bring down her fever. It should be noted that midwives have strong disincentives to openly admit any role they might have in abortion care and that these responses may understate their degree of intervention.

Reasons for minimal treatment of abortion by midwives include their lack of knowledge regarding appropriate action to take, the fact that previous workshops in which they have participated have emphasized referral as the only course of action, and the midwives' fear of being labeled "abortionists" and suffering legal consequences. Midwives also noted that when they do accompany women to a health center or hospital, regardless of the health problem, providers often ignore them or treat them as if they are unqualified to provide any sort of care to women. Feelings of ostracism and condemnation make contact with the formal health system uncomfortable and difficult, exacerbating the divide between traditional and institutionalized health services treating women with abortion complications.

In general, the ethnographic fieldwork illustrated the necessity and feasibility of programmatic efforts that would improve midwives' willingness and ability to stabilize and refer women with abortion complications to the nearest hospital where they could be treated. Such training would need to utilize midwives' own concepts of abortion and abortion care, address their punitive attitudes toward women experiencing abortion, and develop trust between the midwives and hospital staff so that midwives would feel comfortable making formal referrals of women to the hospital.

Midwives' Knowledge of Abortion and Treatment Practices: Findings from a Questionnaire

Midwives throughout Morelos gather for bimonthly meetings to coordinate efforts with the state's health program and to discuss questions and issues of common interest. These midwives have participated in a variety of training events. During the meeting held in June 1996, project team members from the INSP applied a closed-ended questionnaire to the 64 midwives in attendance. Items included in the questionnaire ranged from definitions of different types of abortion to specific actions taken by midwives in the case of infection or hemorrhage. Midwives who were able to read and write filled out the questionnaire on their own, while the questionnaire was administered verbally to those midwives who were not literate.

Results from the questionnaire highlight some important needs. Midwives have limited knowledge of the different types of abortion and their accompanying signs and symptoms (Tables 9.1 and 9.2; definitions of abortion from Benson 1983). The technical skills needed to stabilize women with abortion complications vary. Ninety-three percent of the midwives interviewed knew how to give an injection and 45 percent knew how to insert an intravenous line (Table 9.3). Midwives also engage in

TABLE 9.1
Midwives' knowledge of different types of abortion: Morelos, 1996

Type	Percentage of midwives who defined correctly (N=64)
Abortion	80
Threatened abortion	75
Inevitable abortion	23
Incomplete abortion	75

Threatened abortion: previable gestation is in jeopardy, but the pregnancy continues.

Inevitable abortion: spontaneous abortion will take place; characterized by cervical dilation, rupture of membranes, bleeding for more than seven days, persistence of cramps, and signs of termination of pregnancy.

Incomplete abortion: portions of the conceptus have already been passed, but tissue remains in the uterus.

TABLE 9.2
Midwives' identification of signs and symptoms of different types of abortion: Morelos, 1996

Type	Percentage of midwives who identified correctly (N=64)
Threatened abortion	14
Inevitable abortion	11
Incomplete abortion	44
Molar pregnancy	19

Molar pregnancy: degenerative disorder of the chorion; fleshy mass forms in the uterus.

practices that can present risks to women's health, including using oxytocin (6 percent) and ergometrine (17 percent), manually removing tissue from the uterine cavity (6 percent), inserting cotton or gauze into the vagina in cases of heavy bleeding (28 percent), and inadequately disinfecting equipment used during exams (73 percent).

Infrastructure for stabilization and referral is inadequate for most midwives. Only 28 percent of the midwives who completed the questionnaire had the minimal equipment needed to stabilize a woman with abortion complications, including examination table, lamp, speculum, blood pressure cuff, stethoscope, scissors, and sterile gloves. Only 55 percent could count on some form of transportation to promptly refer and transfer women to a clinic or hospital.

TABLE 9.3
Technical skills of midwives: Morelos, 1996

Technical skill	Percentage of midwives who have specified skill (N=64)
Give an injection	93
Perform a vaginal exam	87
Take temperature	72
Take pulse	72
Take blood pressure	58
Insert an intravenous line	45
Do all of the above	47

Clearly, midwives face limitations in terms of knowledge, practice, and infrastructure that make it difficult for them to provide safe and prompt stabilization and referral services to women experiencing abortion complications.

Intervention Component: Training Traditional Midwives to Stabilize and Refer Women with Abortion Complications

Cuautla Hospital is one of the main health facilities in Morelos to which midwives can refer women who are experiencing abortion complications. Physicians and nurses in this hospital noted in a focus group discussion and in individual interviews that midwives could play an important role in identifying women with abortion complications and referring them to the nearest facility for emergency services. Building on this support and in an effort to create a trusting and positive relationship between the medical staff of Cuautla Hospital and the midwives who were to be trained, SSA directors selected a group of nine health care providers from the hospital to work as facilitators for the course provided to midwives. To sharpen their communication and group facilitation skills, the providers attended two three-day sessions on didactic, adult-learning methodologies prior to the midwife training course.

At the same time, a training curriculum was developed by the SSA, INSP, and Ipas that covered the following topics (SSM and Ipas 1997):

- identifying types of abortion;
- recognizing signs and symptoms of abortion complications;
- obtaining a clinical history from the patient;
- knowing the effects and contraindications of medications often given to women with abortion complications;
- identifying high-risk practices often employed by midwives;
- providing information to and counseling postabortion patients; and
- identifying the appropriate health system and personnel for referral of women with abortion complications.

Findings from the ethnographic work with midwives prior to the training course were incorporated into the curriculum. Terms and concepts frequently used by midwives when referring to abortion and abortion complications were utilized in presentations and materials.

The 11 midwives from Yecapixtla who had previously received training from the INSP on topics related to pregnancy, vaginal delivery, and care of the newborn attended a five-day, 20-hour PAC course at the end of January 1997. Those trained were chosen by the project team because of their inclusion in the ethnographic fieldwork conducted in the initial phases of the program and their prior participation in other SSA/INSP reproductive health courses. Thus, they are not necessarily representative of all traditional midwives in Yecapixtla and Cuautla.

Participants ranged in age from 35–74 years (mean, 57 years) and had varying levels of previous training. Six of the midwives could not read or write and two had severe hearing difficulties, yet they were selected because they had high profiles within the community. In 1996 these 11 midwives attended 5–78 births (mean, 32). Clearly some have significantly more clients than others.

Various didactic methods were used throughout the course, including lectures, guided discussions, sociodramas, case studies, brainstorming, review of clinical records, and small-group discussions. Many of the themes addressed also required one-on-one discussion between midwives and trainers where instructors could evaluate midwives' progress and address specific questions.

Major Findings from the Training Course

Evaluation of Basic Skills

Physicians and nurses who served as trainers for the course conducted pre- and posttraining evaluations of the participants by using a prestructured checklist of skills. Midwives dramatized caring for a patient while the trainer scored them on items such as taking the clinical history of the patient, hand-washing, taking vital signs, and providing information to the patient about her reproductive health. Each midwife was evaluated by a different trainer in the pre- and posttraining periods in an effort to eliminate scoring bias. In general, midwives improved their scores minimally in all skills observed. Trainers documented the following areas as needing further strengthening: taking a clinical history, documenting vital signs, assessing signs of fever, treating infection and shock, and making referrals to the hospital.

Implementing an Effective Referral System

During the first day of the course none of the midwives was willing to discuss the experiences they had had with women who came to them with bleeding or other signs of an abortion, noting that women did not come to them seeking care because they knew that midwives could not attend to their needs. As the course continued, a degree of trust developed between the trainers and the participants. Midwives began to talk about women who had come to them bleeding or after aborting. Most noted that they did not participate in the women's care but rather referred them to nearby health facilities that were geographically and economically accessible. Fears of being called an abortionist and of subsequent legal repercussions were mentioned by some midwives as reasons for not attending to these women. Those midwives who did discuss the care they provided to women couched their explanations in terms of actions that needed to be taken during emergencies when immediate access to a physician was necessary but not possible. In such cases midwives engaged in a range of practices, as outlined above. One midwife summarized, "We all do what we can for these women because there's no one else in the community who will help. Sometimes the families have no money or they refuse to bring the woman to a health institution."

Creating a viable referral system has been among the most difficult tasks throughout this project. Midwives remain fearful of legal repercussions if they refer a woman to the hospital and are even more hesitant to accompany her. Many women resist seeking care at the hospital, and families may actually refuse to allow this.

Conclusions Regarding the Training

Objective evaluation of skills was difficult because of differences in terminology, concepts, and frameworks employed by traditional midwives and by hospital personnel. For example, taking a pulse was noted as performed correctly when the midwife counted the number of beats per minute. However, for many midwives the actual number of beats was irrelevant, while the strength of the pulse was viewed as significant and labeled as slow, weak, or rapid, according to the type of "shadow" that follows the woman. Furthermore, most midwives did not own or use watches, making the medical method of taking a pulse difficult or impossible.

The lack of common terminology and a framework for measuring levels of midwives' newly acquired skills was a challenge that was not overcome in the training. This speaks to the need to incorporate midwives more fully into the design and implementation of future training sessions. While findings from the ethnographic fieldwork and questionnaires were included in the content of the training materials developed, midwives themselves were not involved in defining the methodology, content, and form of their training. Nor were they included in shaping the evaluation indicators in a way that would be most useful to all of the participants.

In sum, the training course was successful in broadening the discussion about abortion and abortion complications among midwives and hospital-based providers and in recognizing the terminology and practices that midwives currently use when women with abortion complications come to them for care. However, significant limitations and challenges remain:

- The training course was brief and included a great deal of technical information about abortion complications, stabilization, and referral that was, in large part, new to the midwives.
- Differences in concepts of health and health care exist between midwives on the one hand and physicians and nurses on the other. The different ways of framing a health problem and its resolution created a gap in communication between these two groups of providers.
- Follow-up mechanisms must be clearly established so that midwives and their health system counterparts fully understand their mutual expectations and the systems for coordinating care of women experiencing abortion complications.

The training course described here must be viewed as a critical initial step toward opening the conversation about abortion among physicians, nurses, and midwives, a topic rarely discussed among these health care providers. It served to formally recognize the important role that midwives play in ensuring that women with abortion complications receive prompt care. It also contributed toward building solid relationships between midwives and the formal health care system so that effective referral can take place.

Actions Following the Training Course

After the training course, coordinators of the state midwife program within the SSA of Morelos began incorporating the monitoring of PAC activities into their routine responsibilities and began planning to extend PAC training to all midwives in the state program. It should be noted that as of July 1997, the trained midwives had not reported any treatment or referrals of women with abortion complications. The dearth of reported activities in the area of abortion care warrants further investigation to determine whether midwives are not seeing women with abortion complications or whether they are not reporting such instances of care.

In addition, during the training, project collaborators identified various information needs at the community level. Women, their partners, and their families should be educated about the need for prompt treatment of abortion complications, how to recognize complications, and where to go for treatment. Radio spots were developed for popular local stations in Morelos, and these have been shared, along with the research results and training materials, with various coordinators of midwife training programs and safe motherhood efforts throughout Mexico.

Conclusions

Women throughout the world continue to depend on the services of midwives and other community-based providers for their reproductive health care. Yet, to date, little work has been done to incorporate them into the process of ensuring that women receive prompt postabortion care. The results presented here show that research regarding traditional midwives' understanding of and practices surrounding abortion and abortion care is critically important before providing training for these providers. Qualitative research conducted by trained investigators who have close personal experience with traditional midwives proved to be invaluable in obtaining an in-depth understanding of their beliefs and practices regarding the usually taboo topic of abortion. Future work that attempts to incorporate midwives into the delivery of postabortion care should utilize similar research techniques so that trainers can use appropriate concepts and language in courses for both midwives and hospital-based physicians and nurses. In essence, the need exists for training and evaluation models that are different from those traditionally used to teach hospital-based personnel how to deliver PAC services. These new models need to be driven and informed by carefully conducted research.

The negative attitudes that midwives harbor toward women experiencing abortion complications, whether from induced or spontaneous abortion, have widespread implications for the care they provide. The intimacy and confidence that characterize many women's relationships with midwives during pregnancy and birth do not seem to be present after an abortion. Programs and training interventions should address these attitudes so that women experiencing abortion complications are not reluctant to seek care from a local midwife or health service.

Women, their families, and traditional midwives in the community need to engage in mutual education to develop an understanding of obstetric emergencies, to recognize the signs and symptoms of abortion complications, and to develop a plan for emergency care and transport. Sibley and Armbruster (1997) note in their recent work with midwives to decrease maternal mortality that women, their families, and community providers need to be aware of decisionmaking processes that cause women to delay seeking care and in actually arriving at a facility for help. Referral networks and emergency transport systems need to be strengthened so that delays in arrival at a facility with emergency services are avoided.

It is vital to create and reinforce formal, officially recognized links between midwives and institutionalized health sectors so that an effective referral process can be developed. To accomplish this, communication and understanding between midwives at the community level and providers within the formal health sector will need to be established. Conducting periodic joint training workshops on various aspects of maternal health care might be one approach. This would allow both groups to establish personal contacts, listen to each other's views and experiences, and work to improve overall care and access, including postabortion care.

Finally, PAC strategies should be incorporated into a statewide safe motherhood program that is fully sanctioned by local and state leaders and health systems authorities. This will lower the risk that midwives run of being targeted for punitive actions, and it will reduce their fear of legal repercussions when they stabilize a woman with severe bleeding, accompany her to the health center or hospital, or otherwise assist her in obtaining lifesaving care.

Acknowledgments

We would like to acknowledge the John D. and Catherine T. MacArthur Foundation whose generous grant and vision regarding women's health in Latin America helped to make this work possible. We would also like to thank the following individuals for their valuable collaboration during the process of ethnographic fieldwork: Nicté Castañeda, Dolores González, Ana Rosa Maldonado, and Laura Rodríguez. Finally, we thank all the traditional midwives and hospital-based health care providers whose collaboration made this project a success.

Notes

1 The term "midwife" can be confusing since it is used in the literature to describe health care providers with varying levels of skill. Klein (1995) distinguishes among three general categories: (1) traditional midwife: a traditional or trained birth attendant (TBA) who learns her skills through experience or from other TBAs and works in the community; (2) auxiliary midwife: a midwife with some medical training who works in the community, maternity centers, and hospitals; and (3) nurse midwife: a midwife with medical/nursing training. In this project we worked with midwives who best fit the traditional midwife description.

According to the Grupo de Trabajo para el Mejoramiento de la Atención de la Salud Materno Infantil por Parteras Tradicionales [Working group for the improvement of maternal and infant health care by traditional midwives], the traditional midwife is "someone who emerges from her own community and by tradition, camaraderie, or vocation dedicates herself to attending births and addressing other health problems, in agreement with the habits and customs of the region. As such, she is recognized by the community as a natural and accepted leader. In some communities her work may have religious or mystical origins" (SSA 1994: 5).

2 Risk factors include parity, interval since previous birth, previous birth outcomes, previous illnesses, extreme age or youth, strong headaches, and abnormal fetal position.

References

Benson, Ralph C. 1983. *Handbook of Obstetrics and Gynecology*, 8th ed. Los Altos, Calif.: Lange Medical Publications.

Castañeda, X., C. García, and A. Langer. 1996. "Ethnography of fertility and menstruation in rural Mexico," *Social Science and Medicine* 42(1): 133–140.

Castañeda, X., L. Guzmán, and A. Langer. 1991. "Una alternativa para la atención perinatal: Las parteras tradicionales en el estado de Morelos" [An alternative for perinatal care: traditional midwives in the state of Morelos], *Ginecología y Obstetricia de México* 59: 353–357.

Castañeda Camey, X. 1992. "Embarazo, parto y puerperio: Conceptos y prácticas de las parteras en el estado de Morelos" [Pregnancy, labor, and postpartum: concepts and practices of traditional midwives in the state of Morelos], *Salud Pública de México* 34: 528–532.

Castañeda Camey, X., C. García Barrios, X. Romero Guerrero, R.M. Nuñez-Urquiza, D. González Hernández, and A. Langer Glass. 1996. "Traditional birth attendants in Mexico: Advantages and inadequacies of care for normal deliveries," *Social Science and Medicine* 43(2): 199–207.

García Barrios, C., X. Castañeda Camey, X. Romero Guerrero, D. González Hernández, and A. Langer Glass. 1993. "Percepción de las parteras sobre factores de riesgo reproductivo" [Perception of midwives regarding reproductive risk factors], *Salud Pública de México* 35: 74–84.

Instituto Nacional de Salud Pública (INSP). 1992. *Atención Tradicional al Embarazo, Parto, Puerperio y Enfermedades de la Primera Infancia en Morelos* [Traditional care during pregnancy, labor, postpartum, and illnesses of early infancy in Morelos]. Mexico: INSP.

Klein, Susan. 1995. *A Book for Midwives: A Manual for Traditional Birth Attendants and Community Midwives.* Palo Alto, Calif.: The Hesperian Foundation.

Langer, A., B. Hernández, and R. Lozano. 1994. "La morbimortalidad materna en México: Niveles y causas" [Maternal morbidity and mortality in Mexico: levels and causes] in *Maternidad Sin Riesgos en México* [Safe motherhood in Mexico], eds. Ma. del Carmen Elu and Ana Langer. Mexico City, Mexico: IMES, pp. 23–30.

Lezana, M.A. 1999. "Evolución de las tasas de mortalidad materna en México" [Evolution of maternal mortality rates in Mexico], in *Una Nueva Mirada a la Mortalidad Materna en México* [A new look at maternal mortality in Mexico], eds. Ma. del Carmen Elu and Elsa Santos Pruneda. Mexico City, Mexico: UNFPA, Population Council.

Maine, D. (ed.). 1997. *Prevention of Maternal Mortality Network,* supplement to *International Journal of Gynecology and Obstetrics* 59(suppl 2).

Marcos, S. and M. Avilés. 1996. "Entre la medicina y la tradición: Las parteras de Morelos" [Between medicine and tradition: midwives of Morelos], in *Maternidad Sin Riesgos en Morelos* [Safe motherhood in Morelos]. Mexico: Comité Promotor por una Maternidad Sin Riesgos en México, pp. 115–135.

Mellado, V., C. Zolla, and X. Castañeda. 1989. *La Atención al Embarazo y el Parto en el Medio Rural Mexicano* [Pregnancy and labor care in rural areas in Mexico]. Mexico City: Centro Interamericano de Estudios de Seguridad Social.

Rosenfield, A. and D. Maine D. 1985. "Maternal mortality—A neglected tragedy: Where is the M in MCH?" *Lancet* 2: 83–85.

Secretaría de Salud (SSA). 1994. *El Pérfil de la Partera Tradicional en México* [A profile of the traditional midwife in Mexico]. Mexico City, Mexico: SSA.

———. 1997. *Servicios de Salud en el Estado de Morelos* [Health services in the state of Morelos], internal report of Dirección General de Salud Reproductiva.

Secretaría de Salud de Morelos (SSM) and Ipas. 1997. *Borrador del Manual del Capacitador: Curso para Parteras Tradicionales sobre Atención y Referencia de Mujeres con Aborto* [Draft training manual: course for traditional midwives on care and referral of women with abortion] Mexico City, Mexico: Ipas.

Sibley, L. and D. Armbruster. 1997. "Obstetric first aid in the community—Partners in safe motherhood: A strategy for reducing maternal mortality," *Journal of Nurse-Midwifery* 42(2): 117–121.

World Health Organization (WHO). 1995. *Complications of Abortion: Technical and Managerial Guidelines for Prevention and Treatment.* Geneva: WHO.

10

Ethical Issues in Postabortion Care Research Involving Vulnerable Subjects

Karin Ringheim

Based on certain assumptions, improving the quality of postabortion care received by women in developing countries can be viewed as a moral and ethical obligation. The knowledge is available, the technology is inexpensive, the successful transfer of this knowledge and technology has been demonstrated in numerous settings, and the international community agrees it is essential.[1] To determine how best to implement the new technology and train providers, operations and survey research is often undertaken. In the process, ethical dilemmas have arisen on how to conduct research in a manner that assures that the rights of the patient are protected while the care she receives is improved.

The International Ethical Guidelines for Biomedical Research Involving Human Subjects suggest that research involving "vulnerable" subjects must meet "particularly stringent review requirements" (CIOMS 1993: 11). Vulnerability is defined as "a substantial incapacity to protect one's own interests owing to such impediments as lack of capability to give informed consent, lack of alternatives to obtaining medical care . . . or being a . . . subordinate member of a hierarchical group" (CIOMS 1993: 11). Although the guidelines do not specify what these more stringent requirements are, subjects typically defined as vulnerable include pregnant and lactating women. One could certainly surmise that women who have developed medical complications from a spontaneous or induced abortion are also in a vulnerable state.

Patients are particularly under duress if they must seek medical assistance following a pregnancy termination. If induced abortion is illegal, the patient may fear legal as well as physical repercussions, and extra precautions are warranted. However, the illegal status of abortion only adds to, but does not define, the vulnerability of the postabortion care patient. A woman may be as vulnerable (e.g., to physical or emotional abuse) if she has had a legal abortion, but without the knowledge or consent of her husband, or of her family if she is an adolescent. Sensitivity surrounding a woman's sexuality and reproductive capacity creates a heightened potential for stigmatization of the patient, whether or not the procedure is legal. Postabortion care research, by virtue of its focus on women who are in a vulnerable state, necessitates more than ordinary attention to ethical standards. In applying both biomedical and social science protocols to a vulnerable patient population, researchers need to exercise more than ordinary caution in assuring that patients' rights to privacy, confidentiality, and autonomy are strictly observed. Although failure to attend to ethical standards in making biomedical decisions may have greater life-threatening consequences for the patient, lack of adherence to the ethical dimensions of social science research may also result in physical and emotional harm to the patient (Ringheim 1995).

This chapter outlines a set of principles developed by ethicists with specific reference to reproductive health that may help to meet the objectives of a rigorous ethical review called for in the case of vulnerable women during postabortion care. Research on how best to provide postabortion care raises a host of ethical issues, from defining the appropriate behavior for the investigator who witnesses a violation of aseptic procedures, to the extent of the researcher's obligation to assure a sustainable supply of instruments for the continued provision of manual vacuum aspiration (MVA) after the study has ended or to lobby for reform of laws that restrict the reproductive rights of women. This chapter relates these principles to a limited set of issues raised by researchers in the field, with attention to the enhanced vulnerability of the patient.

The three topics to be discussed are: (1) the responsibility of the investigator for assuring adherence to informed consent and confidentiality procedures by those in direct contact with the patient; (2) the role of the investigator in securing the patient's right to adequate pain control; and (3) guidelines and special considerations regarding adolescent subjects in postabortion care research. While the chapter raises questions, it attempts to broaden awareness of ethical principles that have a bearing on postabortion care research and to interest researchers in addressing the challenges suggested by such principles.

Ethical Principles Governing Research with Human Subjects

The Helsinki Declaration, formulated in 1964 and amended by the World Medical Assembly, most recently in 1996, states that the rights of patients should prevail over the interests of science and society. This declaration has formed the basis for standards of ethical research that have become increasingly stringent (CIOMS 1993).

Most researchers are familiar with the fundamental ethical considerations by which research on human subjects is commonly judged: respect for persons, which includes both protection of the right to self-determination and protection of persons with impaired autonomy; beneficence, the obligation to maximize benefits and minimize harms or wrongs; and justice, the requirement to distribute the burdens and benefits of research to subjects in an equitable manner and to extend to them any benefits of the study (Beauchamp and Childress 1983; CIOMS 1993).

Consensus is lacking that adherence to these criteria alone is sufficient to judge that ethical standards of research have been met. For example, ethicists have noted that the extent to which health research has been directed toward men violates at least one of these fundamentals, justice, in that those who conduct or fund research have not equally addressed the health problems of women (Macklin 1993). The ethics of research on postabortion care are clearly linked to women's reproductive rights, as it is the absence of self-determination, or of respect for the right to bodily integrity (Harrison 1983), that precipitates the special vulnerability of women who seek care for complications of abortion. It has been argued from a feminist perspective that "women's well-being is the primary concern in all reproductive ethics" (Hunt 1992: 1, derived from Harrison 1983).

Were women able to exercise these rights in the context of legal and safe abortion, the rate and severity of complications would be minimal. Therefore, improving the quality of care for treatment of postabortion complications must not be an end in itself (Berer 1997). The ultimate goal must be to address the root causes that create the special vulnerability of women receiving postabortion care.

Prior to the International Conference on Population and Development in 1994, Columbia University's Development Law and Policy Program and UNFPA sponsored a roundtable on ethics, population, and reproductive health. As a result of this meeting, 36 ethicists, theologians, women's health advocates, and family planning and human rights activists issued a Declaration of Ethical Principles (Development Law and Policy Program 1994). The declaration embodies respect for persons, beneficence, and justice in defining ethical principles for reproductive health, which are particularly relevant to the topic of ethics in postabortion care research. By going beyond what was endorsed by the Belmont Report (National Commission for the Protection of Human Subjects of Biomedical and Behavioral Research 1988) and by the World Health Organization (CIOMS 1993) in terms of explicitly defining the ethical obligations of those working in the field of reproductive health, the Declaration of Ethical Principles offers a framework for the more stringent review of programs relating to vulnerable subjects. The Declaration states:

1. Because reproductive health is an important social good, promoting reproductive health and improving conditions for its attainment are an ethical obligation. Ethical obligation may be seen as context-based, dependent largely on what a community or society can achieve for itself. Universal health insurance, for example, is a social good that is within the capacity of some societies, but not others, to provide. Whether or not a society assumes more obligations as the social and financial capacity to achieve greater social good increases is an ethical issue. As societies progress materially and develop the capacity to promote social good on a broader scale, attention to the principles of justice and beneficence requires that if a prevention, cure, or clearly superior treatment exists, its availability should not be circumscribed by inability to pay. In the case of improving postabortion care, however, the primary constraints are social and political rather than economic. Since appropriate medical care for women with complications of abortion is not more expensive than inappropriate care, the greater roadblocks to quality of care and treatment with dignity are failure to acknowledge the political circumstances surrounding abortion, characterization of abortion as a social problem, and tolerance of abusive behavior toward those who have violated social norms.

If reproductive health is an important social good, women whose reproductive health is compromised by complications following an abortion, whether legally restricted or unrestricted, spontaneous or induced, must be helped. This principle can be seen as the rationale for all postabortion care research and training: to restore the reproductive health of women in the most expeditious manner, and with a high standard of quality of care. The ease of access to care for complications may vary significantly depending on the social context of and desire for the pregnancy. Serious complications from abortions conducted under safe conditions are rare. Women may not avail themselves of safe services, however, if they fear reprisal, breach of confidentiality, or are ashamed of either the pregnancy or the decision to abort. It is difficult to establish definitively whether pregnancy loss is induced or spontaneous. Especially in a legally restricted context, women have reason to conceal the particulars of their pregnancy termination from providers if their complications resulted from an induced abortion.

The Helsinki Declaration states that when medical research is combined with clinical care, "every patient should be assured of the best proven diagnostic and therapeutic method" (CIOMS 1993). Research on postabortion care has already established the superiority of new treatments over standard treatments in terms of health outcomes. Not only are these the better procedures, but the technology to implement them everywhere is available. The ethical obligation to promote reproductive health and improve conditions for its attainment would also apply to providing postabortion care patients with information about the rapid return of fertility and access to methods of family planning.

2. Justice in reproductive health requires an equitable allocation of benefits and responsibilities related to reproductive decisions, including decisions about whether or not to have children. When applied to those who have lost or terminated a pregnancy, this principle implies that all women are entitled to equal status and care in receiving reproductive health services. This may be the most controversial of the ethical statements because of conflicting beliefs over the "right to" and morality of abortion. Women with complications of abortion may not receive treatment equal to what other obstetric patients receive. They may be the last served and least well-served, based on the provider's lack of respect for the patient's right to self-determination. In addition to the principle of justice, "the principle of 'respect for persons' is also violated when women who seek abortions or come for medical help after a botched abortion are treated punitively by physicians or other health care providers" (Macklin 1993: 25). Medical procedures for treating complications of spontaneous and induced abortion are the same, and women who involuntarily lose a pregnancy may be as much the subject of the provider's disdain as those who have induced an abortion.

With particular relevance to adolescents, the declaration states that no groups or individuals should be denied reproductive health services based on age or other criteria. "Information relating to reproductive health and the availability of services must flow freely and be widely disseminated and adequate general education must be provided to all members of society" (Development Law and Policy Program 1994: 5).

3. For actions and practices to be ethical, persons must be treated with respect, and the autonomy of individuals must be respected. The autonomy of women seeking postabortion care is diminished because of physical trauma and their emotional state, and potentially by the illegality of presumed actions. Such patients are dependent on medical personnel to an extent that may compromise their ability to exercise self-determination.

Researchers must recognize that patients who have violated laws or acted without the knowledge or consent of their partners are in need of special protection, and extra attention must be paid to confidentiality and privacy. The Declaration of Ethical Principles states that:

> Societal recognition that women have the capacity for making informed choices despite their poverty or lack of education is necessary for implementing respect for persons in reproductive health programs. Paternalism is inconsistent with respect for persons. Religious and cultural traditions cannot be used as an excuse to countenance violations of respect for persons. (Development Law and Policy Program 1994: 6)

This principle goes to the heart of the investigator's responsibility to obtain a valid informed consent, which must sometimes overrule the health care provider's insistence that individual consent is not necessary.[2] In addition to protecting the patient, confidentiality is also essential to the validity of the study, as those who do not trust that their answers to highly sensitive questions will be held in strict confidence are likely either to refuse to participate or to be less than forthright in answering questions.

Respect for persons also requires recognizing the autonomy of the individual woman to participate in her own treatment and honoring her preference for the type of treatment employed. This includes the patient's right to dictate her own level and type of pain medication, a subject that will be discussed further. Women unaccustomed to making demands upon a medical system or to acting autonomously on their own behalf in any public sphere require education to understand their rights and to request the care they want and to which they are entitled. Given the gender and status power imbalances involved, the creation of a demand for rights and dignity may be a process requiring much nurturing, but is one the researcher can initiate with both clients and providers.

4. Ethically sound reproductive health programs and policies are ones that result in a balance of desirable consequences over undesirable ones. In the medical setting the benefit–risk assessment "obligat[es] physicians to recommend the treatment plan with the most favorable [balance of] benefit–risk for the patient" (Macklin 1993: 26). There is evidence to support the statement that the transition from dilation and curettage (D&C) to

MVA improves health outcomes for patients (Winkler, Oliveras, and McIntosh 1995). Similarly, the increased risk of morbidity and mortality associated with general anesthesia strongly suggests that a procedure that can be done under local anesthesia need not and probably should not be done under general anesthesia. Of course, an ethical obligation cannot be imposed on providers who have no training or instruments to perform the procedure with the most favorable benefit–risk ratio for the patient. As with any new technology or treatment that is clearly superior to the standard, those who have the means are ethically obligated, according to the first principle in the declaration, to make this new technology as widely available and accessible as possible.

The fourth principle embodies the ethical principle of beneficence. Desirable consequences include the complete and rapid recovery of the patient and the prevention of future unwanted pregnancies. The roundtable participants noted:

> Disagreements may occur about such matters as the provision of family planning services to unmarried persons . . . and the availability of abortion services. However, these disagreements do not challenge the principle that every program or policy should maximize desirable consequences and minimize undesirable ones to the greatest degree possible. (Development Law and Policy Program 1994: 8)

Researchers may debate the ability or necessity of routinely considering or upholding the higher standards implied by these four principles, but when research involves a patient population as clearly vulnerable as women who seek postabortion care in an environment in which abortion is legally or normatively prohibited, these more explicit guidelines may be useful in helping researchers meet the challenge of a "particularly stringent ethical review" (CIOMS 1993).

Ethical Training for Interviewers and Providers

The third principle of the Declaration states that "for actions and practices to be ethical, persons must be treated with respect, and the autonomy of individuals must be respected." One of the most difficult questions facing principal investigators, agencies, and donors is how to ensure that ethical standards are being observed by interviewers and providers during their interactions with clients. The principal investigator has responsibility for the welfare of the study participants, but in most studies the interviewer and/or the doctor, nurse, or midwife provide the interface between investigator and subject. The investigator may have the highest of ethical standards, but unless these have been conveyed to and internalized (or at least agreed to) by those directly interacting with the subject, the patient's rights to privacy, dignity, and consent may easily be violated. Such violations may range from a misplaced emphasis in asking interview questions (e.g., "If you didn't want to get pregnant, why were you not using contraception?") to endangering the client through carelessness in protecting the privacy of her records. Protocols for protecting confidentiality and obtaining valid informed consent do not typically draw attention to the importance of interviewer selection, and guidelines for conducting the ethical training of interviewers and providers are notably lacking.

Respecting Human Dignity

The concept of informed consent may be difficult to grasp for those providers who routinely, although perhaps unwittingly, abrogate patients' rights to privacy and human dignity. Many visitors to developing-country hospitals and clinics have witnessed medical procedures being performed without the patient's consent. Providers often dismiss the notion that the patient should have the right to refuse observation. Providers are also probably correct in their insistence that the woman would not (or would not dare) refuse. The balance of power in provider–client relationships is heavily skewed in favor of the provider. In some cases the requirements imposed by the funding agency may be the only reason that providers understand that compliance with informed consent is not "optional."

Educating and empowering consumers to exercise their rights to humane treatment in a medical setting is difficult in the best of circumstances, given the tremendous status differential between patients and physicians. Women who have undergone an illegal or socially forbidden procedure such as pregnancy termination are unlikely to make demands or to report abuses. This is all the more reason for the researcher to educate and sensitize providers about their ethical obligations to the patient as part of postabortion care, and to monitor the behavior of providers throughout the project. Changing a lifetime pattern of paternalism toward women where the provider believes that he or she knows best is not easily accomplished. More particular to the provision of postabortion care is how to alter the hostility and negligence that may await clients, based on providers' negative attitudes toward abortion. A number of studies have documented that these attitudes have a direct bearing on the quality of patient care, including waiting time, pain control, and physical and verbal treatment (Djohan et al. 1999; Langer et al. 1997; Paiewonsky 1999). It has been suggested that those interviewing and otherwise interacting with clients need "empathy training," in order to put themselves in the shoes of the client and develop compassion and understanding for her plight (Terence H. Hull, personal communication, March 1997). When there is the possibility to influence the medical school curriculum to include modules on postabortion care and family planning, the opportunity to train physicians and medical personnel about the rights of human subjects and respect for human dignity should not be lost. Such training should reach practicing physicians through postgraduate and refresher training and through the attention of the medical societies to which most belong.

Informed Consent and Confidentiality

That staff protect confidential information is particularly critical because of the interest that persons with power and authority over the subject may have in this information. Women, for example, must be protected from any pressure on the part of husbands to learn of their responses to questions, such as whether anything was done to induce the abortion. When the possibility exists that access to information about the patient may be obtained by others, or when the research design involves other family members such as a husband, the informed consent procedure should specifically acknowledge and obtain consent from the woman for these conditions, and should articulate precautions being taken to protect the patient's right to confidentiality.

Follow-up of postabortion patients and their families after they have left the hospital represents a particular challenge. It is difficult to determine when informed consent for such follow-up is best obtained. Prior to treatment the patient may be fearful and emotionally distraught. After the procedure the patient may be in pain or discomfort. The researcher must avoid unintentional coercion in approaching a woman who is not capable at that moment of deliberating about her personal goals, as the principle of respect for persons requires. Women who agree to return to the health care setting often do not return, and those who agree to a home visit may later regret it. It may be difficult to conduct the interview in private, out of earshot of others. A recognition that the rights of the patient take precedence over the interests of science should lead to forgoing the gathering of information if an attempt to obtain it would jeopardize a woman's wellbeing.

Monitoring Interactions Between Providers and Clients

It is critical that procedures for obtaining informed consent that assure confidentiality and lack of coercion are made explicit to all those involved in the research. Despite commitment to ethical standards of service delivery, such as providing an environment of free and informed choice, the interaction that actually occurs between provider and client may not be what was envisioned during the training of staff. Supervision and close monitoring of provider–client interactions are necessary to ensure that interviewers and providers adhere to these procedures and do not abuse their power to influence and subvert client choice.

Many agencies that conduct research have prototypes for informed consent that contain all of the necessary information for validity, and some have institutional review boards that examine both the scientific and ethical merit of studies under their auspices. The Evaluation Project, funded by the United States Agency for International Development, developed indicators for measuring the impact of reproductive health programs, including indicators for compliance with provisions for maintaining confidentiality, for obtaining informed consent, and for protection against coercion. The report notes that "the procedures manual [used with providers] should include actions taken when health care personnel breach clients' confidentiality [or] . . . do not properly obtain consent or forgo this step altogether. Consequences should be detailed in the manual" (Evaluation Project 1995: 128–129).

That there are consequences for violating these important requirements is an essential message in training interviewers and service providers, from the highest level to the lowest and from the most accessible to the most remote of service sites. The researcher's responsibility for assuring compliance does not end with training. Interviewer and service provider compliance should be monitored closely, and predetermined action should be taken when violations occur. This requires that the supervisor is fully cognizant of ethical standards of the research project and the rights of the client for informed choice and informed consent and has agreed to abide by them.

Researchers in the field have noted, however, that the situation is further complicated by the fact that there may be repercussions for the person who observes and reports negative behavior, particularly that of a physician. The ethical obligation to protect persons extends to protecting the research staff from harm.

Role of the Researcher in Adequate Pain Control

The second topic to which the Declaration of Ethical Principles with regard to reproductive health (Development Law and Policy Program 1994) will be applied concerns how pain is managed, both during and subsequent to a research study, and whether there is an ethical obligation on the part of the researcher to assure that the patient receives requested and adequate pain control medication.

The clinical literature contains few studies that report on pain control and perceptions of pain from the woman's point of view (Kinoti et al. 1995). Recently, researchers have documented perceived levels of pain among women undergoing MVA (Fuentes Velazquez, Billings, and Cardona Perez 1998), and others have qualitatively recorded recollections of severe pain during D&C (Zhou et al. 1999). In a study that took place in Kenya, where only 3 percent of women who had MVA and 44 percent of those who had D&C received pain medication, nearly all patients were found to have experienced pain, and 60 percent described it as extreme (Solo and Billings 1997). This and other studies suggest that the treatment of pain, particularly the lack of such treatment, is an ethical issue that researchers of postabortion care need to consider (Girvin 1999).

The WHO (1994) guidelines for the clinical management of abortion complications recommend assessing a woman's need for pain control and administering it as needed as the first step in MVA. This step, however, is often overlooked or ignored, sometimes due to the punitive attitude of the provider. If the,patient is viewed by the provider as having committed a crime, the provider may be uninterested in alleviating her pain, believing it is her due. At the other extreme, some doctors prefer, unnecessarily, to use general anesthesia with MVA so the patient will be less troublesome (Girvin 1999; Dale Huntington, personal communication, 1998).

Appropriate, client-directed pain control and comfort and reassurance from the attending medical staff should be the standard for all postabortion care. When interventions are being tested as part of a study, the pain management, or lack of it, that women actually receive becomes an ethical issue for researchers.

The fourth principle of the declaration states that "ethically sound reproductive health programs and policies are ones that result in a balance of desirable consequences over undesirable ones" (Development Law and Policy Program 1994). The transition from D&C to MVA clearly meets the criteria for beneficence, the ethical obligation to promote good consequences over bad. MVA has been shown to be a less invasive procedure than D&C, and one that reduces waiting time, recovery time, and cost. Beneficence, however, incorporates nonmaleficence (meaning "do no harm"). In the case of postabortion care research in which D&C under general anesthesia is being replaced by MVA using a local anesthetic, the evidence suggests that some physicians perform MVA without local anesthesia. Clearly this is an undesirable consequence for the patient. What is the obligation of the researcher to influence health care practices and provider attitudes so that women are treated with compassion and given the right to direct their own pain management?

The American Psychological Association was the first of the social science professional associations to adopt an ethics policy (Fluehr-Lobban 1994). Its guidelines state:

> The ethical investigator protects participants from physical and mental discomfort, harm and danger. . . . Where research procedures may result in undesirable consequences for the participant, the investigator has the responsibility to detect and remove or correct these consequences (American Psychological Association 1981: 633–638).

Administering pain medication is a responsibility of the clinician. The role of researcher is generally to document rather than intervene, even when clearly inferior practices are observed. However, if the researcher is responsible for having introduced a new technology and observes it being implemented in a manner detrimental to the patient, a more proactive response is mandated by the above guideline. Limits to the obligations of the researcher are based in part on protecting the scientific validity of the study. Where the objective of postabortion care research is not to describe the patient's state of being, it should not violate the integrity of the study to intervene on behalf of the patient. At the least, the investigator should reiterate in meetings with providers that WHO or other guidelines are to be followed with regard to pain control. Following from the Helsinki Declaration, respect for persons, autonomy, and beneficence dictate that pain medication should be administered as needed and requested by the patient, recognizing that she is best qualified to judge her own subjective level of pain. The safest form of pain management for the patient is the preferred treatment.

What, if any, is the moral obligation of the researcher to assure the ethical treatment of patients in the future with respect to pain management? The argument has been forcefully made that to be ethical, research must go beyond description and analysis to social responsibility for action (Schoepf 1991). Research and training activities may, for example, succeed in institutionalizing the practice of MVA. If, however, MVA is conducted without availability of pain control, the principles of autonomy, to control pain as needed, and beneficence, to minimize harm, are being violated. To the extent possible, a researcher assumes responsibility for assuring that technology transfer includes the complete treatment and does not leave pain medication to the discretion of medical personnel.

Research Involving Minors

The second principle implies that "justice in reproductive health requires an equitable allocation of benefits" without regard to age. In some settings, many postabortion care clients are unmarried adolescent women. It may be especially difficult to convince local authorities and providers that these young women should be able to participate in postabortion care research or offered methods of family planning.

The guidelines for adolescent participation in research developed by ethicists for the Human Reproduction Programme of WHO state that before undertaking research involving adolescents, investigators must ensure that the information to be gained could not scientifically be obtained from adult subjects, that a goal of the research is to obtain knowledge relevant to the health needs of adolescents, that the risk presented by interventions having no direct benefit to the individual is low and commensurate with the importance of the knowledge to be gained, and that the interventions intended to provide direct benefit are at least as advantageous to the individual subject as any available alternative (WHO Special Programme of Research Development and Research Training in Human Reproduction 1994). In the case of postabortion care research in which MVA is being introduced to treat complications, the benefits to be derived by the client, in terms of safety and reduced recovery time, apply equally to both adolescents and adults.

Parental Consent

Because of their vulnerability to physical or psychological harm if their pregnancy and/or termination is disclosed, attention to confidentiality must be especially stringent where adolescent subjects are involved. The Council on Ethical and Judicial Affairs of the American Medical Association proposed that where an adolescent's sexuality is involved, development of policies requiring parental notification for health care must be mindful of the adolescent's need for privacy and the effect that a parental notification policy may have on her health care seeking behavior (Smith-Rogers, D'Angelo, and Futterman 1994). It is safe to say that parents should not be consulted about adolescent participation in research on postabortion care unless they are present with the adolescent at the hospital and fully aware of her condition. The National Commission for the Protection of Human Subjects of Biomedical Research (1977) contends that the legal ability of adolescents to obtain medical treatment without parental consent can be used as an indicator that the adolescent is capable of giving her own consent to participate in research. This document does not make specific reference to postabortion care research, nor does it recognize that in such a case, medical treatment and research are inseparable. The WHO guidelines state that "unless specific legal provisions exist, consent to participate in research should be given by the adolescent alone. Capacity to consent is related to the nature and complexity of the research. If adolescents are mature enough to understand the purpose of the proposed study and the involvement requested, then they are mature enough to consent" (WHO Special Programme of Research Development and Research Training in Human Reproduction 1994: 3). In the United States, the "mature minor" doctrine (Sigman and O'Connor 1991) provides for informed consent from the adolescent alone when no more than a minimal risk is involved in the research. However, local laws and customs may override this capacity.

Community Involvement

In lieu of parental consent, investigators may consult with key community constituents, including parents, adolescents, and youth advocates, from the area in which the study is to be conducted. It has been argued that in no other research arena is it more critical for researchers to communicate with community members than in adolescent research (Smith-Rogers, D'Angelo, and Futterman 1994). Community involvement may be especially appropriate in postabortion care research, where seeking parental consent could be harmful to the participant. Such community involvement may take the form of, or under some circumstances take the place of, a local ethical review board. By outlining the ethical principles that govern their research and by giving community representatives an opportunity to review the purpose, procedures, safeguards to protect the privacy and confidentiality of subjects, and the proposed dissemination and use of study findings, researchers thereby address the need for a more stringent review of research involving vulnerable subjects. The research may also gain broader acceptance in the community through the support of these constituents, defusing strong local opposition and increasing the likelihood that study results are applied in local programs (Smith-Rogers, D'Angelo, and Futterman 1994).

Postabortion care is a package that includes provision of family planning information and methods. The greatest difficulty in working with adolescents may arise in attempting to counsel them about and provide them with methods of contraception. A study in Sri Lanka, for example, found that providers were personally opposed to offering contraception to adolescents (Hewage 1999). It may be impossible to win the approval of the community or the local medical facility to provide contraceptive services. What, then, is the obligation of the researcher to the adolescent? Is counseling for abstinence the best that can be offered? How does one address the likelihood that the aborted pregnancy resulted from sexual coercion or violence? Clearly there is a need for the investigator to attend to the ethical requirements of autonomy, justice, and beneficence in the design and implementation of the study and to prepare interviewers and providers during training to deal with emotional crises and vulnerable patients through appropriate counseling and referral mechanisms.

Conclusion

By virtue of its focus on a vulnerable population, research on postabortion care is subject to stringent ethical review. Whether or not the research is subject to outside review, researchers must recognize the vulnerability of their subjects through more than ordinary attention to the ethical principles of respect for persons, justice, and beneficence. The Declaration of Ethical Principles with regard to reproductive health, issued by prominent ethicists and others working in the field of reproductive health, calls explicitly for a higher standard of conduct. This language is offered as a point of reference for addressing these more rigorous demands.

It is recommended that the researcher who designs a study that considers the exceptional vulnerability of the postabortion care patient assures that the confidentiality and privacy of patients is paramount; provides ethical training to all personnel who will interact with the patient; closely monitors such interactions for compliance with requirements for respect for persons and informed consent, taking appropriate action where breaches are found; instructs the patient as well as physicians and other care providers on the rights of the patient to direct her own pain management and ensure that pain management is appropriate; involves community members in decisions to include adolescents in postabortion care research; and informs the community about research findings for the benefit of its members.

The issues discussed above are based on concerns expressed by researchers in the field. Recognizing that these and other ethical dilemmas have neither simple nor unequivocal solutions, the development of ethical guidelines for postabortion care research and reproductive health research will benefit more broadly from the further input of those who confront the issues and attempt to apply the guidelines in their work. Until women obtain the right to self-determination and reproductive choice, ethical treatment of women will be compromised, and women who require postabortion care will remain vulnerable.

Views expressed do not necessarily represent those of the United States Agency for International Development.

Notes

1 The 1994 International Conference on Population and Development (ICPD) in Cairo maintained that everyone has "the right to attain the highest standard of sexual and reproductive health." More specifically, the ICPD also prescribed that "in all cases, women should have access to quality services for the management of complications arising from abortion. Post-abortion counselling, education and family-planning services should be offered promptly . . ." (ICPD Programme of Action, paragraph 8.25).

2 Elements of valid informed consent and guidelines for maintaining confidentiality are provided elsewhere (Beauchamp and Childress 1983; CIOMS 1993; Ringheim 1995) and are not discussed in detail here.

References

American Psychological Association. 1981. "Ethical principles of psychologists," *American Psychologist* 36: 633–638.

Beauchamp, T.L. and J.F. Childress. 1983. *Principles of Biomedical Ethics,* 2nd ed. New York: Oxford University Press.

Berer, M. 1997. "Abortion: Unfinished business," *Reproductive Health Matters* 9:6–9.

Council for International Organizations of Medical Sciences (CIOMS), in collaboration with the World Health Organization. 1993. *International Ethical Guidelines for Biomedical Research Involving Human Subjects.* Geneva: WHO.

Development Law and Policy Program. 1994. *Declaration of Ethical Principles,* presented at Roundtable on Ethics, Population, and Reproductive Health, Columbia University, New York, 8–10 March.

Djohan, E., R. Indrawasih, M. Adenan, H. Yudomustopo, and M.G. Tan. 1999. "The attitudes of health care providers towards abortion in Indonesia," in *Abortion in the Developing World,* eds. A. Mundigo and C. Indriso. New Delhi: World Health Organization and Vistaar Publications, pp. 281–292.

Evaluation Project. 1995. *Indicators for Reproductive Health Program Evaluation, Final Report of the Subcommittee on Safe Pregnancy,* USAID Contract DPE-3060-00-C-1054-00, Washington, D.C.

Fluehr-Lobban, C. 1994. "Informed consent in anthropological research: We are not exempt," *Human Organization: Journal of the Society for Applied Anthropology* 53(1): 1–10.

Fuentes Velazquez, J.A., D.L. Billings, and J.A. Cardona Perez. 1998. "Women's experience of pain during the postabortion period in Mexico," paper presented at Global Meeting on Postabortion Care Operations Research, The Population Council, New York, 19–21 January.

Girvin, S., 1999. "Increasing access, improving quality: Lessons learned from postabortion care programs," AVSC presentation at the Postabortion Care Workshop, JHPIEGO, Baltimore, Md., 20–21 May.

Harrison, B.W. 1983. *Our Right to Choose: Toward a New Ethic of Abortion.* Boston: Beacon Hill Press.

Hewage, P. 1999. "Induced abortion in Sri Lanka: Opinions of reproductive health care providers," in *Abortion in the Developing World,* eds. A. Mundigo and C. Indriso. New Delhi: World Health Organization and Vistaar Publications, pp. 321–336.

Hunt, Mary E. 1992. "RU486/PG and ethics: Women's moral property not for sale," *FIRE ETHICS, Newsletter of the International Feminists Interested in Reproductive Health,* 1(1): 1.

Kinoti, S.N., L. Gaffikin, J. Benson, and L.A. Nicholson. 1995. "Monograph on complications of unsafe abortion in Africa," Reproductive Health Research Programme of Commonwealth Regional Health Community Secretariat for East Central and Southern Africa.

Langer, A., C. Garcia-Barrios, A. Heimburger, K. Stein, B. Winikoff, V. Barahona, B. Casas, and F. Ramirez. 1997. "Improving post-abortion care in a public hospital in Oaxaca, Mexico," *Reproductive Health Matters* 9:20–28.

Macklin, Ruth. 1993. "Women's health: An ethical perspective," *Journal of Law, Medicine and Ethics* 21(1): 23–29.

National Commission for the Protection of Human Subjects of Biomedical and Behavioral Research. 1988. *Belmont Report: Ethical Principles and Guidelines for the Protection of Human Subjects of Research,* publication no. GPO 887-809. Washington, D.C.: Government Printing Office.

National Commission for the Protection of Human Subjects of Biomedical Research. 1977. *Research Involving Children: Report and Recommendations,* DHEW publication no. (OS) 77-0004. Washington, D.C.: United States Government Printing Office.

Paiewonsky, D. 1999. "Social determinants of induced abortion in the Dominican Republic," in *Abortion in the Developing World,* eds. A. Mundigo and C. Indriso. New Delhi: World Health Organization and Vistaar Publications, pp. 131–150.

Ringheim, Karin. 1995. "Ethical issues in social science research with special reference to sexual behaviour research," *Social Science and Medicine* 40(12): 1691–1697.

Schoepf, B.G. 1991. "Ethical, methodological and political issues of AIDS research in Central Africa," *Social Science and Medicine* 33(7): 749–763.

Sigman, G.S. and C. O'Connor. 1991. "Exploration for physicians of the mature minor doctrine," *Journal of Pediatrics* 119(4): 520–525.

Smith-Rogers, Audrey, Lawrence D'Angelo, and Donna Futterman. 1994. "Guidelines for adolescent participation in research: Current realities and possible solutions," *IRG, A Review of Human Studies* 16(4): 1–6.

Solo, J., and D. Billings. 1997. "Creating linkages between incomplete abortion treatment and family planning in Kenya: Baseline findings of an operations research study," report. New York: The Population Council.

Winkler, J., E. Oliveras, and N. McIntosh (eds). 1995. *Postabortion Care: A Reference Manual for Improving Quality of Care.* The Postabortion Care Consortium.

World Health Organization (WHO), Maternal Health and Safe Motherhood Programme, Division of Family Health. 1994. *Clinical Management of Abortion Complications: A Practical Guide.* Geneva: WHO.

WHO Special Programme of Research Development and Research Training in Human Reproduction. 1994. *Guidelines for Research on Reproductive Health Involving Adolescents.* Geneva: WHO.

Zhou Wei-jin, Gao Er-sheng, Yang Yao-ying, Qin Fei, and Tang Wei. 1999. "Induced abortion and the outcome of subsequent pregnancy in China: Client and provider perspectives," in *Abortion in the Developing World,* eds. A. Mundigo and C. Indriso. New Delhi: World Health Organization and Vistaar Publications, pp. 228–244.

11

Conclusion

Nancy J. Piet-Pelon

Abortion is the "clash of absolutes."[1] Long before it became the subject of intense public and political debate in the United States, abortion had been a societal dilemma. A woman's decision to have an abortion is fraught with conflict. Even when she is convinced it is her only solution for unwanted fertility, the abortion itself is not a happy event. Women, their partners, families, and caregivers all struggle as they make and implement the decision.

It was perhaps easier to make an abortion decision when the debate was not so public. A woman and her caregiver alone could determine what was "right" or "best" for her. Now, however, it seems impossible to make an individual decision. Women in the United States who attend abortion clinics often run a gauntlet of protesters who publicly—and often threateningly—fight for a life they do not know but believe they have a right to preserve. Women who seek abortions are subject to the pressure of public debates that influence their private agony. In other countries an individual decision is often governed by stringent laws. Women face imprisonment or fines through judicial systems that rule on their private actions. Caregivers fear rigorous punishment, fines, or professional censure if they assist in abortion cases when abortion is outside the law of the land.

There are no easy answers. Even those who strongly support a woman's right to choose how she controls her fertility envision abortion as a "last option," a backup for contraceptive failure. It is impossible for most to accept abortion as simply another clinical procedure, along with care for pregnancy and childbirth, reproductive tract infections, and reproductive health-related cancers. Abortion services have both social and legal dimensions that are pervasive, unlike other women's health services.

Who needs postabortion care? Often we make the mistake of assuming that women who need postabortion care are only those who live in countries where abortion services are restricted and women use illegal, usually injurious methods to terminate their pregnancies. This is not the case. Legalizing abortion does not completely remove the need for postabortion services. In countries where abortion is legal, three other groups of women will still commonly require postabortion care services. Women who do not have access to appropriate abortion services—either because they are unaware of their availability or lack the resources to use them—may use a method of pregnancy termination that causes health complications. A second group of women suffer spontaneous miscarriages. If this is a repeated experience, these women are in particular need of sensitive care. Repeated miscarriage can place women in vulnerable positions within their families, especially in communities where the ability to produce children is considered a woman's full responsibility and miscarriage is her personal failure. The third group requiring postabortion care are those who have complications from incomplete induced abortions. Even when abortion service is legal, service quality may not be uniform, and patients may be in need of postabortion care.

Data in support of postabortion care are compelling. Without this care, thousands of women die needlessly each year or experience lifelong morbidity. Women are also subject to a repeat abortion when their postabortion care is inadequate and their immediate return to fertility—unprotected by contraceptive use—causes another unwanted pregnancy.

Each study in this book reminds us of several critical issues that compel us to improve postabortion care services. First, we are reminded of the magnitude of the problem. From Mexico, Deborah L. Billings and Ana Langer and colleagues report that abortion constitutes the third or fourth most important cause of maternal mortality, while in Ghana, Billings and colleagues found it to be the first cause of maternal death. Nahla Abdel-Tawab and colleagues state that one of every five admissions to

OB/GYN wards in Egypt is abortion-related. In Bolivia, Juan Díaz and colleagues attribute 27–35 percent of all maternal deaths to complications from abortion.

In spite of these alarming statistics, these authors also remind us that complete data are not available. Unlike other reproductive health services, abortions are performed in both formal and informal settings. Even a complete health information system will not capture those services provided in informal settings. Thus, accurate national data are usually not available and estimates of abortion prevalence are limited to hospital-based statistics. There are two main reasons for this: Both providers and clients are reluctant to talk freely about abortion where the procedure is illegal, and many women never reach facilities where abortion statistics are routinely gathered. For example, Díaz and colleagues point out that an estimated 95 percent of abortion-related deaths in Bolivia occur in the client's home.

The second issue is the incredible complexity of providing postabortion care services. Each study was conducted within a cultural, legal, social, and religious framework that needed to be taken into account. Although high-quality postabortion care requires appropriate clinical services, introducing this fundamental element was only a small part of the total intervention. Researchers had to educate themselves regarding provider attitudes toward clients who have abortions and to manage their work even where negative attitudes were prevalent. The negative attitudes toward these clients were most pronounced among traditional midwives in Mexico who expressed their belief that all women who experienced either spontaneous or induced abortions were defective in some way and blamed the women directly for their situation. They expressed the belief that induced abortion was "murder" or a "grave sin." Yet even better-educated providers have strong prejudices against women who have induced abortion. In Bolivia, the researchers had to overcome the prejudice of physicians and other caregivers in a hospital setting about women who induced abortions. Prior to the intervention study many caregivers believed women who had abortions were delinquent and deserved punishment for their actions. In both of these countries, providers also feared legal sanctions. Researchers had to address both the prejudices and the fear of legal sanctions while conducting their work.

Directly related to the complexity of providing postabortion care services are legal and ethical issues. The legal status of abortion varies in the countries where the studies were conducted. In spite of legal restrictions, however, abortion is common. As Tietze and Bongaarts contend, "Regardless of its legal status, abortion is used with similar frequency in all countries that have similar patterns of marriage, contraception, and fertility" (Tietze and Bongaarts 1975: 119).

When caregivers are subjected to strict abortion laws, they are often unable to provide the required care to clients—either for a requested pregnancy termination or for postabortion care. If they fear legal sanctions, many caregivers will find a way to avoid providing essential services. Yet, as Karin Ringheim establishes in her chapter on ethics, improving postabortion care is a moral and ethical obligation. Ringheim bases this on the facts that the knowledge to provide high-quality postabortion care is available, the technology is inexpensive, and the successful transfer of this knowledge and technology has already been demonstrated. One of the remaining unanswered questions is how to deal effectively with legal sanctions where these limit the care that providers can give.

Each of these issues must be addressed when new research is undertaken. Future research must be based on an appreciation of the magnitude of the abortion problem in the study setting; a recognition of the complexity of providing services; and the legal and ethical issues that both caregivers and clients face.

Lessons Learned

The studies presented in this book have taught us fundamental lessons and should encourage us to continue to push for solutions to the complex issues that postabortion care services present.

Understanding Our Research Environment

Postabortion caregivers do not operate in a clinical vacuum. They are the products of their own moral, ethical, and legal backgrounds that often constrain their willingness to provide abortion services and, unfortunately, also influence their disposition toward providing high-quality postabortion care. As the studies illustrate, many providers feel that clients who require postabortion care are personally to blame for their predicaments. Generally there is little sympathy or concern for the woman's situation. Her decision and subsequent condition are treated with a level of contempt that influences the care she receives. Clients requiring postabortion care services are also not free from environmental influences. In situations where they are aware that abortion is illegal or where they are simply fearful of how they will be treated, women often delay their arrival at the hospital and can obfuscate when asked about the cause of their condition.

The studies, particularly those from Bolivia and Oaxaca, Mexico, show that proper training can temper some of the contemptuous attitudes of providers. When providers in Bolivia were trained to treat women requiring postabortion care services simply as clients in need of services and were freed from worry of legal sanctions, they were able to overcome their own concerns about moral and ethical issues. At the same time, clients became more open and attentive to counseling advice when they were treated more humanely. Thus, the hoped-for results of both improved care and increased family planning acceptance were realized. In the Oaxaca study, the emphasis on value-free counseling also proved to be effective.

Overcoming negative provider attitudes through training did not work effectively in Mexico with traditional midwives, however. Although Billings and her colleagues addressed the issues in the training of providers, they were unable to overcome the midwives' fears of legal sanctions sufficiently. The authors do not explain why their program was not more successful in changing attitudes. One possible reason is that the researchers did not sufficiently address the midwives' expressed worries about legal sanctions or their concerns that they would be labeled "abortionists" if they assisted or referred women. Another possibility is based on reported hostile treatment the midwives received from trained medical personnel on the preintervention occasions when they had accompanied referred clients. Clearly these midwives need much more encouragement and reassurance before they will willingly provide services.

Comprehensive and Extensive Training of All Caregivers

A common assumption is that effective postabortion care begins with high-quality clinical services. The essential elements include use of manual vacuum aspiration (MVA) to replace dilation and curettage (D&C), pain management throughout the clinical procedure, and adequate supplies of essential drugs and safe blood supplies. Good postabortion care also requires prompt treatment in an infection-free setting. The importance, and the difficulty, of providing appropriate training to ensure that these clinical elements are all in place and operating at the highest level of quality cannot be underestimated. In each of the studies described in this volume, a significant level of effort was required simply to train for provision of high-quality clinical services.

But this is not enough. Díaz and colleagues in Bolivia and Abdel-Tawab and colleagues in Egypt realized the importance of addressing the essential elements of interpersonal communication between caregivers and clients, including other family members. In both studies, training stressed the importance of treating clients with dignity and establishing the rights of clients for treatment, even when their abortion was induced and, consequently, abhorrent to some caregivers. Through intensive training, the research teams in Bolivia and Egypt developed a cadre of skilled caregivers who provided not only appropriate clinical services but also treated each client with dignity, respect for her privacy, and a sympathetic understanding of her ordeal. Counseling training for all caregivers is another critical element highlighted in the reported studies. It is unfortunate, but apparently true, that most caregivers are not previously trained to counsel clients about their reproductive health. Abdel-Tawab and her colleagues in Egypt broke new ground by providing counseling not only to clients but also, after their informed consent, to their husbands. This greatly increased the counseled couples' family planning acceptance and enhanced clients' postabortion recovery.

In the most successful research work, training is not a one-time event but rather a continual process. In Mexico, Langer and colleagues' training efforts began only after a thorough preintervention phase. Based on the presentation to caregivers of their findings of inadequate postabortion care services, the caregivers themselves requested certain steps to improve services. These included modifying hospital procedures to reduce waiting time, improve pain management, and address issues of client privacy; instructing all caregivers in the use of MVA; training staff in provider–client relations; and developing informational materials for both providers and clients. Following this guidance from providers, successful training programs were developed.

Team training, as outlined in the work of Billings and colleagues in Ghana, is another useful model. Here midwives from primary health care facilities were trained with their supervisors, who worked at the referral points. Through team training, the midwives and their physician supervisors gained an appreciation of one another's work and developed a collaborative spirit in the provision of services.

Related reproductive health services are another element of high-quality postabortion care. Each client should receive counseling on and be provided family planning services and any other reproductive health services she may require. When they are provided in the same setting, as illustrated by Julie Solo and her colleagues in Kenya, clients are more effectively served.

If any of the aspects of clinical services or interpersonal skills are ignored, the quality of the service is in jeopardy. Several of the studies in this book show that when these elements are simultaneously introduced and appropriately combined, clients receive all aspects of care they require. However, improved clinical practice demands sufficient training of providers so that they achieve technical competence in MVA and pain management and an uninterrupted source of essential supplies.

Supervision as a Built-in Component

Most of the studies reported here were dependent on supervision of the postabortion care intervention by the research team. Díaz and colleagues, however, built high-quality supervision into the existing system. This has greater potential for sustainability of services and high quality. Billings and colleagues in their work with Ghanaian midwives also created an effective supervision system. By encouraging cooperation between trainers in referral facilities and midwives practicing in primary health care facilities, they created an environment that encouraged collaboration. In future operations research, supervision from within the clinic setting should be built in, even while research is ongoing and supervision is being provided by the research team. This will serve to ensure sustainability after the research is completed.

Supplies Ensured for Appropriate Clinical Practice

Each of the hospital-based research projects described here included the use of MVA equipment and appropriate pain management. Supplies were often provided for the purpose of research. Clearly more work and research are required in support of the commercial registration and distribution of MVA equipment, as its uninterrupted supply is critical to the provision of appropriate postabortion care.

Appropriate family planning method supplies were also sometimes provided as part of the research. As these are also critical elements of an effective postabortion care clinical service, the continued provision of these supplies must be addressed before research is concluded.

Essential Elements for Future Research

Legal Dimension

While it may be impossible in some settings to ignore the legal dimension of abortion, researchers have an obligation to help caregivers make some critical distinctions. Postabortion care is a health service. Therefore, in all clinical settings it is possible to provide critical care and avoid legal confrontations that are imbued with social polemics. The act of the abortion, even where it is legal, has been done outside of the purview or control of the postabortion caregiver. Thus service providers are not responsible for what has already happened. They are responsible, however, if they do not provide appropriate care to a client who comes to them with a complication from an abortion. The hospital-based studies reported here do an excellent job of helping caregivers make this distinction.

It is beyond the scope of postabortion care research to address the preexisting legal environment; however, it is critical to recognize it and to understand the potential constraints that caregivers feel. It is important to establish that even in the most restrictive legal environment for abortion services, postabortion care is a straightforward medical service to which all women have an equal right. Where caregivers are particularly uncomfortable with abortions and even postabortion care, it is critical for researchers to stress the value of appropriate family planning services. This essential element of the postabortion care constellation of services will decrease future need for abortions in all settings.

Regulatory approvals are also required to govern the importation and use of MVA equipment. The studies described in this volume confirm two findings: (1) MVA equipment and training ensures increased safety for the client; and (2) postabortion care services are more cost-effective when MVA equipment is used. Future operations research should include testing methods that ensure the continued supply of MVA equipment after the research is concluded. This will require work with policymakers responsible for the provision of equipment to their programs. It is critical that they understand why traditional methods of postabortion care can be effectively replaced by MVA.

Decentralizing Services

As Billings and her colleagues showed in Ghana with midwives at the primary health care level, it is possible to provide postabortion care services in decentralized settings. Midwives can be trained to effectively provide emergency care and to refer clients who need further treatment. The elements that made this system successful were the linkages firmly established between the midwife at the primary care facility and her supervisor at the referral facility (who was also her trainer for postabortion care). This system can be replicated in settings where trained midwives are available at the primary care level.

Other settings where postabortion care can be made available are district hospitals or clinical facilities where MVA equipment and pain medication are available. In every research program that attempts to decentralize postabortion care services, it is critical to ensure that referral links are clear and that service providers at referral sites are ready to receive clients on an emergency basis.

The decentralization of services to the level of traditional midwives is a much more complex undertaking, as Billings and her colleagues found in Mexico. Training these traditional caregivers in postabortion services proved to be difficult. Their willingness to associate themselves with any aspect of the abortion process was complicated by their traditional beliefs and also by their lack of acceptance by clinical caregivers. It is important for future research to continue to examine possible linkages with traditional caregivers, though this will be less fruitful in the short term than decentralizing postabortion care services through primary health care midwives linked to the formal health system.

Counseling Family Members and Social Support Systems

The groundbreaking work of Abdel-Tawab and colleagues on counseling husbands of postabortion care clients is very encouraging. There has been considerable discussion in the past few years about more effectively including men in order to improve women's reproductive health status, yet few service programs have done so. Involving husbands or other concerned family members (e.g., parents of unmarried adolescents who require postabortion care services) is certainly worthy of further study. The caution used in the Egypt study must also be replicated. Great care must be used to protect the client's right to privacy. Even if the client is an unmarried adolescent, those accompanying her should not be informed about her abortion unless she agrees. Training caregivers to seek this informed consent without coercion is not easy. But it is essential if the client's rights are to be protected.

None of the research reported here included data on the effect on women's health of educating or informing the community. This is an area for future research work. The stigma attached to women who undergo abortion prevents many from seeking the postabortion care they need in a timely manner. Their suffering is exacerbated by their reluctance to expose their abortions. Research that addresses community needs for education and information on postabortion care could be very useful in removing barriers for women who need care. It could also increase accessibility of services simply by publicizing where postabortion clinical care is available.

Supply of MVA Equipment and Essential Medications

We could successfully argue that it is not necessary to prove again that MVA is cost-effective. Nor is it necessary to further study the appropriate use of medication for pain management. However, it is important to continue to address the value of regulatory approvals of MVA equipment through the appropriate authorities in each country. It is also important to work within health systems to set regulations for the use of MVA equipment; to publicize pain management protocols; and to develop a systematic and uninterrupted supply of equipment and medications. These supplies are the basis for the development of a high-quality clinical program. Without a commitment to provide these supplies in every setting where postabortion care is provided, a health program is remiss in its responsibilities to improve reproductive health services.

Linkages with Other Services for Repeat Miscarriage Patients

Women who have repeat miscarriages may have other health conditions that affect their ability to have a successful pregnancy outcome. They need complete physical checkups that go beyond basic reproductive health services. In addition, they may require counseling regarding their lifestyles:

It is possible that overwork or extremely inadequate nutrition is negatively influencing their pregnancy outcomes. Such women may also be under great stress from other family members who consider them to have failed in their childbearing obligations. Thus, a complete package of services for repeat miscarriage patients would include all needed health services, counseling, and information and education for their partners. This is a neglected area where relevant research could guide the development of much-needed services.

Prevention of Unsafe Abortions

The number of women who suffer when they experience a pregnancy termination method is the most compelling reason to continue to improve the appropriate provision of family planning services. It has been demonstrated that improved access to family planning contraceptive services leads to a reduction in abortion (Westoff, Sharmanov, and Sullivan 1998).

In their early book on abortion, Potts, Diggory, and Peel (1977) also warned that even when strong family planning programs are present, abortion will be necessary. They commented:

> Organised family planning services have an important contribution to make in accelerating the switch from induced abortion to contraceptive practice but two limitations have to be recognised. First, the reversible methods of contraception at present available are not sufficiently predictable, even when well and consistently used, to control fertility over a lifetime and meet the goals of family size set in modern industrialised nations, and therefore in the foreseeable future the resort to abortion cannot be eliminated. Secondly, the input necessary into a family planning service in order to achieve an immediate decline in birth rates from the high level found in developing countries, without any transitory rise in the abortion rate, is very much larger than has been contemplated in any national family planning programme. It may well represent a use of health resources which it would be difficult to justify if the overall needs of the community for health care are reviewed objectively. (p. 496)

There are some embedded warnings for family planning programs in the research presented. Langer and colleagues report that 19 percent of the clients in their postabortion care study reported contraceptive use at the time they became pregnant. In Bolivia, lack of information about contraception was cited by nearly half of women as the reason they had a mistimed pregnancy. In Kenya, 22 percent of the preintervention clients reported contraceptive use at the time they became pregnant. This lack of access and appropriate use of contraception must be addressed mainly by the family planning service programs directly. However, it can also be addressed by improving postabortion care family planning counseling and contraceptive services. While it may be impossible to prevent all need for abortions, the frequency can be significantly reduced through higher quality family planning counseling.

Remembering the Rights of Women to Reproductive Health Care

All women who require postabortion care are entitled to it. The care should be of high quality and the following elements must be ensured:

- emergency health services (treatment of complications of spontaneous or unsafely induced abortion);
- postabortion family planning counseling, referral, and services; and
- linkages to other reproductive health care services.

In addition to these services, there is the need to treat clients holistically. It is inappropriate to provide high-quality family planning services simply as an add-on to poor-quality postabortion care. In fact, to achieve desired results, there can be no substandard elements in reproductive health care services. All have to be at the highest clinical standard and augmented by counseling and caring interpersonal relations with the client. At the same time, all reproductive health services that the client requires should be included during postabortion care. Improved clinical services require the use of MVA and appropriate pain management. Services should be available on an emergency basis and include all necessary drugs to ensure immediate and follow-up care. Postabortion family planning counseling and immediate service are also essential. As much as possible, family planning services should be provided to clients before they leave the facility.

Many women who experience an abortion are in need of referral for other reproductive health services as well. It is essential that these are provided at the same time as the postabortion care. Any referral to other facilities for related services carries a risk that women will not return for that essential service.

Linking Community Caregivers to Referral and Training Points

Billings and colleagues in the Ghana study provide an effective model that links the midwife at the primary care level with referral points. These linkages are critical to ensure that the first caregiver feels comfortable with the referral system and will help her client gain access to the system. If the linkage is not firmly established, many primary caregivers will refuse to assist clients who may be in need of the services only a referral center can provide. As Billings and colleagues found in Mexico, these linkages are not easily formed. It is critical to address the barriers that limit access to referral points for primary caregivers. Clearly future studies of postabortion care could usefully examine the process of women's care—from their first contact with a primary caregiver until they reach the referral facility. This will enable programs to develop required linkages between caregivers.

Conclusion

The studies presented in this book teach us several important lessons that provide direction for future work in operations research and in implementing services. When caregivers are trained to provide postabortion care services, and when legal issues are resolved, the results are positive. Women do receive appropriate care, including emergency services, appropriate pain management, counseling to prevent subsequent unwanted pregnancy, and contraceptive services that are timely and effective. When women know that postabortion care services are available, they appear to come to services earlier and readily accept the counseling and contraceptive services provided. The inclusion of traditional birth attendants in postabortion care services potentially increases clients' access to caregivers.

These reasons alone should encourage us to expand our research and postabortion care services.

The studies should be seen as first steps. Many of these steps bear repeating in other countries until the most successful models for providing postabortion care emerge. It will take time and substantial effort to achieve the desired outcomes for postabortion care services. But each proven model that effectively overcomes barriers to service and establishes legal and ethical precedents should be welcomed. Through these critical services the reduction in maternal mortality and morbidity can be directly influenced.

At the same time, those who are concerned with postabortion care must advocate for increased services based on what is already known. As Langer and colleagues remind us, we are all to be held responsible if this work is neglected. We cannot elude responsibility for the deaths of many thousands of women if we do not use what we already know to establish effective services.

Note

1 This phrase is taken from the title of a book by Laurence H. Tribe, *Abortion: The Clash of Absolutes* (New York: Norton & Company, 1992).

References

Potts, Malcolm, P. Diggory, and J. Peel. 1977. *Abortion*. London: Cambridge University Press.

Tietze, Christopher and John Bongaarts. 1975. "Fertility and abortion rates: Simulations of family limitation," *Studies in Family Planning* 6: 114–120.

Westoff, C.F., A.T. Sharmanov, and J.M. Sullivan. 1998. "The replacement of abortion by contraception in three central Asian republics." Washington, D.C.: Population Resource Center, the Futures Group.

Contributors

Kathlyn P. P. Ababio is Director of Pat's Maternity Home in Koforidua, Ghana. She is also President of the Ghana Registered Midwives Association and an Ipas master trainer in postabortion care.

Nahla Abdel-Tawab is a physician with a specialty in public health. She joined the Population Council as an operations research country fellow in December 1995. She is the Egypt Host Country Advisor for the Frontiers in Reproductive Health Project.

Colette Aloo-Obunga is Ipas Consultant to East Africa.

Fernando Alvarez is Professor of Obstetrics and Gynecology at the Universidad Mayor de San Andrés, La Paz, Bolivia. At the time research for this volume was completed, he was Director of the Women's Hospital in La Paz.

Victor Ankrah is a Program Officer at UNICEF in Ghana. Previously he served as Senior Medical Officer for Public Health in the Ministry of Health for the Eastern Region in Ghana and as District Director of Health Services in the Ministry of Health in Ghana. He has worked with Save the Children on the development of a health management information system.

Traci L. Baird is Director of the Regional Desk for Europe and North America at Ipas. She previously managed abortion and postabortion care programs in Ghana, Nigeria, and Vietnam.

Vilma Barahona is Chief of Pathology at the Dr. Aurelio Valdivieso General Hospital and Founding Member of the Casa de la Mujer Rosario Castellanos in Oaxaca, Mexico.

Deborah L. Billings is Deputy Director of Health Systems Research at Ipas and Adjunct Assistant Professor at the University of North Carolina School of Public Health, specializing in health behavior and health education. During her time at Ipas she has conducted operations research on postabortion care in Ghana, Kenya, and Mexico.

Julia Blanco Muñoz is a physician and Associate Professor at the National Institute of Public Health in Mexico. She has conducted research on primary health care, traditional medicine, gender issues, and epidemiological methodologies, particularly with rural populations in developing countries.

Carlos Brambila is Program Associate with the Population Council in Mexico and previously was a demographer at El Colegio de México. His main research interests are fertility, family planning, and migration.

Virginia Camacho is in charge of the Safe Motherhood Program for Latin America, PAHO, Washington. At the time research for this volume was completed, she was head of the Women's Health Program of the Ministry of Health of Bolivia.

Lourdes Campero is a researcher in the Division of Health and Population at the National Institute of Public Health in Cuernavaca, Morelos, Mexico.

Xóchitl Castañeda Camey is a medical anthropologist and Hewlett International Fellow at the University of California in San Francisco. She was previously head of the Department of Sexual and Reproductive Health and Associate Professor at the National Institute of Public Health in Mexico.

M. Virginia Chambers is Director of the Regional Desk for Latin America and the Caribbean at Ipas. She has been working for 15 years to improve women's reproductive health at the national, state, and community levels in Latin America and the United States.

Juan Díaz is Professor of Gynecology and a member of the Reproductive Health Unit of the Women's Hospital of the University of Campinas, Brazil. He is Senior Medical Advisor for Latin America and the Caribbean and Representative in Brazil for the Population Council.

Mohammed Naguib Abdel Fattah is Assistant Professor in the Biostatistics and Demography Department of the Institute of Statistical Studies and Research at Cairo University. At the time research for this volume was completed, he was a country fellow with the Population Council's Asia and Near East Operations Research and Technical Assistance Project.

Cecilia García-Barrios is Director of Medical Education and Training for the Ministry of Health of Mexico City and has been a consultant for the Population Council for many years.

Ezzeldin Osman Hassan is Professor of Obstetrics and Gynecology at Mansoura University and Executive Director of the Egyptian Fertility Care Society, a nongovernmental organization that specializes in research on family planning and reproductive health. He is the principal in charge of postabortion care work that was done jointly by the Population Council's Asia and Near East Operations Research and Technical Assistance Project and the Society from 1995 to 1998.

Angela Heimburger is Regional Staff Associate at the Population Council, Regional Office for Latin America and the Caribbean.

Dale Huntington is Senior Program Associate with the Population Council, assigned to the Regional Office for South and East Asia in New Delhi, India, as Associate Director for the Frontiers in Reproductive Health Project. He has lived and worked in sub-Saharan Africa, the Middle East, and Asia for over 20 years.

Ana Langer is the Population Council's Regional Director for Latin America and the Caribbean. A physician specializing in pediatrics and neonatology, her main areas of interest are reproductive health, quality of reproductive health care and its psychosocial aspects affecting pregnancy and delivery, the design and evaluation of interventions, and linkages between research and policymaking.

Máriel Loayza is a physician who specializes in public health and a researcher in sexual and reproductive health and postabortion care. She has recently completed consultancies with Pathfinder International and UNICEF, and is initiating consultancies with GTZ and the Population Council in La Paz, Bolivia.

Oscar Lora is a gynecologist in the Department of Obstetrics and Gynecology of the Women's Health Hospital in Sucre, Bolivia.

Margaret Makumi is Program Manager in Reproductive Health in the Division of Primary Health Care for Kenya's Ministry of Health.

Laila Nawar is Program Associate at the Population Council and Regional Advisor for the Frontiers in Reproductive Health Project for West Asia and North Africa. At the time research for this volume was completed, she was Egypt Host Country Advisor for the Population Council's Asia and Near East Operations Research and Technical Assistance Project. From 1987 to 1992 she was Director of the Population Policy Analysis Unit at Egypt's Central Agency for Public Mobilization and Statistics.

Stephen Ntow is Health Promotion Specialist and National Training Coordinator in the Human Resource Development Division, Ministry of Health, Accra, Ghana. Previously, he worked as a Regional Health Education Officer in the Ministry of Health, Eastern Region.

Achola Ominde is Regional Reproductive Health Advisor with the Commonwealth Regional Health Secretariat, based in Arusha, Tanzania. At the time research for this volume was completed, he was Program Manager in Reproductive Health in the Division of Primary Health Care, Ministry of Health.

Nancy J. Piet-Pelon is an independent consultant in reproductive health and family planning. Her work in this field began in 1970 in Indonesia and continued in Bangladesh, Nepal, and other countries in Asia. She is a former Director for Asia of AVSC International.

Karin Ringheim is a social scientist in the Office of Population of USAID Washington, where she helped found the Postabortion Care Working Group. She served as technical advisor to the Population Council's Asia and Near East Operations Research and Technical Assistance Project and now advises the Men and Reproductive Health Committee of the Interagency Gender Working Group.

Xóchitl Romero Guerrero is a physician who is currently conducting research in reproductive health for the National Institute of Public Health in Mexico, the Mexican Institute of Social Security, and Ipas, Mexico.

Andrea Saldaña Rivera is a public health nurse with training in research and management. She is Director of Ipas, Mexico, is a member of the National Safe Motherhood Committee of Mexico, and serves on the Board of Directors of the Midwifery School, CASA, in the state of Guanajuato.

Julie Solo is Program Officer with Reproductive Health Alliance Europe, an independent nongovernmental organization based in the United Kingdom and affiliated with AVSC International. She was based in Nairobi, Kenya, for four years with the Population Council's Africa Operations Research and Technical Assistance Project II.

Karen Stein is Associate Director for Clinical Operations at Pasteur Mérieux Connaught.

Joseph E. Taylor is an OB/GYN specialist and Medical Director for the Ministry of Health, Eastern Region, in Ghana. He is Superintendent of the Central Hospital in Koforidua, Ghana, and the regional medical advisor for Ipas. He has been involved in the Life Saving Skills Program, the Safe Motherhood Program, and the postabortion care program in Ghana.

Yamile Torres de Yépez is Professor of Obstetrics and Gynecology at the Catholic University of Bolivia in Santa Cruz. At the time research for this volume was completed, she was Director of the Maternidad Percy Boland in Santa Cruz de la Sierra. Currently, she is head of the emergency room at the hospital.

Patricia Voorduin is an obstetric nurse who participates in training and reproductive health research in the Secretariat of Health, where she is also head of the Traditional Midwives Training Program in Morelos, Mexico.

Beverly Winikoff is Program Director for Reproductive Health and Senior Medical Associate at the Population Council, New York. She was principal investigator of the acceptability component of the U.S. trials of mifepristone and directed the Council's studies of mifepristone in India, Cuba, China, and Vietnam. Her work has focused on issues of reproductive choice, contraception, abortion, and women's health.

Hala Youssef is a public health physician, Assistant Professor in the Department of Public Health at Cairo University, and Consultant to the Frontiers in Reproductive Health Project. At the time research for this volume was completed, she was the project coordinator for three postabortion care studies carried out jointly by the Population Council's Asia and Near East Operations Research and Technical Assistance Project and the Egyptian Fertility Care Society.